Crystals for Self-Care

Also by the author

Lunar Living
The Lunar Living Journal

Crystals for Self-Care

The ultimate guide to crystal healing

KIRSTY GALLAGHER

First published in Great Britain in 2021 by Yellow Kite
An imprint of Hodder & Stoughton
An Hachette UK company

3

Illustrations by The Colour Study © Hodder & Stoughton 2021

A CIP catalogue record for this title is available from the British Library

Hardback ISBN 978 1 529 36023 3
eBook ISBN 978 1 529 3602 40

Typeset in Celeste by
Palimpsest Book Production Ltd, Falkirk, Stirlingshire

Printed and bound in Great Britain by Clays Ltd, Elcograf S.p.A.

Hodder & Stoughton policy is to use papers that are natural, renewable and recyclable products and made from wood grown in sustainable forests. The logging and manufacturing processes are expected to conform to the environmental regulations of the country of origin.

Yellow Kite
Hodder & Stoughton Ltd
Carmelite House
50 Victoria Embankment
London EC4Y 0DZ

www.yellowkitebooks.co.uk

For everyone following their True North,
this book is for you.

Contents

Part 2:
Making Crystals a Part of Your Life

Introduction

Welcome! I'm so excited to share the magical world of crystals with you. For those of you who haven't met me yet, my name is Kirsty Gallagher and I'm a moon mentor, soul-alignment coach, yoga and meditation teacher and crystal lover.

I remember getting my first crystal in my early teens, around the same time that my fascination with astrology started. It was a tiger's eye, one of the crystals for my zodiac sign. From then on, I was never far from a crystal and used to carry them around in my pockets or even in my bra!

I started working intentionally with crystals to make changes in my life around 20 years ago, long before they were a trend. I could not believe the support, guidance, clarity, focus, transformation and healing I gained from working with them in a conscious way; for me, it was – and still is – a true act of self-care. I took a course to become a crystal healer in my early

20s and over the years I have undertaken numerous other training courses and workshops to learn more about these magical gifts. And still, to this day, I will gaze at a crystal in total awe that it came from the earth.

Nowadays I work with crystals daily, whether I'm simply wearing one to be in tune with the energies of the crystal or consciously meditating or manifesting with one. Crystals, to me, are loving, loyal friends, offering me invaluable support, and I will often refer to them as such throughout this book to explain the effects and benefits of working with them.

Over the years, I have shared my love of crystals with anyone who will listen. When I was working in a corporate environment, I ensured that almost all my colleagues had one on their desk; and as I moved from that world into teaching yoga, I would gift everyone who came to my workshops a crystal to amplify the work we were doing together.

In *Crystals for Self-Care* I want to share what I have learned over the years with *you*, so that you, too, can feel supported by crystals in the same way I do. As with all my work, I want to make the topic of crystals accessible and relatable – to strip away the confusion around working with them and give you the confidence you need to start (or continue) your crystal journey.

We begin, in Part 1, with a look at what crystals are and how they work, before going on to choosing, caring for and programming them and, of course, how to go about using them. Then, in Part 2, we go deeper into the many areas in which crystals work their magic, whether you need to strengthen relationships, improve your sleep, be supported in your work or business, and so much more.

My aim is to support, guide and empower you in many different areas of your life. But, as the title of the book suggests, I also want you to treat the time you spend with your crystals as an act of self-care – a conscious undertaking to look after your own wellbeing and deliberately take care of your physical, emotional, mental and spiritual health. You are worth the same love, care and attention you give to everyone else around you and I want you to remember and honour that.

Block out the time you allocate to working with your crystals in the same way that you would a meeting. Commit to healing, growing and making improvements and changes in your life, wherever they are needed. You might choose to dedicate ten minutes a day to your self-care with crystals, or perhaps an hour once a week. Try working with the same crystals and areas for a few weeks before moving on, so that you can go deeper each time and really start to feel the benefits.

If you wear or carry your crystals daily, take a moment to connect with them as you put them on or into your pocket. See this in itself as an act of self-care as you allow them to infuse you with their energies all through the day.

◆ Keeping a Crystal Journal ◆

You may choose to keep a crystal journal so that you can make a note of the crystals you use and wear, grid with and manifest with for self-care. This will help you to notice any changes and magic taking place.

Finally, one thing I want to make clear right from the outset is that you are your own authority, and you know what is best for you. With crystals having grown in popularity, you will find countless well-meaning people telling you a thousand different things, but your journey with crystals is yours and yours alone. And while it's extremely useful in the beginning to take advice on things like the crystals that may be best for you or how they should be worn, over time, you will learn to trust in your own intuition and work with them on a much deeper, more personal level in a way that is right for you. I am here to help you with these things and more. This is where the real magic starts.

PART 1:

The Enchanted World of Crystals

In my experience, the thing that prevents many people from starting to work with crystals is the feeling that they don't understand what they are, how they work or what they should do with them. I want to answer all of those questions – and more – here, in Part 1. I will provide you with the basics about choosing, caring for, cleansing, charging and, ultimately, working with your crystals. I'll also share with you my go-to crystal kit and explain some of the terminology used in these pages, so that you will have a good understanding of all things crystals.

Let the journey begin . . .

Crystals: A Quick Guide to What They Are and How They Work

In simple terms, crystals are an established batch of molecules and atoms that bond in a repeating pattern. They form over millions of years in a chemical process, during which movement in the earth's crust forces molten magma, liquids and gases towards the surface where they cool, solidify and crystallise. Crystals exist in many different shapes and colours, determined by their chemical components and bonds.

Did you know that it's a crystal that helps your phone, watch and TV to work? With very few legitimate studies done, science has yet to back the healing properties of crystals but what science can agree on is that crystals such as quartz produce energy. It's what's known as piezoelectricity and was discovered in 1880 by Jacques and Pierre Curie when they put crystals such as quartz, topaz and tourmaline under pressure and created electrical energy.

Science also agrees that everything is made of energy. Right now your energetic system is receiving and responding to all of the vibrations of energy not only in but around you.

◆ Crystal Energy ◆

I will talk about energies a lot in this book. If this is new to you, let me explain what I mean in brief, so that you can deepen your understanding of your own energies and, in turn, how the energy of crystals works.

Everything in the world is made of energy – you, your thoughts, your emotions and beliefs – and it is all vibrating to a particular frequency. Crystals, too, are made up of energies and, similarly, vibrate at a certain frequency. Working with them allows us to match our own energies and frequency with theirs, so that we can take advantage of their therapeutic properties, helping to soothe our emotions, calm our minds and bring ourselves back into balance and alignment.

When we speak of your energetic system, we are referring to your aura and your chakras.

◆ About Your Aura ◆

Have you ever just known that a friend is off or not feeling great without them saying anything, even when they try to tell you that everything is ok? That is you picking up on their subtle energy. Your aura reflects your emotions, thoughts, moods, energy levels and overall vibe. It is felt, rather than seen, and it is often someone's aura that we pick up on when we first meet them.

The aura is made up of seven different layers, each associated with different qualities (physical, emotional, mental, astral, spiritual, causal and true self).

◆ About Your Chakras ◆

Often described as your inner universe, your chakras are energy centres in the body that are constantly receiving and processing information from the world around you. There are seven main chakras, each relating to a different area of the body and aspect of our being. They are: root (safety), sacral (emotions), solar plexus (power), heart (love), throat (communication), third eye (intuition) and crown (connection). They are explained in more detail in Chapter 6 ('Crystals for . . . the Chakras').

◆ The Power of Crystals ◆

When the energies in our physical, energetic, mental, emotional or spiritual bodies become blocked, stagnant, stuck or overactive, we begin to feel out of alignment and disconnected, and things in our lives don't seem to flow or work as well as they could. This is where the power of crystals comes in.

Every crystal has its own geometric pattern that is repeated over and over, so that each one holds its own energy and vibrates to a specific frequency. Whereas our human energies are in a constant state of flux, the energy frequency of crystals is stable, i.e. they emit the same energies at all times. So when we work with them, they can help to heal and restore balance in our own energies, lowering or raising our vibrations to match theirs, absorbing, transforming and releasing stuck energies and bringing us back into alignment and balance where needed.

It is the unique energetic blueprint of each crystal that enables them to offer support, guidance and healing in different areas of your life. Some will work with the energy of your heart and any healing that needs to take place there; some will clear blockages you have around money and abundance; some will help you to find your voice and speak your truth; and some will soothe your anxieties and work to keep you calm in challenging situations. Certain crystals will bring you strength and protection, while others will help you to be more open and receiving. Again, it is useful to think of crystals as friends who are on your team and want to help you in the best way that they can.

We all have our own skills and strengths and things we are naturally good at as part of our energetic make-up, and it's the same with crystals. We choose or are drawn to (you might say chosen by) the crystals we need to balance our energies.

Holding, wearing and placing particular crystals on your body and around your home allows you to connect to their energies, enabling them to do their work of aligning and regulating your energies and supporting you in the very best way that a crystal knows how.

◆ Your Go-to Crystal Kit ◆

Before we go any further, here are my crystal must-haves:

Clear quartz
Known as the master crystal, this is one of the most popular and versatile crystals and is known for its high vibrations. Clear quartz helps to amplify (thoughts,

words, intentions and more – whatever you ask it to work with), and so it's amazing to use for manifesting or intention setting, and when you want to raise your own vibration. Clear quartz can balance all the chakras and bring mental, spiritual and emotional clarity, aiding you in getting clear on the direction of your life.

Clear quartz can be used and programmed for just about anything, and so if you don't have any of the crystals mentioned in Part 2 of the book, you can use a clear quartz in their place and program it to do the work you want it to do. It's also good for enhancing the energy of other crystals, so keep a clear quartz tumbled stone or point with any other crystals you are working with to increase their energy and power.

Rose quartz

The crystal of universal, unconditional love. Everyone needs to own a rose quartz. Rose quartz will lend a helping crystal hand in all matters of the heart. Whether that's finding self-love and self-worth, healing or opening your heart, embracing forgiveness, discovering a new relationship, healing from on old one or deepening the love in an existing one, rose quartz will help to invite more love into your life.

Moonstone

Given my love affair with the moon, this is obviously one of my favourites! As its name suggests, moonstone helps us to connect to lunar cycles, the feminine realms of intuition and the understanding that life is all about cycles and rhythm and flow. Moonstone can calm the emotions and is known as the crystal of new beginnings – it is powerful in any times of change.

Citrine

The crystal of abundance, citrine is your go-to when it comes to manifesting, prosperity and wealth. Highly energising, it's good for confidence, inner power and self-esteem. It's like the joyous friend who immediately lifts your mood and makes you smile and believe in yourself.

Amethyst

Bringing peaceful and calm vibes and a whole host of magical superpowers, amethyst needs to be on your team. It will support you through difficult emotions, calm and bring clarity to your mind, help with sleep issues and connect you to higher guidance.

Black tourmaline

One of the best crystals for grounding and protection, black tourmaline can energetically shield and protect you, cleansing you and your environment. It will help to ground and connect you to the earth in any times of mental or emotional anxiety and release any heavy or unwanted energies.

Ethical crystals

As crystals have gained in popularity over the last few years, much more has come to light on how they are mined and also on their environmental impact (crystals are a non-renewable source and their extraction has been linked to labour issues and damage to the environment). If you already have some crystals, I would encourage you to work with those before rushing out to buy more; the crystals you have chose you for a reason, and you only need a small collection to get big results. When you do purchase crystals, please look for ethical suppliers; a good one should be able to tell you exactly where the crystals have been sourced from and many nowadays will only deal with mines they can visit. Ethical crystals may cost a little more, but by purchasing them, you ensure that you are supporting ethical mines and practices.

It's better to have five sustainably sourced crystals to work with than a houseful of hundreds of cheap and more readily available ones.

Key crystal terminology

Here is a list of some of the terminology used in this book:

💗 **Intention setting:** the act of stating what you intend to achieve, accomplish, create and bring into your life.

💗 **Manifesting:** the art of creating what you want in life through your actions, thoughts, beliefs and emotions.

💗 **Vibrations:** all things in the universe vibrate with energy and to a certain frequency, including us and all our thoughts, emotions and attitudes – and crystals, too, of course. The more positive the energy, the higher the vibe, so things like love, gratitude or kindness vibrate at a much higher frequency than fear, anxiety or doubt.

💗 **Crystal grids:** the placing of crystals in an intentional way to direct the energy towards a specific intention or focus.

💗 **Altar:** a sacred space that is dedicated to your personal growth or spiritual work; it becomes a visual focus for your intentions, manifestations and energy and a place you can go to daily to check in.

15

❖ **Corners:** the practice of feng shui holds that there is an energy map in your home connected to different areas or aspects of your life; depending on your intentions, you can add more power to them by setting up a crystal grid in specific spaces (it is not recommended to work with more than two or three areas at once).

CHAPTER 2:

Choosing Your Crystals (or Letting Them Choose You)

There are two ways to select your crystals: either you choose them or they choose you!

If you are seeking out crystals, you will likely have a specific purpose in mind for them, and so you would find ones that hold the properties you are looking for. Part 2 of the book goes into much more detail about this and should help you with all that you need to know about choosing the crystal that is right for you.

The other approach is to let the crystal pick you. It can sometimes take a little longer to get comfortable with this method, as it requires tuning into and trusting your intuition. The more you work with crystals, the more you will connect to that part of yourself and the easier this method will become.

You may find that as soon as you enter a crystal shop, a certain one just jumps out at you (figuratively, that is) and you just know that's the one. Otherwise, take a few long, slow, deep breaths. Open yourself up to 'feeling' the crystals and allow yourself to wander around and explore. You may be drawn to a certain colour or shape or you may feel that a particular crystal 'speaks' to you. Try holding a couple in your hand, one at a time. As you hold each one close your eyes and ask yourself how each one feels to you. Does it seem warm or heavy? Can you feel any differences between them – in their texture or energies? Some people feel a tingle in their hands or a warm feeling in their heart; or, for you, it may be a little voice that says 'Yes'.

For me, as soon as I hold a crystal, I know whether it's for me or not. If it's right, holding it feels like home; it feels as though it was always meant to be mine. You know that feeling you get when you meet someone, and you just know that you like their energy and vibe, and that they will be good for you? Well, it's the same with crystals.

It's also possible that in the beginning you feel nothing at all – and that's ok, too. Keep working with sensing crystal energies and it will become much more familiar over time.

One tip here is to get to know the feeling of your own energy first – and especially the energy in your hands:

❤ Rub the palms of your hands together, until they feel warm.

❖ Next, close your eyes and move your palms to about shoulder-distance apart, facing each other.

❖ Slowly move your palms closer together, until you feel a slight resistance between your hands – this is your energy field.

❖ You can experiment with moving your hands closer together and further apart to really feel this or imagine you are making an energy ball by moulding the energy between your hands into a ball shape.

Try your hand

You can also begin to tune into which hand is your receiving hand and which is your sending hand. Typically, your dominant hand (the one you write with) tends to be the one through which you release and send energy out into the world. Your non-dominant hand would be the hand through which you receive energies, and the one with which you would hold crystals to sense and accept their powers. Try holding a crystal first in one hand and then the other to see how it feels. It helps to know this for when you are meditating with your crystals, so you can hold the crystal in the relevant hand, depending on whether your intent through meditation is to receive energies, advice and guidance or to release stuck energy, emotion or fears. (See 'Crystals for Meditation', p. 38.)

You can apply a similar process when buying crystals; online. Take some time to look through the different images and see which one seems to jump off the page or keeps drawing you back. Once you have selected your crystal type, feel free to message the supplier and ask for pictures of different ones. So if you know, for example, that you want a citrine point, you can ask for pictures of five different ones, so you can choose the particular one that you want. This is how I buy crystals online and any good supplier should agree to this, so that you can see which speaks to you most.

Be discerning with where you purchase your crystals; there is no such thing as a 'bad' crystal, but there can be less-than-ethical suppliers (see p. 11). I tend to choose dedicated crystal shops and I generally find that as soon as I enter a shop or see a crystal stall or supplier online, I know if they seem legitimate. I want to buy from someone who is passionate about crystals and treats them well, and you can tell a lot from how the energy of the crystals and the shop feels – they should feel alive and vibrant, rather than numb or lifeless.

It's also worth remembering that it's always better to

start off with fewer crystals – say, three to five – and to do the work with them, instead of buying and trying to work with lots and lots, which can become overwhelming. You may try working with your chosen crystal for 30 days to really deepen the relationship and get the benefits, rather than swapping and changing every day. The more you connect to and spend time with your crystals, the more magic you will create together.

◆ Crystals as Gifts ◆

Gifting crystals to others is a beautiful thing to do and I'm often asked how to go about it.

Try holding the person in your mind's eye and feel into your heart what you would like the crystal to help them with – what is the purpose or intent behind this gift? You may want to look through the various chapters in this book and choose crystals based on what is going on in that person's life or keep them in mind when you are crystal shopping and then trust in your intuition.

I sometimes find that when I am crystal shopping, a certain person will come so clearly into my mind when I am near or holding a particular crystal and I will just know that it is intended for them. I have also bought crystals for myself in the past, got them home and realised they were not for me, after all, because our energies just didn't blend together, but that I knew just who they would be better suited to.

I often gift crystal pouches that contain four or five tumbled (see p. 23) stones for different purposes, so that the person can use different crystals at different times, based on what they are feeling drawn to.

◆ Crystal Shapes and Colours ◆

Crystals come in many different forms, shapes and sizes that will determine how you can use them.

Colour me beautiful

We'll explore more on colours and the chakras and how you can use different-coloured crystals in various areas of your life in Part 2, but for now, here is a rough guide to what the colours of crystals mean:

❖ **Black** – grounding and protection

❖ **Brown** – support and nourishment

❖ **Red (root chakra)** – energy and action

❖ **Orange (sacral chakra)** – change and creativity

❖ **Yellow (solar-plexus chakra)** – power and optimism

❖ **Pink (heart chakra)** – love and acceptance

❖ **Green (heart chakra)** – growth and abundance

❖ **Light blue (throat chakra)** – communication and wisdom

❖ **Deep blue/indigo (third-eye chakra)** – clarity and intuition

❖ **Violet/purple (crown chakra)** – awakening and spirituality

❖ **White or clear (all chakras)** – cleansing and purifying

Shaping up

When it comes to crystal shapes, some are natural and others are man-made and have been cut to shape. Here are some of the most common:

❖ **Tumbled:** The most common and versatile type of crystal, this is when small crystals are polished in a special machine until they become smooth and

23

shiny. These can be carried, held or used in grids or for just about any purpose.

❖ **Raw:** Sometimes known as chunks, these are often larger pieces of crystal in their natural form. Raw crystals are frequently used in grids, within rooms to help with the environment or are held during meditation.

❖ **Cluster:** A number of smaller crystals (usually points) in their natural form that join together and are attached to the same matrix. Clusters are good for radiating energy into a room or environment.

❖ **Points:** Usually naturally occurring, with a rough base where the crystal has been removed from its matrix. They can focus and direct energy and are great to use when meditating or manifesting.

❖ **Spheres:** Shaped into a sphere or a circle, as the name suggests, these are a good focal point for meditation or to soothe in times of stress. They bring harmony and allow energy to radiate in all directions, while creating a sense of wholeness and a reminder that you are connected to something greater – like you are holding the whole world in your hand.

❖ **Pyramids:** Shaped into a pyramid, these are amazing for manifesting what you want and connecting to high-vibration energies and higher consciousness.

❖ **Wands:** These are usually pointed at one end and rounded at the other, although you can get double-terminated wands with a point at each end. Wands are used for healing and to release negative energy or bring healing energy into the body.

❖ **Towers:** Usually carved/polished into shape, so that they stand up, these are similar to a point in that they help to direct and focus energy.

Now that you've chosen your crystal/s, it's time to go a little deeper . . .

CHAPTER 3:

Caring for and Programming Your Crystals

With your crystal collection under way, it's time to learn how to take care of them. Crystals tend to be fairly low-maintenance but, just like people, a little TLC is needed to get the best out of them.

◆ Cleansing and Charging Your Crystals ◆

Your crystals may have been on quite a journey to get to you, often crossing continents and passing through many hands. So the first thing you'll want to do with your new crystals is to cleanse them.

As we've learned, crystals hold vibrational energy. If you imagine your crystals as an air filter, they are working to cleanse, purify, transform and raise the quality of the vibrations all around them, while filtering out all the lower or unnecessary ones. Just as an air filter needs changing every once in a while, to do its best work, the same goes for your crystals.

It is important to mention that there is a difference between *cleansing* and *charging* your crystals. While cleansing helps to remove unwanted energies from your crystals, at times, they might also need a bit of charging; just like your mobile phone or laptop battery, your crystals' energy may drain if they've been hard at work, so remember to charge them up once in a while.

Here are some ways to treat your crystals to some cleansing/charging care:

❦ **Moonlight:** The light of the full moon will not only cleanse, but also charge your crystals, bringing them back to their full power. On the night of a full moon, simply lay your crystals outside if you can – they especially love to be on the earth. If that's not possible, a window ledge or balcony where they can soak up the moonbeams will do just fine. It doesn't matter if it's a cloudy evening, or even if you can't see the moon, they will still absorb the lunar vibes. And it also doesn't matter if you miss the night of the full moon; the night before or after will also work.

❦ **Sunlight:** Most people tend to charge their crystals by the moon, but there is nothing nicer than putting them out on a warm, sunny day. Just like the moon, the beams of the sun will cleanse and charge your crystals, filling them with more light and life. Place your crystals on the earth outside for a little sunbathing time or, again, on a window ledge or balcony. Just be mindful that some crystals can fade and/or crack if placed under intense direct sunlight for too long (pink and purple ones especially), so don't leave them out all day – an hour or so of sunshine should be more than enough.

❖ **Water:** You can soak or run your crystals under running water, while visualising washing them clean of any energy they no longer need. I often used to take my crystals to a local stream and treat them to fresh running water. Please be mindful, however, that many crystals are water-soluble and so should not be placed in water. As a general rule, those that end in -*ite* should not get wet (for example, selenite, hematite, celestite, malachite, angelite, etc.).

❖ **A crystal bed:** Place your crystals on a bed of amethyst or clear quartz. Every night, I put the crystal jewellery I've worn on a large bed of amethyst, so that it can be cleansed overnight.

Selenite is also amazing for charging other crystals, so you can keep your other crystals by a piece of selenite.

❧ **Smudging/smoke:** Use sage, Palo Santo or incense and waft the smoke over and around your crystals, visualising the smoke cleansing away any unwanted energies.

❧ **Energy healing:** You can use energy healing such as reiki to cleanse and charge your crystals. You would first hold the crystal with the intention of using reiki to cleanse it. Once you feel this has happened, you can charge the crystal back up using your healing vibes.

❧ **Earth:** Every now and then, you may find a crystal that wants to go back to the earth for a while, especially if you have been doing deep healing work together. If this happens (and it's usually just a feeling you get), bury your crystal in the earth for a few weeks to cleanse and charge it. Again, be mindful of water-soluble crystals, as they will likely get wet in the earth.

In the same way that we need to take care of ourselves, so that we have the energy to be able to help take care of others, our crystals sometimes need a little self-care and time out. After the initial cleansing when you get your crystals home you may want to cleanse/charge your crystals once a month or every so often. As you get to know them better, you'll know when it's time – when mine start to feel or look a little 'dull', I know it's time to treat them to some care.

◆ Programming Your Crystals ◆

With your crystals cleansed and charged, it's time to program them, so that they can heal, balance, align and amplify your own energy.

When I first get a crystal, I hold it in my hands and ask it to work with me for my highest good and the highest good of all. I do this out of respect for the crystal. In my opinion we don't own anything from the earth and crystals come to us to work *with* us, not *for* us. This needs to be a partnership and, just like human inter-actions, there needs to be a mutual respect. I like to treat my crystals as living vibrational beings who are going to work alongside me.

I then ask my crystals to be self-cleansing and self-charging – this does not mean that they don't ever need cleansing or charging, but just that they tend not to need it as often.

I also ask my crystal not to take on the energies of anyone else. This is particularly important, as you'll notice, especially when you are doing powerful work with a crystal, that people are drawn to it and want to hold it. This ensures that your crystal is protected from other people's energies.

CHAPTER 4:

How to Work with Crystals

You've chosen your crystals and they are cleansed, programmed and ready to go. So now what?

As we've explored, crystals already come with a purpose and the properties they are best used for, but it really helps to add to the energy and power of working with a particular crystal if you program it for what you especially want to use it for, adding an intention to working together (to help bring you love, soothe your anxiety or bring you your dream job, for example). This can focus the energy and allow the crystal to support you even more.

◆ One or Many? ◆

A frequently asked question is whether it's ok to use more than one crystal at a time, and the answer is yes . . . and no!

In truth, it depends on what your intention is for working with a number of crystals. If you are working to cleanse and balance your chakras, and you want a crystal for each one, then absolutely – as each will have its own purpose and job to do (and the same applies to crystal grids). You may want to meditate with a crystal in each hand or with one on your third eye (your forehead) and one on your heart. Again, this is more than ok, as each crystal will have its own purpose and is able to work with you in its own special way.

If, however, it's simply that you feel more is better and you want to throw all the crystals at a situation, that may not be the best idea. It's a bit like when you have more people working together, the energy may be more powerful – especially if they share similar working methods or goals; but if you have a roomful of people all wanting to make their voices heard and do things their own way, you may find it becomes more of a struggle than anything else and the bigger workforce is not beneficial at all.

If you do decide to work with more than one crystal, it's more useful either to choose a different crystal for each specific purpose (as with the chakras – see Chapter 6) or to find ones that complement each other energetically and will, together, bring more power to the work you are doing with them.

Just having crystals around your home is enough to benefit from them, especially if you set an intention on them (see below), as they will keep amplifying the intention and sending their vibes out into your environment. But you will likely want to go deeper – and so you should. As I said earlier, crystals are like friends and the more time you spend with them, the deeper the connection will be and the more you will benefit from their magic. We will cover more on specific meditations, intention setting and grids for different areas of your life in Part 2, but for now, here's a guide to the many ways you can work with your crystals daily.

◆ Intention Setting with Crystals ◆

I love to set intentions with my crystals and use them to help me to manifest what I want. When you set an intention with a crystal, it will continue to amplify the energies of that intention, working to draw it more quickly into your life.

I usually set intentions around the lunar cycles as it holds more power (see Chapter 13) but you can set intentions at any time.

I'm not sure if my publisher knows this, but I used intention setting with a crystal to manifest my first book, *Lunar Living*, when it was being presented to the wider team for a final decision on whether we would go ahead. The day before the presentation, I held a moonstone and asked for its assistance in getting the book deal. I visualised not only the 'Yes', but also how it would feel to have my book out in the world. I asked for help to spread the word of my passion for living in alignment with lunar cycles and moon magic, filling that little crystal with all my hopes and dreams for the book and asking it to please send these energies to everyone involved in making the decision. I then hid the moonstone in the bushes outside my publishing company Yellow Kite's offices. I must admit, looking back now, the sight of a girl skulking around, trying to hide a crystal in the bushes must have been so strange. But it worked! They said yes, *Lunar Living* was brought into the world and it became a *Sunday Times* bestseller. And to this day, there is a crystal hidden in the bushes outside my publisher's offices sending out good vibes! If you want to try this same intention-setting magic for yourself, here's how to do it:

1. Take some time to consider why you have chosen the particular crystal you are using, and the support you really want from it. Get as specific as you can. For example: if you want to bring love into your life, what kind of love would that be? If you want help with a new job or a career choice, what would that look or feel

like? Maybe you want to feel calmer and more relaxed, and that would come through not over-thinking or worrying about the future quite as much. The clearer you can be on what you want your crystal to work on, the better.

2. Next, try to distil this into a sentence or two. For example:

   ❧ 'I ask that you please help me to find a love that is honest and true. I ask that you help release any blocks or fears around receiving love and open me up to the right person coming into my life.'

   ❧ 'I ask that you help me to find a job that is fulfilling and satisfying. A job where I can best use my skills and experience and be appreciated for all that I do.'

   ❧ 'I ask that you please help bring more peace and tranquillity into my life. I ask that you help me to calm my mind and remain more focused in the present moment.'

When you have come up with your sentence/s, hold your crystal in your hand (either or both hands) or even against your heart, and say your intention out loud or whisper it from your heart.

3. You can then wear your crystal or keep it in a special place or on an altar, where it will continue to emit the relevant vibrations for you at all times, even when you're not together; and each time you hold, meditate or work with your crystal, the same intention will be amplified.

◆ Crystals for Meditation ◆

Crystals can transform your meditation experience. There are a number of ways and reasons for choosing to meditate with crystals, from helping to quieten your mind and connecting you with your deep inner wisdom to accessing your higher self, manifesting or amplifying your intentions and working to shift your energies if you are overwhelmed, stressed or feeling like you need a little more get up and go. Your crystals will guide and support you in what you need.

◆ Three easy ways to ◆ meditate with crystals

1. **Hold them in your hand/s:** Feel the energy exchange between you and the crystal and allow it to work with you during your meditation

practice. Hold the crystal, close your eyes and visualise it doing the work of helping you to release or draw to you what you need. You may remember that we talked earlier about discovering your sending and receiving hands – see p. 20.) This comes in really useful during meditation with crystals, as it will help you to direct the energies even more powerfully. If I have been feeling stressed, anxious and overwhelmed and my intention during meditating with my crystals is to release those feelings, I will hold the relevant crystal in my releasing hand and allow it to support me in letting go of anything I don't need. If I am working on manifesting something, or needing to receive extra energies or guidance, I will hold the crystal in my receiving hand to allow these energies to come into my being.

2. **Place them on your body:** You may feel that your heart needs a little healing, that your throat needs opening (if you've been struggling to

39

communicate your needs) or that you want to add a little more power to your solar plexus (if you've been giving away your power and not maintaining clear boundaries). If so, lie down, place the relevant crystals over the relevant places on your body (see p. 58) and close your eyes, while the crystals do their work. Stay like this for ten minutes, or until you feel a difference in the area/s concerned.

3. **Create an energy field:** You might want the energy and support of your crystals, but not want to hold or place them on your body. In this case, you can place them in a circle around you, or just one in front of and one behind you, so they can still hold and support you in their energies. Sit or lie for as long as you would do your usual meditation while you soak in their energies.

It's also powerful to meditate with crystals that you have set intentions on to keep amplifying them, and you may find guidance coming to you through the meditation. You can use any of the above options to do this or sit in front of the special place or altar where you have placed your crystals and tune into their energies before and after the meditation.

◆ Crystal Grids ◆
and How to Use Them

Put simply, a crystal grid is an arrangement of crystals used with intention to manifest a desired result. As we learned in the intention-setting section above, when you set an intention on crystals, they continue to amplify this, and when you grid them it creates an even more powerful energy vortex. Using crystal grids is exceptionally effective, as your crystals continue to work on your intention at all times and, as such, they should definitely be part of your work with crystals.

Traditionally, crystal grids were used with sacred geometry an ancient science that explores the energy patterns and shapes that exist in nature all around us, as it was believed this increased their power. In some cases, I have found this to be true, while in others, I prefer to follow my own guidance. You can have crystal grids around your house for protection, love or abundance, or you may set one up before a big interview or date. Before I appeared on *This Morning* over Skype, for example, I gridded my laptop with crystals to ensure that my message of moon magic would be delivered to the nation in the best way possible.

There really is no right or wrong with crystal grids, and as you get more confident with using them, you'll realise there are no limits to how they can be utilised. Use them for just about any dream, goal or intention that you want to manifest to know that you have crystal power right behind you. On the Leo New Moon Lionsgate Portal in 2021 I set an intention to start to let myself shine and be seen in my business so that I could make more of a difference in the world, placing my written intention under a crystal grid. Two weeks later, on the full blue moon, my book became a *Sunday Times* bestseller again. I'll let you know when the other intentions under my crystal grid come true, as I am sure they will, but this is the power of setting your intentions with a crystal grid, especially with a little moon magic thrown in too.

Your ten-step beginner's guide to setting up a crystal grid

1. The most important thing is the intention behind your grid and holding that clear intention as you set it up. So get very clear on what this is – I would suggest you write it down. As long as your intention/s is/are there, the grid will work as it is intended.

2. Choose a centre crystal. It's a good idea to ensure this is one that resonates with the intention of your grid (i.e. love, abundance, communication) – or you can use a quartz point for directing your intention. This is also known as the anchor stone, as it anchors the intention of your grid.

3. Choose the rest of your crystals based on the purpose and intention of your grid, but also feel free to add any extra crystals that you are drawn to using.

4. You may also want to add quartz points to your grid to activate the flow of energy. Points facing in will bring more of what you intend in, while points facing out will help to release anything in the way or that needs to go.

43

5. Cleanse your crystals and the space you are going to set up the grid using Palo Santo, sage, incense or energy healing.

6. Place your centre/anchor crystal in the middle of your grid. You can also place the piece of paper you wrote your intention on underneath it.

7. Place the rest of your crystals in your chosen shape or sacred geometric pattern (you can – but don't have to – purchase special boards or cloths for this) around your central crystal. Keep your intention in mind as you do this and feel as though all the crystals are connecting to create one big energy grid. A simple beginner's grid would be a circle of crystals placed around your anchor crystal and then possibly an outer circle around that. As you get more confident with gridding, you will be guided by what feels right.

8. If you feel you want to, you can add candles, flower petals, leaves, images, statues or anything else that represents what your grid is all about.

9. Activate your grid. I like to use a quartz point for this. Starting at the centre, touch your point to your anchor crystal, then using the point

energetically, draw a line from crystal to crystal to join them all to each other – a bit like connect-the-dots.

10. Leave your grid in place for as long as you want. I usually recommend at least one lunar cycle, but I have grids that remain in place all the time (for things that I want to keep in my life – like abundance or protection).

Have a play around with different crystals and ways of setting up your grid, until it feels right for you, and enjoy the process of discovery.

◆ Self-Care Crystal Grids ◆

For some deep healing self-care time, you can also create crystal grids on and around your body. I would suggest lying in a grid of crystals with one at your crown, one by your feet and, perhaps, others by your shoulders, hips and knees. You can also place crystals on your chakras or hold them in your hands to really soak in their healing qualities. A crystal grid will surround you with powerful energetic healing, working on you physically, mentally, emotionally and spiritually. Different ways of doing this will be covered in Part 2.

45

◆ Wearing Your Crystals ◆

One of the simplest ways to connect with the energies of your chosen crystal daily is to wear it, most commonly in the form of jewellery like necklaces, rings and bracelets. I find it so comforting to wear my crystal every day and often find myself holding it without realising, especially when I need guidance or support. You can buy jewellery ready-made or purchase little wire holders that you can place any crystal in yourself. Alternatively, many crystal shops and suppliers can wire wrap your chosen crystal for you. You can even wear them in your bra if you want them to be really close!

◆ Holding Crystals for Support ◆

Finally, you can choose to simply hold crystals and take a few long, slow, deep breaths to connect with their energies whenever you need to. I have a piece of lemurian quartz to allow me to connect to a higher wisdom and knowledge, and I hold it when I record a meditation or deliver a workshop, Instagram Live or coaching session. Other times, I may hold a piece of rose quartz if I need to connect to my heart or black tourmaline if I need to ground. Those few moments of purposefully connecting your energy with your crystals may be all you need to set you up for the rest of the day.

CHAPTER 5:

Time to Say Goodbye

Just as with any relationship in life, there may be times when your work with your crystal is done and your journey together has come to an end. Crystals often know much sooner when this is than we do; as humans, we are never very good at endings and letting go. When this happens your crystal may break, or just simply disappear. It is sad, but please don't see it as a sign of anything bad. Your crystal just loved you enough to know when it was time to let go.

I used to have a piece of angelite that would regularly disappear on me for months at a time and turn up in the strangest of places, like a dressing gown pocket, for example. It would always seem like it had showed up at exactly the right time as a reminder to reconnect back to my guides for the answers I was looking for. So if a crystal disappears, don't panic. It may be that it has done its work and taken itself away, or that it will show up again when you need its energy the most.

Crystals are often like little guardian angels turning up at just the right time, and in just the right way.

If a crystal breaks clean in half or into useable pieces, please continue to use it, trusting that it was meant to be in different pieces to do its best work. I once bought a beautiful, large pink amethyst geode and as soon as I took it out of the packaging, it leaped out of my hands, on to the table, and broke into two pieces. I had a human moment of being so upset, but then I realised that's how this crystal had always meant to come to me. It looked perfect in its two parts and I could no longer imagine it whole. Now I have one piece in the bedroom and one in the living room, so its energies fill more of my home.

If a crystal completely shatters, I see it as a sign that the work we did together is completed, the lessons are learned, the blockages are released, the issues have been worked through. Even if you can't see any physical manifestation of the work just yet, trust and believe that the work this crystal was doing with you has happened. And please don't panic, thinking that a broken crystal means that any areas of your life you were working on with it are broken, too; they are not. It just means that the crystal has done what it needed to do in relation to that life area and it may be that you now need another one with a slightly different purpose to take you further, or just that you need to be patient and allow the magic to unfold. It is the crystal's time to return to the earth, so I give love and gratitude for the work we did together and bury broken crystals back in the ground.

Alternatively, it might be you who feels as though your journey with a crystal has come to an end. You may not be drawn to hold or use your crystal any more or feel the same vibes from it as you once did, and this too is ok. In fact, it's more than ok, as it shows that on some level you know you have healed or learned or experienced what you needed to with this crystal.

Crystals come in and out of our lives to teach us what they need to teach us. When this happens, consider gifting your crystal to someone else. Just because it has finished its work with you, that's not to say it doesn't still have work to do with someone else. You may sit and hold the crystal and see who comes to mind or notice if any of your friends speak to you about issues you know this crystal would be beneficial for. Very often, the crystal/universe will help you to guide it to exactly the right place. Then cleanse your crystal, take a moment to give thanks for the journey and maybe even reflect on any lessons learned, before sending it with love to its new home to continue its magic.

◆ ◆ ◆

Now we've learned all we need to know about choosing, caring for, cleansing, programming and, of course, working with your crystals, let's move on to Part 2 to see how you can bring the power and magic of crystals into all the different areas of your life.

PART 2:

Making Crystals a Part of Your Life

Next, we are going to move into how to use the magic of crystals to support you in all different spheres of your life.

This section covers all the main life areas that I am asked frequently about, along with those that I have personally used crystals in over the years. Within each section I offer suggestions for the different crystals and recommended colours to use, as well as the related chakras to work with. I also provide ideas for meditations, visualisations, affirmations, grids and ways in which to deepen your crystal magic in each area.

There may be days when you need gentle soothing and other days when you need a little more of a kick in the right direction, and you will learn which crystal holds the energy for what you need. You will also find that the more you work with your chosen crystals, the deeper your connection with them and the more they can work with you. Over time, you will learn to trust in the wisdom of your body, energy and intuition and begin to know the best crystal for you in times of need.

Remember that it's better to begin with just a small selection of crystals (see p. 33). And with this in mind, I have tried, where possible, to use the same crystals in a few different sections, so that you can get the most out of them. Each holds a number of properties and so can be used for different things, depending on your needs.

CHAPTER 6:

Crystals for . . . the Chakras

We've touched on chakras already, but here we're going to go much deeper into what they are and how we can work with them. So let's get a brief understanding of them before we go any further.

Chakras are energy centres within the body. Often described as a spinning wheel of energy that is continually receiving, processing and expressing information from the world in and around us, there are seven main chakras in the body, and each relates to a different physical, emotional, psychological and spiritual aspect of our being.

The chakras are our inner universe and help to keep us balanced in body, mind, heart and soul. Just like crystals, each chakra vibrates to its own energy frequency and spins at its own pace. When our chakras are balanced and aligned, we feel connected to ourselves and in flow with life. However, they can begin to spin out of balance and, when they do, we tend to feel stuck, stagnant or closed off in certain areas of ourselves and our lives. Using crystals is a wonderful way to balance the energies in your body and bring your chakras back into alignment.

If you are feeling out of alignment in any of the areas associated with a particular chakra, it may be time for a little crystal TLC. Each chakra is associated with a different colour, and so one of the simplest ways to use crystals with your chakras is by using one that's the same colour as the chakra you want to balance.

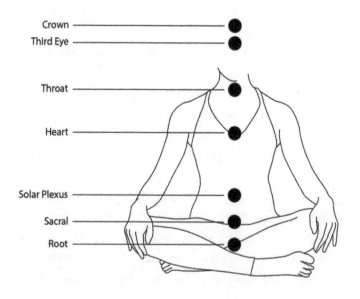

Or, if you want to go deeper into a particular area, you could also use crystals specific to what each chakra is associated with. We will cover all this in more detail in the following chapters. For now, here are some suggested crystals and a bit more information about each chakra to get you started.

Root chakra
Located: at the base of the spine
Colour: red
Associated with: feeling grounded, safe and secure in life; having all of your basic needs met – from physical to financial and emotional; feeling connected to your physical body and the earth
Crystals: red crystals, such as red jasper, bloodstone or garnet

Sacral chakra
Located: just beneath the belly button
Colour: orange
Associated with: emotional wellbeing and regulation; the ability to feel and process your feelings; relationships and sexuality and how we relate to others; creativity, pleasure, play and enjoyment of life
Crystals: orange crystals, such as carnelian, fire opal or amber

Solar-plexus chakra

Located: just beneath the rib cage

Colour: yellow

Associated with: your personal power, beliefs and identity; drive, willpower and taking control of the direction of your life and being able to trust and follow your own guidance

Crystals: yellow crystals, such as citrine, tiger's eye or yellow jasper

Heart chakra

Located: in the centre of the chest

Colour: pink or green

Associated with: all forms of love, from self-love to love for others; acceptance and forgiveness; connection to life and the world around you

Crystals: pink crystals, such as rose quartz or kunzite; green crystals such as jade and aventurine

Throat chakra

Located: at the base of the throat

Colour: light blue

Associated with: communication and your ability to express yourself and your needs and desires; staying true to yourself and speaking your truth

Crystals: blue crystals, such as blue lace agate, lapis lazuli or kyanite

Third-eye chakra

Located: on the forehead, just above and between the eyebrows

Colour: indigo

Associated with: intuition and spiritual awareness; being able to 'see' beyond what the physical eyes can see and vision the future; inner wisdom and knowing

Crystals: indigo crystals, such as sodalite, azurite or labradorite

Crown chakra

Located: at the crown of your head

Colour: violet

Associated with: consciousness and connection to higher guidance, the universe and divine (or whatever name you give to it) unity

Crystals: violet/purple crystals, such as amethyst, sugilite and lepidolite

Note: clear/white crystals, such as clear quartz, selenite and apophyllite, are also sometimes associated with the crown chakra, but can also be used to balance all of the chakras.

◆ Crystal Chakra Meditation ◆

One of the simplest ways to bring your chakras back into balance using crystals is to enjoy a crystal chakra meditation. Simply choose a corresponding-coloured crystal for one or every chakra, lie down comfortably and place the relevant crystal on the appropriate chakra, as follows:

- ❖ **Root:** just above the pubic bone or off the body between the legs

- ❖ **Sacral:** between the hip bones, just beneath the belly button

- ❖ **Solar plexus:** between the lower ribs and belly button

- ❖ **Heart:** at the centre of your chest

- ❖ **Throat:** at the base of your throat

- ❖ **Third eye:** between the eyebrows

- ❖ **Crown:** off the body right above your head

You may follow a guided meditation, set a timer for 10–15 minutes or play some relaxing music, as you focus on your breathing: take really long, slow, deep breaths, following the flow of your inhale and exhale; visualise bringing energy into your chakras with each inhale and releasing anything that is blocked or stuck with each exhale. You could also visualise each chakra – one at a time, for a few breaths from the root to the crown – and feel the healing energy of the crystals doing their work and each chakra cleansing and balancing.

If a crystal falls off during the meditation, don't worry – it doesn't mean it's not working. Just replace it, if that feels right, or leave it. It's your choice; you can't get this wrong. However, I would say that if you replace it and it falls off a second time, it's best to leave it and trust that the energy and crystals know what they are doing and that chakra has got what it needed.

Make sure that you cleanse your crystals (see p. 27) after you have finished. You can enjoy this meditation as often as and whenever you like (maybe make it a weekly act of self-care), but especially when you feel out of sorts, out of balance or not aligned in yourself.

Crystals for . . . Love and Relationships

Crystals are one of your greatest companions when it comes to the journey of love. Whether it's for self-love, healing from love, welcoming love or deepening existing love, there is a crystal out there just waiting to support you.

I am going to give you lots of crystal ideas for love in this chapter, but you'll hear me mention rose quartz a lot, as it is the crystal of universal, unconditional love and is one of the best for whatever you need when it comes to love. You can also work with any pink and/ or green crystals, paying attention to or placing or wearing your chosen crystal over your heart chakra.

◆ Self-love ◆

It's impossible to truly love anyone else or allow anyone else to truly love you until you love yourself. If you ever struggle with self-love or lack of self-worth, self-care or not feeling worthy or deserving, rose quartz needs to become your best friend.

Rose quartz

Rose quartz carries a beautiful, loving, feminine energy that helps to heal and open your heart and allow love in. I would always suggest wearing rose quartz, especially when you begin your self-love or crystal journey, so that you can connect to those loving vibes at all times. If you can find a necklace that goes over your heart, even better.

Another powerful way to work with rose quartz is to hold a piece while repeating self-love affirmations, and if you can look at yourself in the mirror while doing this, it will be even more powerful. Set an intention on your piece of rose quartz for self-love and then hold it as you repeat your affirmations daily. These might include the following:

❧ 'I love and approve of myself.'

❧ 'I am perfect just as I am.'

❧ 'I am enough.'

Carry your rose quartz with you as a self-love reminder or put it in a special place throughout the day – perhaps even over a picture of yourself or in a grid (see p. 41 and below) – where it will continue to amplify your self-love vibes and bring you more self-love each time you connect with it.

Hold a piece of rose quartz in your receiving hand while you meditate and sense the energy of love flowing into and filling your entire body. Or lie back and place a piece of rose quartz on your heart chakra and feel the crystal lovingly and gently open your heart to more unconditional self-love.

Magnesite

One of my all-time favourite crystals is magnesite, a crystal that is so powerful for teaching you about self-love. It can remind you of your value and worth and instils a sense of confidence in you, allowing you to believe in and love yourself enough to create anything you desire in your life. It helps you to get to know and love the authentic you and, in doing so, ensures that you don't abandon or lose yourself – especially when it comes to relationships (this makes it an exceptional crystal for those of you who tend to do that). Carry around a piece of magnesite to feel the power of this soothing, loving crystal.

Self-love grids

In times when you really need to be infused with self-love you can create a self-love grid by surrounding yourself with pieces of rose quartz, magnesite, some quartz points and any of the crystals in this section. Place a piece of rose quartz over your heart and the others around your body, even holding one in each hand. I would suggest having some of the quartz points facing inwards to direct the flow of loving energy towards you, and you could even place a few turned out for releasing anything that stands in the way of you loving yourself fully and completely. Lie down within this grid for as long as you need to, soaking in the loving vibes. See this as time well spent, truly taking time for *you*, as an act of self-love and care.

Other crystals for self-love: rhodochrosite, rhodonite, carnelian and pink tourmaline.

◆ Healing from Love ◆

If you know that you have closed off your heart and that you have some healing to do from past relationships and hurts, crystals can help you not only to heal, but to provide powerful insights that will allow you to move on. You can carry any of the suggested crystals with you, holding them in times of need, or meditate with them to take advantage of their powerful healing properties.

In times of real heartbreak or when you need some deep heart healing, lie down within a healing grid (as described in the self-love grid) but this time using the suggested crystals below. Place your quartz points facing out for the release of heartbreak, hurt and emotional wounds. As you lie there, bring your awareness to your heart and feel as though you are breathing in and out through your heart. Absorb the healing energies of the crystals into your heart with each inhale and, as you exhale, soften your heart, allowing any hurt, pain, anger, sadness or resentment to release and dissolve. Visualise the crystals holding and supporting you, surrounding you in healing and love and soothing your pain.

Rhodochrosite

If you find yourself in the same situations in love, over and over again, rhodochrosite will help you to learn your lessons. It's a wonderful crystal for moving on after rejection and working through any painful emotions without closing off your heart. This is also a powerful crystal if you need to forgive. Remember that forgiveness does not mean that you are saying what someone did was ok, but rather that you are no longer willing to carry it around in your heart. Rhodochrosite will help you to release the pain and open your heart to forgive both others and yourself, if needs be.

Malachite

Malachite is a powerful crystal for grief and heartbreak. It works with your heart, bringing deep emotional healing. It can also keep you out of the past and constantly wandering down the relationship memory lane, so allowing you to let go. Known as the transformation crystal, malachite will encourage you to take your heartbreak, learn from it and open your heart to a new relationship adventure when you are ready. It's incredibly powerful, so use with care. Perhaps work first with other, more gentle crystals – such as rose quartz or rhodochrosite (above) – moving on to malachite once you feel a little more emotionally stable and are ready for that push to move you forward into deep healing.

Apache tears

Wonderful crystals for grief, heartbreak or times of emotional crisis, ancient legend has it that apache tears were formed by a group of strong women mourning a huge loss, and that they cried enough tears for all those who mourn. This crystal brings a comforting, soothing energy, while helping you to heal emotional wounds and grieve the past or, as is often the case when a relationship ends, an imagined future.

Dioptase

This is one of the most supportive crystals for the heart, emotionally and spiritually. It is powerful for healing old wounds and resentment you have held on to when it comes to relationships. It helps you to find compassion (for yourself) and to forgive and let go, especially when there has been betrayal or abandonment. If you feel stuck in terms of love, in particular after past hurts, it is great for moving forward.

Other crystals for healing from love: Rose quartz, morganite, rainbow obsidian or pink amethyst (you may also want to try the letting-go exercise on p. 122).

◆ Welcoming in Love ◆

Crystals can be an incredible wing (wo)man when it comes to attracting love into your life.

One of the simplest ways is to take some time to get very clear on what you want from the relationship in question and write it all down. Then take a raw piece of rose quartz (but tumbled will do if it's all you have), hold the crystal to your heart and read your list to the crystal, asking for help in attracting this love to you. Once you have finished, place your rose quartz (with your love list underneath, if you wish) in the relationship corner of your home or bedroom – this is the farthest right-hand corner as you stand with your back to the door. Your rose quartz will then go to work in helping you to attract this love into your life. You can also create a crystal grid here for manifesting your love to you. To do so, add more rose quartz and/or the suggested crystals below to your central piece of rose quartz and, if you like, some clear quartz points – facing inwards – for drawing the love that you desire to you.

Or try setting intentions on the crystals below, asking them to support you in bringing the love you want and deserve into your life. You can hold them while you meditate to amplify your intentions and call that love into your life, or place them over your heart, feeling them open it, ready to receive this new love. Wearing or carrying them with you somewhere on your body, especially when out in social settings, will open you up more to the love you are looking for.

Pink amethyst

One of my favourite crystals for working with the heart and believing in love is the newly discovered pink amethyst. This beautiful-looking crystal radiates divine love that you can feel from simply looking at it and, to me, it feels as though I get to glimpse into my own heart when gazing at it. Pink amethyst is also linked to the womb, helping you to tune into the wisdom and creative energies of your womb space, drawing new love to you. It is a deeply healing crystal that will enable you to trust and believe in love and allow it into your life and heart once more.

Citrine

If you want to have some fun and explore the dating scene, try wearing citrine to help let your inner light and beauty shine out into the world with confidence. You'll be sure to turn heads.

Tiger's eye and malachite

Tiger's eye is good for boldness and bravery and putting yourself out there in the dating world, while malachite will help you to show up as your authentic self and love yourself enough to know what you deserve, so that you can see immediate red flags.

Jade

Wonderful for attracting love into your life and also friendships, jade is a protective crystal that supports you not only in finding new love, but also in gently opening your heart in preparation, allowing you to become aware of any ways in which you are blocking love from coming in.

Kunzite

Kunzite is a crystal of divine love and holds a loving high vibration for connecting you to the love that is always surrounding you. Love is almost certainly on its way to you when you work with kunzite, as this crystal helps you to awaken your heart, trust in love and to freely express your feelings when it comes to matters of the heart.

Rhodochrosite

This is one of the best crystals for attracting love, and especially for calling in those relationships you need to help teach you important and valuable lessons about love in this lifetime – those soulmate relationships. Rhodochrosite will work to open your heart to possibilities and opportunities in love, and also bring out your flirty and playful side, giving you the confidence to be seen. A must-have for all the singles out there.

Twin quartz

If it is deep, soulmate love that you are yearning for, get a twin quartz. This is a pair of crystals of similar size that grow side by side from the same base (with separate points). As the name suggests, this crystal will help to draw your soulmate to you.

Other crystals for welcoming in love: Larimar, rhodonite, rose quartz or pink topaz.

◆ Deepening Existing Love ◆

Once you've found love, crystals can help you to deepen your connection, encourage loyalty and honesty, open your communication and take your love and romance to ever deeper levels.

Emerald
Often called the crystal of successful love, this is a go-to crystal for faith, loyalty and unity. Helping to bring partners closer together and create a deep love connection, it is wonderful to use in the beginning of a new relationship or when you feel that you want to deepen the connection in an existing one.

Rose quartz
With its loving energy, rose quartz in your bedroom will raise the love vibrations. Place rose quartz by the bedside, or you can 'grid' your bed for love by placing a piece at each corner of the bed or underneath it to keep your love and lovemaking sacred and intimate. Rose quartz can also strengthen communication and trust between partners.

Rhodonite
To overcome any difficulties in your relationship, try working with rhodonite. Sometimes referred to as the

rescue stone, it is known for its emotional healing. Rhodonite works with your heart, so that you can see your partner with love, bringing acceptance, forgiveness, compassion and open, honest communication. Meditate with a piece of rhodonite in your hand or over your heart and ask for the crystal's assistance in overcoming issues and resolving problems with love. You may also hold your rhodonite when in conversation with your partner so that you speak from your heart (rather than reacting from your mind), communicating from a place of love.

Sugilite
Try working with the 'premier love stone' sugilite to deepen your bond with your partner, while allowing you both the freedom to be yourselves. It supports and deepens love and commitment through good times and bad, helping you to grow through the experiences together. It encourages loving communication and deep, true love.

Garnet, red jasper and carnelian
If you want to invite more sexual intimacy into your relationship, keep pieces of the following in the bedroom or as part of a grid around your bed, too: garnet can bring the desire, passion and spark back, while red jasper or carnelian will reignite the flames

of passion and help to recharge the sacral chakra, increasing sexual desire.

Other crystals for deepening existing love: Chrysoprase, amazonite, lapis lazuli or ruby.

CHAPTER 8:

Crystals for . . . Stress and Anxiety

Crystals can be wonderful companions in times when you find yourself overwhelmed, stressed or anxious. Simply holding your chosen crystal and taking ten slow, deep, mindful breaths can often be enough to bring you back into the present moment.

If you find yourself mentally stressed and over-whelmed, work with indigo/dark blue crystals, placing them on your third-eye chakra. If it's your emotions that need some calming, orange crystals over your sacral chakra should do the job. You may also want to include red or grounding crystals on your root chakra to help you ground in times of stress and uncertainty.

Take a look at the calming crystals below and the ways in which you can use them to bring peace of mind, to soothe and balance your frazzled nerves and to bring you calm in times of chaos.

◆ Calming the Mind ◆

Crystals can offer incredible support for those times when you find yourself trapped in your mind, over-thinking, questioning everything or not able to make sense of the jumble of thoughts in your head.

Sodalite

This is one of the first crystals I will always suggest in stressful times of need. Often referred to as the crystal of peace, it helps to calm the mind and is especially useful when you find your thoughts spiralling out of control and you can't make sense of anything. One of the best ways to use sodalite is to carry a piece around with you and hold it in moments when you begin to feel anxious. It's like holding hands with a good friend, and you'll immediately feel its comforting, calming support.

If you know that you are going into a situation or environment that makes you anxious, meditate beforehand holding a piece of sodalite in one hand and focus on your breath as you imagine drawing the calming energies of the crystal in through your hand, up through your arm and into your mind. Feel as though your mind becomes filled with calming, peaceful vibes. You can then send these vibes down into your heart and through your whole body, until your entire being feels calm, peaceful and relaxed. Imagine yourself surrounded by a bubble of peaceful protection.

Fluorite

If you find yourself constantly overthinking every situation or decision, to the point where you end up doing nothing, fluorite is for you. Often called the genius stone, fluorite is great for organising and structuring your thoughts, thinking more clearly and making decisions, especially when under pressure. Try combining it with journaling or a brain dump (where you spill all the contents of your mind out on to paper). Hold a piece of fluorite while writing everything down or when looking back over what you have written, and you may just find its energies will help you to see things much more clearly.

Other crystals for calming the mind: Blue calcite, amethyst, lepidolite or celestite.

Note: at times when you feel your mind is in anxious overdrive, try lying down and placing one of the above crystals on your third-eye area. Lie there for as long as you need to, feeling the energies of the crystal soaking into your mind, bringing calming, soothing, peaceful vibes. Try exhaling out of your mouth, visualising the exhale and crystal working together to release uncertainty, anxiety and the jumble of thoughts in your mind.

◆ Releasing Stuck Thought Patterns ◆

If you find yourself constantly ruminating over the same past events or worrying over an imagined future, stuck in negative thought patterns, crystals can help.

Amethyst

I would suggest using amethyst as a first choice, as it helps release negative thoughts from the mind. If you can use an amethyst point or pyramid, it will be even more powerful. Either sitting or lying down, place your amethyst over your third eye with the point facing away from you. Close your eyes, breathe deeply and visualise the crystal drawing all unwanted and negative thoughts out of your mind. See them floating up into the universe where they will be transmuted and transformed into sparkly new energy.

78

Other crystals for releasing stuck thought patterns:
A clear quartz point, black tourmaline or kyanite.

◆ Soothing the Emotions ◆

In times of emotional turmoil or when you are caught
in a worry or fear spiral, crystals can help you to
acknowledge, accept, process and heal your emotions,
bringing you inner calm and peace.

Moonstone
Moonstone is wonderful if your emotions are spiralling
out of control. With its feminine, nurturing energies,
moonstone works to balance and calm the emotions. In
particular, if you often find yourself emotionally overre-
acting or not being able to make sense of your emotions,
moonstone will help you to process and heal them, rather
than repressing or supressing them to the point that
they become explosive. Moonstone is particularly useful
for balancing hormones and for those times of the month
when emotions seem to become overwhelming.

Carry moonstone with you and hold it whenever you
feel your emotions rising. You can also meditate with it,
either holding it in your hands or placing a piece over
your heart and/or sacral chakra, allowing the calming
effects to soak into your emotional body. As you meditate,

try inhaling slowly through the nose, as deeply as you can, pausing for a moment and then taking a long, slow, deep exhale out of the mouth, visualising the release of pent-up emotions. You may even add sounds – like a deep sigh, hiss or blowing out of your mouth – to consciously breathe out anger, frustration, sadness or any other overwhelming emotions you may be feeling. Place a couple of quartz points pointing away from you around your body to bring a deep, emotional cleanse at times when you feel really emotionally overwhelmed.

Amazonite

Amazonite is another must-have crystal for your emotions, helping to soothe them in times of emotional turmoil or when all you can feel is worry or fear. This calming crystal brings a sense of balance and peace, helping you to flow with your emotions rather than fight with them.

Kunzite

This beautiful pink crystal is a powerful emotional healer. Kunzite will wrap you in a nurturing, calming and loving energy, soothing your head and heart, especially in the heat of the moment or when emotions feel out of control or overwhelming.

Other crystals for soothing the emotions: Morganite, rose quartz, amethyst or howlite.

◆ Releasing Deeply Held Emotions ◆

Very often, we supress, deny or don't deal with emotions and they become deeply held within us. This is when emotional outbursts or uncontrollable reactions happen, or when we tend to find ourselves stuck in the same emotional patterns over and over again. Working with crystals can help you to uncover and release these deep emotional attachments.

Kyanite blades

If you find that you are carrying around a lot of anger or other intense emotions that you can't seem to let go of, try working with kyanite blades. The blade helps to cut through anger, frustration and stress and to remove emotional hooks and attachments. Often, we continue to be sucked into emotions about a certain situation, person or event as we are still energetically attached to it, which keeps replaying the emotions within us.

Lie down with your arms and legs stretched out as much as is comfortable for you. Take six blue or black kyanite blades (or a mix) and place them around your body: one at the crown of your head, one by your feet and one at each elbow and knee. Lying down with your eyes closed, allow yourself to be drawn to wherever in your body you feel the intensity of the emotion you are feeling and/or any energetic attachments. This may be felt as an intense sensation of the emotion itself, a little tingle, warmth or just that you are more aware of this part of your body. As you focus, visualise any energetic and emotional attachments releasing themselves from your body. Feel the power and energy of the kyanite blades drawing them away. You may even see them float off into space or back to wherever they came from.

You may also add crystals to your third eye (see 'Calming the Mind', p. 78) if your thoughts have also been in emotional overdrive, or to your heart (see 'Healing from Love', p. 65) and/or sacral chakra (see above suggestions) to help with further releasing deep emotion.

Other crystals for releasing deeply held emotions: Malachite, kunzite, apache tears or smoky quartz.

Note: see also Chapter 9 ('Crystals for . . . Energy Clearing and Protection') for information on how to cleanse your energy daily with crystals to keep you free from emotional and energetic cords and attachments.

◆ **Grounding on the Earth** ◆

A powerful way to manage any emotions, stress and anxiety is to connect to the support, safety and grounding of the earth and release back to it any overwhelming thoughts and feelings to be healed and transmuted.

To do this, stand with one of the crystals mentioned below in each hand. If you can use a smoky quartz point with the point facing down towards the earth, so much the better, but any grounding crystal will do. Now, close your eyes if that feels good, and take a moment to feel your feet on the earth and notice how you feel. Take a long, slow, deep inhale and, as you exhale, imagine any overwhelming thoughts, emotions, concerns, worries, fears, etc. draining out of your mind, down through your heart, belly, body, and legs and out through the soles of your feet down into the earth beneath you. Continue for as long as you need to – until a feeling of calm comes over you – letting go of anything unwanted. You can also do this seated, but make sure that your feet are on the earth.

Alternatively, create a grounding healing grid by making a circle of any of the crystals mentioned below. Once again, you can use smoky quartz points, if you have any, with the points facing away from you to draw off emotion, anxiety and worry. Once you have finished setting up your grid, sit in the centre of the circle of crystals, holding a grounding crystal in each hand. Close your eyes and, as you stay there and breathe deeply and calmly, feel as though these crystals are lovingly absorbing all your emotions, worries, cares, concerns, stress and anxiety and releasing them into the earth. Feel these crystals creating a defensive barrier around you, shielding you from any unwanted energies. Feel grounded and protected in this safe space.

You can also wear or carry your grounding crystals with you, using them as a touchstone to remind you of the earth's support in times of overwhelm. Or meditate with them daily to help keep you connected to the earth and release unwanted energies, emotions, worries or stress.

Smoky quartz

Smoky quartz is one of the best crystals for helping to release negative energy, stress and anxiety. With its cleansing and detoxing properties, it will encourage you to release mental, emotional and energetic baggage and anything unwanted that you no longer need, gently absorbing them from you. It's a powerfully grounding and protective crystal that anchors you to the earth and provides a sense of stability.

Hematite

One of the best crystals to use at times when life feels chaotic and uncertain and you feel unsettled and overwhelmed, hematite will strengthen your connection to the earth, helping you to build a strong foundation within yourself and making you feel grounded, centred and safe. Hematite will work to protect you, drawing away any unwanted energy and feelings of worry or anxiety.

Other crystals for grounding on the earth: Black tourmaline, red jasper, fire agate or obsidian.

◆ Keeping Your Environment ◆ Calm and Peaceful

Crystals in your environment can be great for soothing the mind, emotions and nervous system – absorbing any negative energies, while sending out positive vibes, so that you feel at once more relaxed and at ease.

Apophyllite

I always have a piece of apophyllite in my living space. It is one of the best transmitters of energy and helps to cleanse a room and raise the vibrations to a high frequency.

Clear quartz

Clear quartz clusters are incredibly healing. Known as the master healer, clear quartz will absorb and regulate the energy, radiating positive energy out into your space.

Amethyst and rose quartz

Try an amethyst cluster or chunks of rose quartz to send loving, soothing, calming vibes through the entire room.

Black tourmaline

If you find that you come home from work (or anywhere else) feeling stressed or out of sorts, place a piece of black tourmaline by your front door. Then pause there as you walk in the house and feel the energies of the black tourmaline capture and release any stresses or anxieties you are carrying, leaving your worries at the door. You may visualise this as a shimmery black waterfall at your door that cleanses and washes your day away.

> **Note**: see also see Chapter 11 ('Crystals for . . . Work and Business') for ways to keep your workplace productive and zen and Chapter 9 ('Crystals for . . . Energy Clearing and Protection') for protecting your home.

Other crystals for keeping your environment calm and peaceful: selenite, celestite, citrine or smoky quartz.

Worry crystals/stones

The origins of these have been traced back to ancient Greece, but they have recently made a comeback and have been termed 'pocket tranquillisers'. They are smooth crystals that have either been shaped or naturally have a thumb-sized indentation in them. Holding the crystal between your first two fingers and thumb, you place your thumb in the indentation and gently rub it across the crystal to calm and clear your mind and ease stress and anxiety.

Keep your worry crystal in your pocket and use it as a physical touchstone any time you need it to remind you to take long, slow, deep breaths and be in the present moment, seeking the support you need from it. Choose your touchstone based on what you most need it for – for example: amethyst is first choice for anxiety and soothing the mind; rose quartz when you want to be surrounded by a loving presence; or tiger's eye for grounding and calming.

I often find that when I am choosing crystals, I pick them for how they feel as I hold them in my hands. I usually naturally find that it's where my thumb fits on the crystal that matters most.

◆ Self-care in Stressful Times ◆

A final reminder here that in times of stress and anxiety we tend to forget all about taking care of ourselves and, as this happens, the feelings of anxiety, stress and overwhelm get worse. In any times of overwhelm, keep some rose quartz nearby to remind you to love and take care of yourself. In times of anxiety, place rose quartz over your heart and take some long, slow, deep breaths to remind you to nurture and care and have compassion for yourself as you work through any difficult thoughts or emotions.

CHAPTER 9:

Crystals for . . .
Energy Clearing and Protection

As we move around through day-to-day life our energies can get out of balance, making us feel disconnected, out of alignment and even down, unmotivated and overly emotional.

When our own energy isn't balanced and protected, we are more likely to leak it and/or take on that of our environments and other people – which is why you can often feel out of sorts or drained after time with certain people or in certain places.

Have a look through all the ways below that you can keep your energy clear and your vibes high. I have also included in this section some crystals that work to protect your home and keep you protected when travelling.

◆ Clear Your Energy ◆

The crystals below will help you to clear your aura and chakras of any trapped or stuck energy or emotions, remove any energetic cords and release anything you are carrying that isn't yours.

Selenite

Using a selenite wand daily will help you to cleanse your aura and remove any energetic or emotional attachments that you have picked up, keeping you balanced, grounded and protected. I usually do this at the end of each day, as though I am clearing the day out of my energy field:

❖ Stand with your feet hip-distance apart, so that you feel deeply rooted and grounded.

❖ Holding your selenite in one hand, close your eyes and take a few long, slow, deep breaths, just feeling into how your energy feels at the end of the day (or whenever you feel out of sorts).

❖ Beginning at the crown of your head, 'comb' the selenite through your energy field, all around the front, back and sides of your body, as though you are brushing your aura clean.

❖ Visualise removing any unwanted energy or emotion, as well as any attachments or cords that have been created through the day.

❖ When you have finished, you can move the selenite down the front of your body, from your crown to your root chakra, to cleanse all your chakras.

Clear quartz

This is another perfect crystal for clearing your energies of any clutter. It will help to absorb and release any unwanted energy, aligning your chakras and energy bodies and bringing your whole being – body, mind, heart and soul – back into a state of balance. Hold a piece of clear quartz (or any of the crystals mentioned below) as you take long, slow, deep breaths, visualising each exhale carrying away anything unwanted in your energy. You can also place clear quartz points around your body, with the points facing away to draw off any stuck or trapped energies.

Other crystals for clearing your energy: amethyst, fluorite, kyanite or black tourmaline.

Note: see also Chapter 6 ('Crystals for . . . the Chakras') for clearing and balancing your chakras.

◆ Protect Your Energy ◆

Once you've cleared your own energy field, you may want to keep it protected, especially when spending time with certain people or heading into situations and environments that can drain you.

Carry any of the crystals mentioned below with you for protection. Or you can use them in an energy grid that you sit or stand inside on days when you know you are going to need some extra protection: placing the crystals in a circle, sit or stand inside the grid, stay here, or even meditate here for 5 to 10 minutes, feeling the crystals create an energetic field that surrounds and protects you.

Black tourmaline

My go-to for protecting my energy is black tourmaline. Wear this crystal when you are out and about or heading into draining situations to create a shield of protection around you that nothing can penetrate. If my energy feels off at any time, I touch the tourmaline to strengthen the protection and deflect any unwanted energy coming my way.

Fire agate

Another amazing crystal for building a protective shield around you and deflecting any unwanted energies, fire agate is particularly powerful if you ever have to head into situations of conflict or when you feel that people are sending unwarranted judgement or criticism your way. Fire agate helps to return any harm to its original source so that the person responsible can learn from it. Wear or hold your crystal and imagine a shield around your energy. You can also place it by the windows of your home if you have issues with neighbours.

Jet

If you find that you often take on other people's moods or energies, jet will act as an energetic filter, working to keep these out of your aura.

Labradorite

Labradorite is powerful for making sure there is a protective boundary between you and other people's emotions and energies. It is especially useful to wear or have with you around those people who always want something from you and drain your energy reserves.

Other crystals for protecting your energy: obsidian, jasper, smoky quartz, hematite or amethyst.

◆ Protection for Your Home ◆

Having crystals around your home will help to keep the energy of your home cleansed and protected. Crystals can also make excellent security guards to help ensure your home is a safe haven.

Selenite
I always have a selenite tower in my home to clear and protect the energy of where I live. Selenite helps to absorb negative emotions and energy and cleanses the environment. Try gridding your room or home with a selenite tower in each corner to create a protective energetic shield around your living space.

Black tourmaline
You can further protect the energy of your home by placing black tourmaline either with your selenite or by itself by your front door. Similar to asking people to take off their shoes to keep your house clean, black tourmaline will work to draw off any negative energy as people enter your space.

Note: you may also try placing crystals by your Wi-Fi router, TV, computers and other electronic devices to help shield you and your home from EMF (electromagnetic fields). I have always kept a piece of black tourmaline next to my TV, selenite by my computer and shungite on top of my Wi-Fi router.

Other crystals for protecting your home: rose quartz, citrine, apophyllite or clear quartz.

◆ Protection for Travel ◆

Crystals make perfect travel companions to help keep you protected, stress-free and calm and relaxed on your journey.

Black kyanite and black tourmaline
I always keep a piece of black kyanite in my car to protect me and keep me safe on the road. You can use black tourmaline, too, which is also powerful for deflecting any road rage sent your way.

Moonstone and amethyst
Moonstone has long been known as the traveller's stone and so is one of your best companions on your travels.

Carry a piece with you at all times to ensure a smooth journey and protection on your travels, especially when travelling over water. It will also help you to overcome symptoms of jetlag more quickly and easily.

If travelling makes you anxious, take amethyst with you to soothe and calm your nerves. A highly protective crystal, amethyst will wrap you in a loving bubble of protection on your journey, working to alleviate travel sickness.

Both moonstone and amethyst will help not only to protect you, but also your luggage, so make sure you pack a piece, too.

Malachite

Malachite is often gifted to airline workers as a talisman to protect them when flying. If you're scared of flying, hold a piece of malachite throughout the journey, or especially at take-off and landing, to keep your fears and anxieties at bay and protect you during the flight.

Other crystals for protection for travel: tiger's eye, rose quartz, smoky quartz or clear quartz.

CHAPTER 10:

Crystals for . . . Manifesting and Abundance

When it comes to manifesting and abundance, crystals are your go-to support squad for supercharging your wishes and bringing abundance in all areas of your life.

Yellow crystals over your solar-plexus chakra can be helpful in lighting up your personal power and making you magnetic to all you wish to manifest. A crystal pyramid is a wonderful choice for manifesting, as the point beams your intentions out into the world, while the base anchors them in reality.

◆ Manifest Your Desires ◆

The crystals below will work with you to make you magnetic to all that you desire and to beam your intentions out into the world, bringing them more easily to life.

Clear quartz

One of your first choices for manifesting should be clear quartz, which, as the master crystal, can be used to manifest anything and everything. Clear quartz amplifies the energy of any intention, dream or wish that is programmed into it and will continue to draw your desires to you, even when you are not consciously thinking about it.

Clear quartz can also bring clarity to your mind and heart, and therefore your intentions. If you are not certain about the direction of your life or what your dreams or desires are, try meditating with a piece of clear quartz for a few weeks to allow any blockages to be removed and to get crystal clear on your intentions.

Once you have decided what it is that you want to manifest, take some time to connect with your clear quartz and set your intentions. Tell the crystal what you would like it to help you to manifest. Be as clear and specific as you can (you may want to look back at Chapter 4 for more information about how to set intentions with your crystals).

Once you have set your intention on your clear quartz, either carry it around with you or spend some time each day holding it and visualising your life as though your dream has already come true; the more energy and power you can give to your intentions, the more quickly they can manifest into your life.

Clear quartz points and towers can be extremely powerful when sending your intentions out into the world and drawing to you what you desire. Try writing your intentions down and placing them under a clear quartz tower, where it will beam them out into the universe for you. Or place quartz points around your intention-charged clear quartz with the points facing in to draw even more power to your manifestations. Clear quartz points can be placed around any crystal or grid or any of the crystals below that you have set intentions on to bring even more power, energy and magic to your desires. You can even try placing clear quartz points in a circle around yourself with the points facing towards you as you meditate on your intentions and desires, visualising them coming true. The quartz points will help draw towards you all that you need to make your dream a reality.

Manifestation quartz

A small crystal encased in a larger crystal, these – as the name suggests – are incredibly powerful for mani-festing your dreams. They are quite rare, and so slightly harder to come by, but if you have a big dream or desire you want to manifest, keep a look out for this one. Set your intentions on one of these and then meditate holding it each day and watch your dreams come true.

Citrine

Your solar-plexus chakra is your place of personal power from where you magnetise yourself to your dreams and desires, drawing them towards you. Place a piece of citrine over your solar-plexus chakra and spend five to ten minutes breathing into this place of power and allowing the energies of the citrine to supercharge you. Feel the abundance, the manifestation, the magnetism, as though you are easily attracting to yourself all that you desire. You can even add some clear quartz or citrine points around your body, points facing towards you, turning yourself into an even bigger magnet for your dreams and desires.

If there is something big that I want to manifest into my life, I meditate holding a citrine point facing towards me to draw to me all that I desire. You can also hold a citrine point and clear quartz point (or any of the crystals below that resonate with what you want to manifest), while repeating affirmations around your intentions and desires. Either create an affirmation specific to your intention ('I easily and effortlessly manifest my business ideas into reality', for example) or a more generic one ('Everything I desire is coming to me now').

Other crystals for manifesting your desires: rose quartz (for manifesting love), pyrite (for manifesting wealth), blue apatite (for manifesting your ideas into reality), green aventurine (for manifesting new opportunities) and amethyst (for manifesting wisdom and self-awareness).

◆ Opening to Abundance ◆

Work with the magical crystals below to help open you up to receiving the very best that life has to offer; it's time to welcome in the prosperity, joy and happiness that you deserve.

Citrine

Citrine is my abundance crystal of choice. This beautiful little ray of golden sunshine has a vibrant energy and has been dubbed the merchant's stone for the prosperity it attracts.

I always keep a piece of citrine in my purse to attract more money and wealth; you can do the same with a wallet or cash register or anywhere you keep money, to ensure a flow of financial abundance.

I also have a grid of citrine and pyrite in the wealth

corner of my house (this is the farthest left corner of your house or any room as you stand with your back to the door). I write out affirmations of abundance such as 'Money comes to me easily and effortlessly' or 'I am magnetic to money, prosperity and abundance' and place the citrine and pyrite over these affirmations to keep drawing more wealth and abundance into my life. You can also place citrine over notes of money or even write yourself an imaginary cheque for however much you want to attract into your life and let citrine help you to open the flow of abundance.

Remember that abundance isn't just about money. It's joy, happiness, laughter, adventure, connection – it's about being open to and receiving all the good things that the universe has to offer you.

Sunstone

As the name suggests, this beautiful little crystal is filled with the energies of the sun, bringing light, life, energy and joy. If life has lost some of its sparkle, meditate with, wear or carry around a piece of sunstone to help you to see the light. Sunstone is also incredible when it comes to shining your light out into the world.

Amazonite

This brings a playful, childlike energy, encouraging you to let go of all you are trying to control and go with the flow of life. You'll feel hope and optimism and a sense of being open to whatever life has to offer when amazonite is around.

Clear quartz
This is great for reminding you that you are part of something way greater. It will connect you to the universe, your higher self, intuition and guides (see p. 152), helping you to feel expansive and connected to the abundant flow of life and the guidance and wisdom that surround you at all times.

Other crystals for opening to abundance: rose quartz, labradorite, malachite or apophyllite.

◆ Removing Blocks to ◆ Manifesting and Abundance

Manifesting and abundance are a state of mind and it all starts with feeling good about and believing in yourself. You have to believe that you truly deserve to have abundance and prosperity, otherwise you subconsciously refuse and block it. If you find yourself blocked from being able to manifest what you want into your life, try working with the crystals below.

Tiger's eye

This will bring you a confidence boost and a reminder of how powerful and capable you are. It will give you the courage to go after what you truly want.

Chrysocolla

This will remind you of your personal power and bring a hit of motivation to make changes in your life.

Carnelian

As well as helping to raise your sense of self-worth and boost your confidence, carnelian also brings the courage to follow opportunities.

Other crystals for removing blocks to manifesting and abundance: hematite, lapis lazuli, black tourmaline or amethyst.

Note: you may also want to look back over the self-love section (p. 62), how to cleanse your chakras (p. 58) or how to clear and protect your energy (pp. 90–3).

CHAPTER 11:

Crystals for...
Work and Business

Whether you're at the interview stage, dreaming of setting up on your own or wanting to expand in your career or company, crystals can make the perfect business partners. They can also work with office environments and protecting your energy.

◆ Attracting the Right Job, ◆ Career and Clients

Call on the assistance of these hard-working crystals when you want to expand in your career and make yourself seen and heard.

Citrine
When it comes to career success, citrine will act as your own personal recruitment agency. Take some time to

get very clear on what you want from your work or job. What would you be doing each day? How would it feel? How would you contribute and make a difference? If you know the exact career path that you want to take, get as specific as you can and go into as much detail about it as possible. Write it all down and place it underneath a citrine tower, so that the crystal can beam your energetic CV out into the world, working to attract the perfect job for you. You can surround this with citrine (or clear quartz) points facing in to help draw this into your life more quickly.

The same thing can also be done in existing businesses where you want to attract more interest. Take your business card or write down details of ways in which you want to develop your business and place citrine, pyrite and rose quartz on top to bring more business your way. If you want to attract a certain number of new clients, get specific on how many you want. Spend some time meditating with your citrine, letting it know these things. Meditate holding your crystal every day and visualise its bright golden energy coming in through your hands and filling your body. Imagine every cell in your body infused with this golden light and your intention to attract your new clients and business; feel the desire in every part of you. Feel as it fills you up and starts to surround and beam out of you, as though you are an energetic lighthouse, calling and attracting your clients. Imagine them easily seeing and following your bright light to find their way to you. Beam your business out into the world.

Chrysoprase

Hold a piece of chrysoprase when completing application forms or business paperwork. This supportive crystal will help you to believe in your talents and abilities, giving you the confidence and courage that you have what it takes.

Pyrite

This will encourage you to believe in yourself and what you have to offer and to know your value and worth in your career and business. It's a great crystal to hold or meditate with in moments of doubt and when you don't feel worthy of work or success. It will enhance your willpower, boost your confidence and inspire you to get things done.

Aventurine

If you need a lucky break, try meditating with aventurine to open you up to new opportunities in your career and business. This crystal will help you to overcome any doubts or fears and shift your perspective to one of hopeful optimism, enabling you to create your own luck and attract the right job or clients to you.

Other crystals for attracting the right job, career and clients: sunstone, jade, rose quartz or malachite.

◆ Acing the Interview Process ◆

Set an intention on any of the crystals below to help you breeze through the interview process. Meditate with your chosen crystal on the morning of the interview and then keep it close at hand, either by wearing it or keeping it in a pocket throughout. After the interview, while you are waiting for the decision, you can place your crystal inside a grid of clear quartz to keep empowering the process and meditate with it daily, visualising getting the job.

Tiger's eye
If it's a boost of bravery and courage that you need, look no further than tiger's eye. Wear this crystal, hold it or keep it in your pocket or close by during interviews to ensure that you remain grounded, bold and brave throughout. Working with the solar-plexus chakra, tiger's eye will ensure that you allow the very best of you to shine, bringing out the most confident and empowered version of you.

Sodalite

Sodalite will not only help to calm your nerves, but also to communicate effectively. As it brings peace and clarity to your mind, it will work to organise your thoughts and help you to speak clearly and confidently when answering questions. As it also encourages you to access your intuitive mind, it is great for bypassing nerves and the monkey mind and accessing your deeper wisdom. Wear or hold throughout, perhaps even taking a moment to hold it to your third eye and throat right before the interview to infuse you with its vibes.

Rose quartz

Rose quartz is an excellent interview crystal as it will keep you connected to your heart and keep reminding you of your value and worth and what you can bring to the position.

Other crystals for acing the interview process: lapis lazuli, labradorite, aventurine or blue lace agate.

◆ Support for Your First Day ◆ at Work or New Business Venture

Crystals can offer you so much support when you are stepping into the new and unknown. Keep your chosen crystals with you at all times as you enter new territories, either by wearing or holding them in times of need.

Malachite

Malachite is often one of my first choices for any kind of new beginning. As the crystal of transformation, it helps you to embrace change and adapt to the new. Its protective energy will be like having a supportive friend by your side, encouraging you on. It works to overcome shyness and nerves and connects you to your heart, allowing your true self to shine through.

Chrysocolla

If you're just starting out on a new job, project or business endeavour, use chrysocolla to bring not only motivation and excitement, but also fresh, new energy, propelling you confidently into change and connecting you to the venture from your heart, drawing to you the people, support and connections that you need to make it a success.

Carnelian

Carnelian will bring the bravery you need to face big, new projects or ventures. Associated with passion and creativity, it is particularly powerful in helping you to get passion projects off the ground. Known as the stone for new opportunities, it will support you in achieving your goals and staying motivated, inspired and creative throughout the process.

Other crystals for your first day at work or new business venture: tigers' eye, green aventurine, jade or moonstone.

◆ Continuing Your Career Success ◆

If you are looking to climb the corporate ladder or expand in your business, these crystals are for you. Work with them close by, placing them in a grid over a business plan or holding them as you repeat affirmations out loud, such as 'I deserve success'.

Sunstone

A go-to for promotion, new opportunities or allowing yourself to expand and shine in your business or career. Meditate daily with sunstone, either over your solar-plexus chakra or in your hands, to feel your inner strength, power and self-belief expand. Sunstone will help you to express yourself, to be seen and heard, to stand in your power and to achieve all that you know you are capable of.

Jade

Jade will help you to achieve your career goals, overcoming any limitations and guiding you to make the right decisions. A crystal of luck and prosperity, keep it close by for formulating long-term goals and continuing to earn, grow and achieve in your business.

Amazonite

Known as the stone of success or of hope, amazonite supports you in getting confidently clear on not only where you want to go, but also how to get there. Working with your heart chakra, it will assist you in believing and trusting in yourself and nudge you to get out of your comfort zone to go after what your heart truly desires.

Other crystals for career success: carnelian, fluorite, tiger's eye or rose quartz.

◆ Keeping Your Workplace ◆ Productive and Zen

Having crystals around you at work can help to raise the energy and vibration of your workplace, provide protection from colleagues, clients and bosses and keep you feeling calm and in control.

Smoky quartz and black tourmaline

If you find your work environment stressful, try keeping a piece of smoky quartz or black tourmaline on your desk to shield you against negative energies and colleagues or even bosses!

Clear quartz and amethyst

A clear quartz cluster in your workspace will work to filter out any negative energies and fill the area with positive vibrations. Amethyst is also a good option for raising your workplace vibrations to a calm, peaceful, loving energy and for finding balance in your mind and emotions in times of stress.

Other crystals for keeping your workplace productive and zen: selenite to cleanse away tense emotions or energies from difficult customers or colleagues; hematite, to absorb draining energies and emotions; rose quartz for remaining in your heart and treating people with compassion and empathy; labradorite to prevent you from absorbing and taking on other people's negative or angry energies; blue lace agate for calm and clear communication.

Note: crystals can also offer powerful protection from technology and EMF (electromagnetic fields). Place a piece of shungite, hematite, pyrite or black tourmaline near your computer to help counteract the negative effects of some of your screen time.

CHAPTER 12:

Crystals for . . . Finding Your Power and Moving Forward

When you need to find and stand in your power, speak your truth and find the courage to set boundaries or let go and move on in your life, crystals are your cheerleading squad.

◆ Standing in Your Power ◆

Standing in your power means knowing who you are and what you are capable of, trusting in yourself, following your dreams and being responsible for your own happiness.

When you are deeply rooted in your own power, nothing and nobody can shake the foundation of who you are. But let's face it: it can be way too easy to give your power away, whether to other people or to your own self-doubt and self-sabotage – especially if this is something you have spent most of your life doing. This is where crystals can be a big support.

Crystals for your solar-plexus and root chakras

Your solar plexus is your place of personal power and so wearing or meditating with crystals such as citrine, sunstone, tiger's eye or carnelian placed here will help you to replenish, strengthen and maintain your source of power.

We also want to be grounded and rooted in our power, so don't forget your root chakra, especially if you struggle to stay in your power for more than fleeting moments. Try meditating with or carrying black tourmaline, smoky quartz, red jasper or bloodstone. Meditate with, carry or simply hold any of the crystals below when you need a crystal-powered boost of energy.

Labradorite

Labradorite is quite simply a magical crystal to work with when stepping into your inner power as that's just what it will support you in doing: believe in your own magic. This stunning crystal will help to reflect back to you the light and power within you, giving you the power and courage to believe in yourself and what you have to offer and allowing you to know and own yourself, so that you are not afraid to show up in the world as you.

Malachite

Malachite will help you to protect and guard your inner power, so make sure that you wear or carry it when you are going into situations that you know test your resolve.

Fire opal

As its name suggests, this crystal brings a fiery energy to light up your inner personal power and keep it ablaze, protecting you against anything that tries to dim it.

Black obsidian

At times when self-doubt is keeping you powerless, obsidian will reflect your inner strength and power back to you, helping you to connect to and know who you are and what you are capable of.

Larimar

When you need to step up and take back power and control over your life, larimar will help you to see and release any self-sabotaging behaviour and limiting beliefs that you use – or allow – to hold yourself back.

Other crystals for standing in your power: charoite, moldavite, black onyx or peridot.

Note: see also Chapter 15 ('Crystals for . . . Connecting to a Higher Power'), as this will help you to strengthen and trust in your inner knowing.

◆ Creating Healthy Boundaries ◆

If you find yourself constantly giving your power away, struggling with setting boundaries and always saying yes when you mean no, these crystals can awaken your inner power.

Sunstone

Sunstone will help you to say no when you mean no and overcome any feelings of fear that come with this. It is also one of the best crystals for awakening your inner power. Place a piece of sunstone over your solar-plexus chakra and visualise the bright yellow inner sunshine of that chakra becoming clearer and stronger as it soaks up the power of the sunstone. As you lie there, imagine that with each exhale you release any guilt or fear of dark clouds of expectation from others that are hanging around you. Once you have done this, and are hopefully already feeling lighter and brighter, begin to fill your body with this sunshine energy, feeling it activate the power and bravery within you to say no.

Feel it filling your aura and creating a healthy boundary around you. Say to yourself 'I have the power to say no; it is safe for me to say no' as many times as you need to, until you feel the force and the truth of these words in your body. Alternatively, try 'I fearlessly activate all of my power', if you want to remind yourself of the power within you.

Amazonite

Use amazonite to set boundaries based on the needs of your own heart and what is best for you, as well as for sticking to them and staying true to yourself and your decisions, releasing any fear of judgement. Keep this crystal close by when you need to affirm, reiterate or strengthen your boundaries or when they are being questioned or pushed by others. Amazonite will also support you in communicating your boundaries from a clear and firm yet loving and compassionate place.

Other crystals for creating healthy boundaries: rose quartz, malachite, chrysocolla or tiger's eye.

◆ Speaking Your Truth ◆

When you need to speak your truth, use crystals to find and amplify your voice, making yourself heard.

Any blue crystals over your throat chakra will help to clear and balance your voice, so try this before any difficult or deep conversations or when speaking in public. Remember that our words carry such powerful vibrations and meaning, so we want to be as truthful and authentic in our interactions as possible.

Or, to open up your communication channels, try holding one of the crystals below in your receiving hand as you journal and use this as an opportunity to convey anything that needs to be said or heard in that moment. Don't overthink it, just allow the words to flow on to the paper (it can be destroyed afterwards, which often makes it easier for us to be more honest about what we write, as there is no fear around it ever being seen).

Lapis lazuli

Lapis lazuli is one of my go-to crystals when I need to find my voice. Not only does it help to open the throat chakra, this crystal of truth also ensures that your words come from a place of deep authenticity and that you can speak your truth, expressing yourself clearly, openly and honestly, so that you say what you mean and mean what you say. Meditate with lapis over your third eye or throat to tune into your deepest inner truth and hold or wear it at times when you need to communicate this. If you have supressed your voice for a long time, this can feel quite intense and too much to begin with; imagine a hosepipe with a kink in it – you want to let the water out gradually, rather than in one big tsunami. In which case, it may be better to begin with blue lace agate . . .

Blue lace agate

This is a soothing crystal for beginning to gently find your voice and express yourself. If you're afraid to speak up, this crystal will hold you in a loving energy, working to calm your emotions and ease any anxiety as you start to find your voice. Wear blue lace agate (particularly near your throat) to help heal your voice and learn to express yourself with confidence and ease.

Other crystals for speaking your truth: blue kyanite, chrysocolla, amazonite or celestite.

◆ Letting Go ◆

If you are always living in the past or are weighed down by emotional baggage and limiting thoughts or beliefs, it may be time to use the power of crystals to heal and let go.

Black obsidian

This crystal is not only good for dissolving away ties to the past, but also for grounding you in the present and bringing your focus back into the moment. Meditate with or hold obsidian, especially when you find your mind wandering back into the past. Black obsidian is also powerful when trying to release limiting beliefs and unconscious thought patterns that cause you to repeat the same behaviours. Wear obsidian when you find yourself stuck in patterns of limiting beliefs or meditate with it daily to help release their grip on your mind.

Selenite and kyanite

You can use a selenite wand or kyanite blade for 'cutting ties' to the past. Sit in a comfortable position and take a few long, slow, deep breaths. Begin to visualise in your mind's eye the person or situation that you still find yourself energetically connected to. You may take a few moments here to say anything to them about any lessons learned and why it's now time to let go. Feel where in your body there is still a connection to this person or situation; your awareness may be drawn there automatically, or you may notice a tingling or sensation somewhere. Then hold your selenite or kyanite over that place in your body and affirm your readiness and willingness to let go. When you feel that it's time, you can either lovingly cut this cord or my preferred way is to use your crystal to unhook and draw it out of your body and see it float back to where it came from.

You can also use a selenite wand or kyanite blade in a similar way for releasing any limiting thoughts or trapped emotional energy. Take your wand or blade and point it at your third eye to free up your mind – or anywhere in your body you feel that you are holding stuck emotions. Circle the wand or blade a few times over the area and then draw it away from you, as though you are drawing out and releasing away the thoughts, doubts, fears or emotions. I often visualise shaking them off the end of the wand or blade and seeing them being released out into the loving energy of the universe to be dissolved and healed.

Amethyst and rose quartz

If you find that you are weighed down by emotional baggage, use amethyst to release this and move on.

Meditating or journaling with this beautiful, soothing crystal is great for working through any painful experiences and emotions, processing why something happened, learning the lessons and letting go. Try meditating with an amethyst point to draw away and release any emotional or painful attachments that are holding you back. Add rose quartz if there is a lot of guilt or resentment involved and to help you to bring love and compassion for all involved, including yourself.

Chrysocolla

If it's limiting beliefs that keep you stuck, chrysocolla is the crystal for dissolving these and, in their place, developing a sense of self-belief and power in your thoughts. Known as a teaching stone, it will encourage you to gently question your thoughts and whether they are true, opening you up to being curious about new ways of thinking about yourself and your life. Wear chrysocolla to help you break through and beyond the limits of your mind, meditate with it when the resistance from your mind is strong and hold it while repeating positive affirmations, such as: 'I know that I am capable of whatever I put my mind to' or 'I believe in myself'.

Other crystals for letting go: moonstone, smoky quartz, carnelian or citrine.

◆ Creating Change ◆
and Moving Forward

One of the main reasons why we hold on to relationships, beliefs, jobs or other things that we know, deep down, are not good for us is fear: fear of change, or of the unknown. Turn to these crystals to realise what changes need to be made and bring you the bravery to make them and move forward in your life.

Rose quartz

If you know changes need to be made in your life, but you're not sure what or how, start by working with rose quartz. The loving, gentle energy of this crystal will help you to connect to your heart and begin to face your fears with love, encouraging you to believe and trust in yourself enough to know that you can face any challenges and changes and get through them. Work with rose quartz daily to uncover the truth of your heart and what you yearn for in your life, so you know where and how to go about changing things. You could do this through meditation or journaling with your rose quartz.

Jet

Jet is powerful for overcoming fear of change and the unknown. So if fear is keeping you frozen in place and preventing you from making any changes or decisions, meditate with jet daily to help keep your fears at bay.

Hematite

If you know you need to make changes, but you don't know how, hematite is the way to go. It's a strongly supportive crystal that will not only reassure you that you've got this and it's all going to be ok, but will also guide you forward into the new experiences that are waiting for you. Meditate with or carry it so it can show you the way.

Tiger's eye

Once you're clear on the changes that need to be made, tiger's eye will bring you the courage and bravery to face your fears with strength. Wear or carry it with you and it will encourage and support you in boldly moving forward with any necessary changes.

Smoky quartz

This crystal will also encourage you to bring any required changes into reality, giving them structure and a clear plan of action. Meditate holding smoky quartz or with a point facing towards you to help bring needed change.

Malachite

And finally, if you're really and truly ready to make change, work with the crystal of transformation: malachite. But be warned – it will bring change and bring it fast. Working with malachite often brings about immediate and big changes, pushing you to take action. It's almost as though everything is falling apart, but, in fact, it's coming together. Anything that is not meant for you will be obvious and clear when malachite is involved in a life review. Make a list of all that isn't working in your life and ask for malachite's assistance in bringing about the necessary changes. Wear or carry it with you to help with taking action, or place it in a grid over your life review to bring changes in any required areas.

Other crystals for creating change and moving forward: rhodonite, carnelian, labradorite or clear quartz.

CHAPTER 13:

Crystals for . . . Moon Magic

As a self-confessed moon child, I had to include a section on how to use crystals with the moon to create a little more moon magic.

Moonstone is the first and most obvious choice to connect with lunar energies. As its name suggests, it is strongly connected to the moon and is one of the best crystals to work with to enhance your moon magic. Selenite is also a good option (named after Selene, the Greek goddess of the moon).

So first, let's look briefly at how we can work with the moon's energies, and then how to use crystals to work even more powerfully with them.

Using the Moon's Energies

Working with the moon has quite simply changed my life. We can learn so much from the moon and her ever-changing cycles, and, in turn, tune into her energies to help us flow with the rhythms and cycles of our own lives. Using the moon's energies to release and let go allows us to create space for new beginnings and amazing opportunities for ourselves, ensuring that we continue to grow and move forward in life, rather than holding ourselves back or staying stuck in the past.

Month by month, moon by moon, working with lunar energies gives us the opportunity to check in with where we are in our lives, and whether that's where we want to be. From there, we get to make conscious change, releasing whatever stands in the way and moving our lives in the direction of our dreams.

The new moon brings the opportunity for new

beginnings and new direction. Use the day of the new moon to identify what you truly want in your life and start to plant the seeds of growth: make wishes, set intentions, dream and imagine all that's possible for you.

During the waxing lunar cycle (when the moon is growing bigger), continue to add energy to the intentions and goals you have set and take any action that you can to help make your dreams a reality.

The full moon is a time of celebrations, endings, completion and letting go. On the day of the full moon, celebrate what you have achieved since the new moon, then use the full-moon energies to identify what stood in the way of you achieving your goals, any areas in which you would like to see change or things you want to release. This can be anything from negative thoughts, grief or anger to relationships or jobs.

Use the period of the waning lunar cycle (when the moon is becoming smaller) to continue letting go of anything that's standing in the way of you manifesting your goals, affirming your willingness to release any obstacles to happiness.

(If you are keen to learn more about moon magic and working with lunar energies, be sure to read my *Sunday Times* bestselling book, *Lunar Living: Working with the magic of the moon cycles*.)

◆ Using Your Moonstone ◆

Moonstone is about new beginnings. It will help you to bring your moon intentions to life, linking you to your intuition and the waxing and waning cycles of the moon.

On a new moon, hold your moonstone and state out loud or whisper in your heart your new-moon intentions for the coming cycle. Ask your moonstone for support, guidance and wisdom in bringing these intentions to life. Then leave your moonstone on your altar or in a special place or grid (see opposite), where it will continue to send out the energetic vibes of your new-moon intentions into the world, helping them to manifest. Once a day through the waxing phase of the lunar cycle, meditate with or hold your moonstone for a few moments, visualising your new-moon wishes and dreams. I often find that during these daily moments of connection with my moonstone, I get intuitive guidance and clarity on things I need to do.

Reconnect with your moonstone on the full moon, meditating with it and looking back over the two weeks since the new moon. What has worked and what hasn't? In what areas did you give the required energy to your new-moon dreams and intentions and where did you get distracted, scared or pulled off track? Use your moonstone now to set your intentions of what you need to release over the waning part of the lunar cycle. Once more, whisper them to your moonstone, asking for help and guidance in releasing whatever stands in the way. Again, place your moonstone on your altar or special place, where it will continue to work with you on releasing and letting go. Once a day over the waning lunar cycle, meditate with or hold your moonstone with the intention of releasing all that you no longer need.

You can also add selenite to this ritual to bring in even more moon magic. Take a look at how to clear your energy on p. 90 and include this moon-time energy cleanse on a new and full moon. Imagine the light of the moon helping you to further cleanse away anything you no longer need.

◆ More Lunar Crystal Magic ◆

Add other crystals to your moonstone to increase the potency of your moon magic. One of the most powerful ways to work with lunar cycles and crystals is to create grids. I begin the grid on the night of the new moon and keep it in place throughout the lunar cycle. I may then refresh it, completely change it or keep it in place for a further lunar cycle if the same intentions need some extra moon magic.

A simple grid is to use clear quartz points around

your moonstone. On a new moon and through the waxing part of the cycle, the points should face in, to keep bringing energy to your new-moon intention. On the full moon and through the waning part of the cycle, the points should be turned out, for releasing and letting go of what no longer serves you. You may include some selenite in this grid to draw in even more lunar energy. And when you are not using or meditating with your moonstone, keep it inside this grid of quartz crystals to keep amplifying your moon intentions.

You can add other crystals to your grid too. Or when you are meditating/visualising daily, hold your moonstone in one hand and another crystal in the other depending on what your new moon intentions are focused around. For example, for love, add rose quartz; for business ventures, citrine; and for being brave and bold, tiger's eye. Black tourmaline is incredible for releasing through the waning part of the lunar cycle, as are kyanite or labradorite. Howlite will support you in setting better boundaries; or try amethyst or labradorite for following your intuition. And take a look through the other chapters of this book for life areas in which you are setting your intentions, adding the relevant crystals for bringing even more power and focus to these and your crystal-moon magic. You can also read up on crystals for the zodiac signs on p. 155 and use crystals relevant to the sign that each new and full moon is in.

Lastly, if you want to wear moonstone as jewellery, it will help with keeping you connected to the energies of the moon and going with the rhythm and flow of life, trusting in what is unfolding for you through the cycle. Just be warned that if you are moon-sensitive, it might feel a bit too much wearing it around a full moon, when the lunar energies peak, so you may need to remove it for these few days.

CHAPTER 14:

Crystals for . . . Sleep and Relaxation

If you have trouble winding down, can't seem to drop off easily to sleep, find yourself in the wide-awake club in the early hours or want to work with your dreams, there is a crystal here to support you.

A Crystal bath

One thing I love to do is take a bath with crystals, and I always turn this into a real act of self-care.

Light some candles, play relaxing music, add some beautiful bath oils and make sure your phone and all tech are out of the room. Choose the crystals you want to work with (always remembering to check that they're not water-soluble) and place them in the running bath water, asking that they help to infuse the water with their vibrational energy for you to absorb.

As you relax in your crystal bath, take long, slow breaths and imagine your crystals drawing all the stresses, worries and anxieties out of your body, while the water cleanses them away. Soak for as long as you need to and when you are done, as you pull the plug, feel all your cares drain away with the water.

Rose quartz
It's rumoured that Cleopatra bathed with chunks of rose quartz, so you may follow her lead and add it for some self-love vibes.

Other crystals for taking a bath
Amethyst (for deep relaxation), clear quartz (for deep cleansing), smoky quartz (for deep healing) or even a crystal for one or each chakra.

◆ A Bedtime Relaxation Routine ◆

An evening routine before bed is great for sleep troubles. This not only lets your mind and body know that the time for sleep is coming, but also encourages you to put aside stresses from your day and create a calm space.

The combined magic of crystals and yoga

One of the best things for deep relaxation before bed is a yoga pose called viparita karani. This deeply restorative pose will help to calm the mind, relieve anxiety and completely relax the entire nervous system. Just add crystals and you're on a one-way street to deep relaxation like never before.

How to do it:

1. Decide which crystals you want to use and have them close by.

2. Sit on the floor with one hip flush against a wall.

3. Gently swing your legs around, until they are up the wall with the backs of your thighs resting against it. Make sure your buttocks are as close to the wall as possible and your arms are down by your sides, palms facing up.

139

4. Place the relevant crystals on your body. You may even cover yourself with a blanket, too, and put an eye pillow over your eyes, if desired.

5. Stay in this position for 10–15 minutes, before slowly lowering yourself down to lie on your back.

While you are here, you may place sodalite or amethyst on your third eye to bring peace of mind, rose quartz on your heart or moonstone on your sacral chakra to soothe your emotions, and even hold a crystal of your choosing in each hand to feel the connection to the healing energy.

You could even turn this into a proper self-care ritual at any time of day by adding a crystal to each chakra (see Chapter 6 – 'Crystals for . . . the Chakras') or by placing your body inside a crystal grid of choice to help with any stresses or issues you may be facing. Burn some incense, play soothing music and relax deeply, breathing all your troubles away.

Selenite

Another powerful ritual before bed is journaling, to get out all the things that would otherwise run through your mind in the middle of the night, keeping you awake. Hold a piece of selenite while you write, and this powerful crystal will work to cleanse all that troubles you out of your mind, body and heart and on to the paper. You can then use the selenite to cleanse your aura and chakras (see p. 90) for a full pre-bedtime cleansing ritual. Keep your selenite nearby through the night, as it also helps with insomnia.

Other crystals for a bedtime relaxation routine: blue lace agate, lepidolite, pink tourmaline or smoky quartz.

◆ Sleeping Soundly ◆

If you struggle to drop off to sleep or you wake in the middle of the night, crystals can become the perfect bed companion to help you sleep soundly. They can also help you to access, remember and work with your dreams.

Amethyst
Probably one of the first crystals that will be recommended for insomnia and sleep troubles, amethyst has serene, calming and soothing vibes that wrap you in a bubble of peace, ready for a good night's sleep. Keep an amethyst geode on your bedside table or a tumbled piece inside your pillowcase or under your pillow for a great night's sleep. Amethyst also helps with nightmares, so if you suffer from these, be sure to have a

piece nearby, so that it can protect you while you are sleeping.

Howlite

Speaking of dreams . . . if you want to encourage the more peaceful kind and work with your dreams to understand their messages, sleep with howlite under your pillow. It helps you to access dream wisdom and allows you to remember it upon waking, so be sure to keep a dream diary by the side of your bed! An incredibly calming crystal, howlite is also powerful against insomnia, encouraging your waking mind to switch off, so that you can drift into a deep, dreamy sleep.

Celestite

Another crystal for dream work – especially for connecting to higher wisdom to gain answers through your dreams – is celestite. It will help your sleep and dreams to be calm and peaceful and is particularly powerful for those who struggle to sleep through the night without waking up. Keep celestite by your bedside to bring tranquillity and peace to your bedroom, so that you sleep soundly through the night.

Other crystals for sleeping soundly: moonstone, lepidolite, rose quartz or chrysoprase.

Note: do be mindful of how many crystals you have in your bedroom. If you are energy-sensitive, you might find that they stimulate your energy, keeping you awake. So try to keep only soothing, calming crystals (any of those mentioned in this chapter) in your bedroom if you do have trouble sleeping.

◆ Staying Wide Awake ◆

For those who find getting up and out of bed in the morning difficult and are constantly hitting the snooze button, try waking up to the crystals below. You can also try taking a few long, slow, deep breaths holding them for an energy boost during the day, rather than reaching for the caffeine when the 3pm slump hits.

Clear quartz

If you struggle to wake up and get going in the morning, try holding a piece of clear quartz for a few minutes first thing, perhaps visualising it filling you with energy, to give you a hit to start your day. This powerhouse of a crystal will raise and amplify your energies, setting you up for the day.

Sunstone and citrine

Try meditating with sunstone or citrine in the morning or carry them with you throughout the day to invite in some uplifting energy, light and life.

Carnelian

Carnelian will boost your energy levels and give you a spring in your step for the day ahead. Again, you can meditate with this in the morning or carry it with you as you go about your day.

Other crystals for staying wide awake: pyrite, tiger's eye, obsidian or bloodstone.

CHAPTER 15:

Crystals for . . .
Connecting to a Higher Power

Whether you want to connect to your own source of inner wisdom and guidance (or those of the universe, guides or angels), hear the voice of your intuition, live a more purposeful life or go into deeper states of meditation, crystals can help connect you to a source of higher power.

Many of the crystals mentioned in this section are high-vibration ones that will work on all the areas mentioned, all of which blend with one another: as you meditate daily, you will naturally connect more to your intuition; as you connect to and follow your intuition, you will naturally uncover your purpose; as you begin to live more on purpose, you will naturally connect to higher wisdom, and so on.

◆ Meditate, Meditate, Meditate ◆

One of the first and most important ways to connect to any kind of higher wisdom or power is through meditation. Meditation will help you to cut through the noise in your head, get beneath the turmoil of your emotions and quieten your world, so that you can hear, connect to and access deeper states of intuition, wisdom, guidance and knowledge.

Clear quartz

My first recommendation for deepening your meditation practice is clear quartz. This master crystal brings clarity to your mind to heal and raise your energies and vibrations, so that you can become more aligned with higher states of energy. Hold a clear quartz in your receiving hand as you meditate daily to deepen your practice and expand your awareness.

Selenite harmonisers

If you are only just starting out with meditation or struggle to clear your mind or find a state of calm in your practice, get a pair of selenite harmonisers (sometimes called rods). These are cylindrical pieces of selenite, and you hold one in each hand as you meditate to clear your mind and your energy field, so that you feel grounded, peaceful, balanced and calm during your practice.

Other crystals to help deepen your meditation practice: apatite, chrysoprase, smoky quartz or rose quartz.

◆ Listen to Your Intuition ◆

If you want to find a deeper connection to your intuition – that deeper wisdom within you that can nudge you along your life path – crystals are here to help.

Crystals for your third-eye and sacral chakras

Meditating with crystals over your third eye – the main portal to your intuition – will help to awaken your innate awareness. Kyanite is one of the most powerful crystals to begin with as it can gently stimulate and open your third eye, strengthening your intuition and inner wisdom.

I often hold a crystal over my third eye when I need answers and guidance, tapping into the wisdom within me. I will allow a situation or question to run through my mind's eye, as the power of the crystal helps me to access my intuitive answers. You may not hear the answer straight away, but trust that the part of you that needs to know knows, and the answers will become clear.

It's also vital to work with your sacral chakra when you want to tap more deeply into your intuition. Think of some of the things we say, such as 'I felt it in my gut' – this describes intuitive guidance and it can very often get lost beneath the myriad emotions that we don't address, listen to or heal. Take a look at 'Soothing the Emotions' (p. 79) or 'Letting Go' (p. 121) for insight on how to heal your emotions, so you can begin to feel your intuition more.

You can harness the intuitive power of both your third-eye and sacral chakras by holding an associated crystal to meditate or by placing the crystals on the relevant chakra. Close your eyes and take deep breaths and imagine a link between your third-eye and sacral chakras, opening up an energetic line of intuition and wisdom that you can begin to tap into. You may imagine the energy moving one way with your inhale and the other way with your exhale. Work with your intuition daily and follow it as often as possible to strengthen it and build trust in yourself.

Other crystals for listening to your intuition: for your third eye: amethyst, moonstone, labradorite or sodalite; **and for your sacral chakra:** citrine, moonstone, sunstone or clear quartz.

◆ Finding Your Purpose ◆

If you're looking to find more purpose and meaning in life, meditate daily with the crystals below or wear them at all times to guide you along your way.

Sugilite

Sugilite is one of the best crystals for finding answers to all the big questions of life, such as who am I and why am I here? A deeply spiritual crystal, sugilite will help you to appreciate who you are and what you have to offer, remind you of your soul purpose and inspire you to live from love and follow it.

Selenite

Another powerful one for connecting with your soul and learning from your life experiences and how they lead you along your path of discovery, this high-vibration crystal will help you to hear and follow messages from the universe that guide you towards your soul's intent and purpose.

Charoite

Charoite will teach you about you and show you your part to play in the world. It will inspire you to be of service, awakening your soul gifts that only you can offer and encouraging you to share these gifts with the world so that everyone can benefit from your magic.

Howlite

Once you have found your purpose in life (and remember this can change over time), howlite will encourage you to remain on your path, committed to the journey ahead. It is also useful at the beginning of your journey. If ever you feel completely lost and directionless, howlite will work with you to find your way.

Other crystals for finding your purpose: clear quartz, labradorite, moldavite or amethyst.

◆ Connection to Higher Wisdom ◆ and Guidance

Whether you call it your higher self, the universe, source or soul, if you are looking for a connection to a higher source of wisdom and guidance, crystals can help to facilitate that, and your crown chakra is where you want to focus for this. Meditate lying down with a crystal above your crown or, if – like me – you much prefer sitting to meditate, hold your chosen crystal and visualise your crown chakra opening to guidance as you meditate.

Lapis lazuli

This stone of communication will not only help you connect to your higher self, but also to differentiate between the voice of your ego and that of your higher self and to be able to listen to and hear the latter more clearly. Meditate with or wear this crystal to stay connected to the wiser, all-knowing, higher part of you.

Blue goldstone

Although man-made, blue goldstone is a powerful crystal for divine connection; you can almost feel your connection to the whole universe just by looking at it. This crystal will help you to understand that everything is made up of energy and vibration and that you are part of the whole.

Celestite

Often associated with divine power, celestite brings higher spiritual awareness and connection to universal energies.

Labradorite

Labradorite is a magical crystal that helps you to communicate with higher guidance, connect to universal energies and explore past lives and the akashic records (vibrational records of all that ever has, is or will happen;

they hold a soul's journey and all the thoughts, feelings and deeds from each lifetime).

Apophyllite

Apophyllite will help to connect you to the spiritual realms and create a conscious connection between the spiritual and the physical.

Moldavite

One of my favourite crystals for receiving messages and guidance from higher realms is moldavite – but please use with caution, as it is incredibly powerful. Created when a meteorite crashed to earth approximately 15 million years ago, moldavite is not of this world and, as such, is said to have been sent here to help with the future of the earth.

Other crystals for connecting to higher wisdom and guidance: selenite, clear quartz or amethyst.

✦ Connecting to Guides and Angels ✦

For those of you with a belief and interest in spirit guides or angelic realms, crystals can help raise your vibration to access these celestial beings.

Try meditating with one of these crystals while being

open to hearing and receiving messages, guidance or signs. Then perhaps open your eyes and immediately begin journaling, seeing what messages flow. Or wear these crystals to remember that you are never alone and that angelic assistance is always nearby; touch your crystal and call on your guides in times of need.

Angelite

As its name suggests, angelite is all about connecting to guardian angels, knowing that they are close and feeling their support. One of my favourite crystals, you maybe remember me mentioning it in a story earlier (see p. 47).

Lapis lazuli

Lapis lazuli will help you connect to and communicate with your spirit guides, receiving their wisdom and guidance.

Danburite

This will help you to access higher levels of consciousness and your own inner guidance, also opening you up to receiving messages and signs from spirit guides and angels.

Petalite

Sometimes known as the angel stone, petalite helps to expand your levels of awareness to connect to your guardian angels.

Other crystals for connecting to guides and angels: selenite, apophyllite, celestite or kyanite.

CHAPTER 16:

Crystals for . . . the Zodiac Signs

Each sign of the zodiac carries different energies, qualities and traits and is associated with different crystals. These associations originate from many different sources, including the month you were born, which was later picked up by astrologers and linked to the zodiac signs, the ruling planet or element of each zodiac sign and how the energies of a particular crystal complement or counteract those of that sign.

Through the year, the sun moves through each sign of the zodiac, staying in each one for around a month, which is known as a season. No matter what our sun sign is (determined by which sign the sun was in at the time we were born), we are all influenced by and can work with the energies and qualities of each particular zodiac season as the sun makes its journey through them all.

Below I have listed some of the best crystals to use

for each sign of the zodiac. You may want to work with these crystals during that particular zodiac season (dates for these are given below) or when the moon is new or full in each zodiac sign (see Chapter 13, 'Crystals for . . . Moon Magic'). You may also want to choose a crystal to work with based on your sun, moon or rising sign, or have a look through some of the qualities that each sign and crystal offer and work with these crystals to invite a little more of this energy into your life.

ARIES
(21 March–19 April)

As the fiery first sign of the zodiac, Aries brings drive, ambition and motivation to get things started.

Carnelian
As a high-energy crystal that encourages creativity, carnelian brings a confidence boost to take the first step towards manifesting dreams and desires.

Bloodstone

Bloodstone helps you to take action in the present moment, which is useful, as Aries can have a tendency to rush off into hundreds of ideas and never complete any of them.

Aquamarine

If you are finding the Aries fire a little too much, this crystal will calm the flames, helping to clear the mind and soothe the emotions.

TAURUS

(20 April–20 May)

Taurus offers grounding, stability and security, bringing things down to earth. It is a sign associated with pleasure and encourages slowing down and self-care.

Rose quartz

Perfect for those self-worth, self-love and self-care vibes, rose quartz will help you to look after yourself and put your needs first.

Black tourmaline

A healing, protecting crystal with strong, earthy energy, tourmaline helps you to ground and feel safe and secure.

Malachite

If you're finding the Taurus vibes slowing you down to a stop or that you're stuck in a stubborn stand-off, malachite will help to get things moving.

GEMINI

(21 May–20 June)

Gemini brings a quick, lively energy that is focused on communication, information and ideas. This sign of the zodiac loves change.

Danburite

A powerful crystal for accessing your own inner guidance and gaining information and wisdom from within, it also facilitates change, helping you to leave the past behind.

Blue lace agate
The perfect communication crystal, this will help you to express yourself and speak your truth, saying what you think and feel.

Chrysocolla
If your mind is brimming with ideas you can't make sense of or you're feeling anxiety or fear of change, chrysocolla will bring order, calm and tranquillity.

CANCER
(21 June–22 July)

Deep, sensitive, nurturing and caring, Cancer is all about the emotions, which can ebb and flow just like the tides.

Rhodonite
A heart-opening crystal, rhodonite has a deeply healing energy that promotes unconditional love, compassion, peace and forgiveness.

Chrysoprase

Chrysoprase brings a nurturing energy that provides a sense of safety and security in which to process emotions and a feeling of deep trust.

Moonstone

Cancer is ruled by the moon, so this is the perfect crystal to help you to allow your emotions to flow, soothing and calming them if they become too intense.

LEO

(23 July–22 August)

Big, bold and brave, Leo energy is childlike and playful, asking you to open your heart, express yourself and shine in life.

Sunstone

Leo is ruled by the sun and, as the name suggests, sunstone is like holding a little piece of sunshine, bringing a sense of joy and happiness and encouraging you to shine.

Tiger's eye

Awakening your creativity and unlocking your true potential, tiger's eye brings Leo-like qualities of courage, power and self-belief.

Larimar

If you find yourself on the verge of a temper tantrum if you don't get your own way, or in a self-sabotage/doubt spiral, this crystal will bring you peace, calm and healing.

VIRGO
(23 August–22 September)

One of the most healing signs of the zodiac, Virgo is practical, logical and hard-working, focused on the finer details and solving problems.

Citrine

The ideal crystal to have on hand when you need to organise your thoughts, analyse information and find solutions to problems.

Sugilite

Also known as the healer's stone, sugilite helps to access deeper wisdom, not only from the thinking mind, but also intuition and a sixth sense.

Howlite

If you find yourself stuck in the self-critical, perfectionist nature of Virgo, howlite will help to quieten the inner critic, bringing compassion and patience.

LIBRA

(23 September–22 October)

Peace, harmony and equilibrium in relationships and life are what Libra is searching for, alongside a sense of justice and fairness.

Jade

A true crystal of tranquillity, harmony and peace, jade is also a bringer of luck in love, helping all of your relationships to flourish.

Apophyllite

One of the most calming crystals around, apophyllite emits tranquil, peaceful vibes, connecting you to love, happiness and higher realms.

Lapis lazuli

For those times when you find yourself in that Libra tendency of being indecisive, lapis will help you to take back control of your life.

SCORPIO

(23 October–21 November)

The alchemist of the zodiac, Scorpio brings transformation, transmutation and a deep dive into the depths of our being to understand ourselves better.

Obsidian

Black obsidian is a powerful crystal that takes us into our shadows and subconscious realms to bring healing and clarity. Snowflake obsidian is gentler.

Labradorite
A magical crystal of transformation, labradorite shines light into hidden truths, bringing what needs to be seen, understood and transformed to the surface.

Amethyst
If you find yourself overwhelmed by deep emotions, especially sadness, anger, fear or grief, amethyst will help you to find a deep understanding of them and the ability to release them gently.

SAGITTARIUS
(22 November–21 December)

The optimistic adventurer of the zodiac, Sagittarius loves to expand horizons and explore all there is to know about the world and life.

Turquoise
Used as a traveller's amulet in many ancient civilisations, this is the perfect companion to protect you as you undertake adventures and explorations.

Azurite

Azurite helps you to find purpose and direction, explore new realities and ways of expanding consciousness. It also helps to reveal truths.

Smoky quartz

If you find yourself running at the first sign of trouble, trying to escape reality or taking on too much, smoky quartz will help to ground and anchor you.

CAPRICORN

(22 December–19 January)

The most ambitious, hard-working sign of the zodiac, Capricorn is focused on reaching goals and succeeding in life.

Garnet

A crystal of commitment, garnet brings the motivation to stay until the job is done, helping to overcome any setbacks and bringing passion to the project.

Amber
Not strictly a crystal but a fossilised resin, amber motivates you to get what you want – if you can see it and believe it, amber will help you to achieve it.

Aragonite
If you are pushing yourself too hard or taking on too much, aragonite will help you to know that you are doing your best and make sure your expectations are realistic.

AQUARIUS
(20 January–18 February)

Freedom-seeking and future-driven, Aquarius is innovative, ingenious and humanitarian-focused, seeking authenticity and liberation.

Angelite
A 'new-age' crystal, known to raise conscious awareness, heighten perception and connect to higher realms, angelite helps you to know and speak your truth.

Apatite
Promoting humanitarian service, apatite shows how you can contribute to the collective good by being and expressing yourself. It will help you to seek freedom, always looking to the future and what's next.

Rhodochrosite
Aquarius can have a tendency to avoid emotions, shutting down and giving the cold shoulder. Rhodochrosite will help keep the heart open and process emotions.

PISCES
(19 February–20 March)

The final sign of the zodiac, Pisces is dreamy, empathetic and highly intuitive, bringing the knowledge that we are all connected and the ability to vision a new reality.

Fluorite
Helping you to strengthen your intuition and connect you to higher spiritual energies, fluorite encourages you to see the bigger picture of your life.

Ametrine

Bridging the gap between the spiritual and physical worlds, ametrine shows you how to bring dreams to action by tuning into your higher awareness.

Hematite

Pisces can sometimes have issues with setting boundaries, taking on and feeling the worries of the whole world; hematite will help you to set energetic and emotional boundaries and keep you grounded.

Conclusion

Thank you so much for taking this crystal journey with me. I hope that you now feel confident in the many ways through which you can invite the magic of crystals into your daily life to help you to care for yourself and bring healing and transformation.

Dip in and out of this book as often as you need to, and enjoy the process of discovering new crystals, as well as new ways of using them along the way. But remember that this is your journey, and that you know best. My greatest wish is that through reading this book and working with crystals you will discover what works for you, as you learn to trust in yourself and your intuition. There is no greater act of self-care. This is a lifelong journey, and crystals will be there for you every step of the way.

I always love to hear from you, so please share your crystal stories, tagging me on Instagram: @kirsty_gallagher_

Enjoy the crystal magic. I can't wait to see where it will take you . . .

Acknowledgements

To my wonderful family: Sandra, Kylie, Kerry, Liam, Stephanie, Soraya, Jake, Chloe, Edward, Isaac and my late Grandpa Donald. I love you all and thank you for always loving and supporting me.

To Sam, for being the best friend a girl could ever ask for, and to my godson, Harley, for loving crystals as much as I do.

My editor, Holly Whitaker – thank you for being the best and for your continual support and encouragement; I love creating books with you! And to all the wonderful people at Yellow Kite who have supported me on this journey, thank you. I am so grateful to Myrto Kalavrezou and Caitriona Horne for your PR and marketing skills, Anne Newman for your editing magic and Jo Myler for creating yet another book cover of dreams.

If you are holding this book in your hands, thank you for allowing me to share the crystal magic with you. I hope it changes your life as much as it has mine.

Eternal gratitude to you if you bought my book *Lunar Living*, as you helped to make it a *Sunday Times* Best-seller, not just once, but three times! Thank you for all your support – you are the best community ever and I appreciate you more than you know.

My Lunar Living online sisterhood: thank you for all your support, lunar love and for being the best sister-hood ever. My never-ending gratitude to my right-hand woman, Helen Elias – nothing I do would be what it is without you.

To all of you who have attended my 'Soul Space' online lunar yoga and meditation workshops, 'Sacred Space' wheel of the year workshops and 'Still Space' meditations, along with all my IG followers; thank you for being a part of this magical community and contin-uing to show up for yourselves and each other. Remember, you are never alone – you've got this, I've got you, we've got each other.

So much love and gratitude to these special people in my life: Becki Rabin, Megan Rose Lane, Wendy O'Beirne, Caggie Dunlop, Emma Taylor, Hannah Holt, Lisa Strong, Rebecca Dennis, Ian Steed – my life would not be the same without you in it.

To my Soul Alignment and Aligned clients: you are the absolute dream to work with. Thank you for your willingness to trust me with your hearts and souls. I love seeing you show up and make such a huge difference in the world. I am so proud of you.

Thank you to everyone at ITV's *This Morning* (especially Holly and Phillip) and *The Chris Evans Breakfast Show* for all your support over the past year and for allowing me to share the moon magic with the nation. Thanks, too, to Fearne Cotton, Warehouse, *You*, *Red*, *Stylist* and *Happiful* magazines and everyone who has invited me on to their podcasts or let me share my work with their audiences.

If I have not named you, it's not because you are forgotten or that I am not grateful. It's simply that I have been blessed to have so many wonderful people touch my life and there are not enough pages to mention you all; it would be another book in itself! If you have ever been a part of my life in any way, thank you.

About the Author

Photograph by Jen Armstrong

Kirsty Gallagher is a moon mentor, soul-alignment and spiritual coach, yoga teacher, meditation teacher and *Sunday Times* bestselling author with an infectious passion for life.

She has been sharing the life-changing benefits of yoga and the moon for 13 years through classes, workshops and private and corporate sessions, and has taught over 80 worldwide retreats. She is author of the *Sunday Times* bestselling book *Lunar Living* and founder of the online sisterhood Lunar Living, which teaches how to weave the secret and ancient wisdom of the moon into modern, everyday life.

Kirsty has created a worldwide community through her Soul Space lunar yoga and meditation classes and her Sacred Space seasonal yoga, meditation and ritual classes. One of her greatest passions is bringing people together, showing us that we are never alone.

Kirsty works alongside women in one-to-one and group mentoring programmes, teaching them to live back in alignment with an ancient cycle, a natural rhythm and flow, so helping them to connect back into their inner wisdom, power, authenticity and purpose. Weaving lunar, nature and divine feminine wisdom with spiritual teachings, astrology and cutting-edge transformational coaching techniques, Kirsty helps women to overcome doubts, fears and self-sabotage to know and trust in themselves like never before and find greater meaning and purpose in life.

Kirsty is a sought-after leading voice in lunar wisdom and has shared moon magic on *The Chris Evans Breakfast Show* and *This Morning*. She has also been featured in *You, Stylist, Red, Women's Health, Soul & Spirit* and *Natural Health* magazines.

Described as down to earth, warm-hearted, compassionate and inspiring, Kirsty is known for bringing ancient mystical practices and wisdom to modern-day life in a relatable way that anyone and everyone can take something from. Find out more at kirstygallagher.com.

If you enjoyed reading *Crystals for Self-Care*,
why don't you read Kirsty's other books,
Lunar Living and *The Lunar Living Journal*?

books to help you live a good life

Join the conversation and tell
us how you live a #goodlife

🐦 @yellowkitebooks
📘 YellowKiteBooks
📌 Yellow Kite Books
📷 YellowKiteBooks

go to Brigade headquarters, which was a short distance further
along the road. These head quarters were in the re___ ___ had
been a good sized house. A little of the walls still stood whole, and
these were strengthened with stacks of sand bags, railway lines, wood
and iron girders, and was like a little fort. The place was like a
bee hive. there was one continual stream of men comeing and going
from it. Telephones rang every few seconds, orders were being given
and written messages sent by the score. Standing about were men
of the signal corps. waiting to be sent off. to repair or make a new
telephone line. Outside on the road, guns. shells. horses. and men were
all pouring along. each going to a aloted place. Enimy shells
exploded on the road frequently, makeing large holes, but
hardly had the smoke cleared away, when gangs of men whould
fill in the hole with stones, taken from the heaps kept at the
side of the road. My officer had gone below some where for orders and
was away some time. When he returned he said "he had nothing to do

HARRY'S WAR

THE VALLEY
VIMEY RIDGE

HARRY'S WAR

Experiences in the "Suicide Club" in World War One

HARRY STINTON

Researched & Edited by
VIRGINIA MAYO

BRASSEY'S

First published in 2002 by Brassey's

A member of **Chrysalis** Books plc

Brassey's
64 Brewery Road, London N7 9NT

Virginia Mayo has asserted her moral right
to be identified as the author of this work.

Library of Congress Cataloging in Publication Data available

British Library cataloguing in Publication Data
A catalogue record for this book is available from the British Library

ISBN 1 85753 317 8

Edited and designed by DAG Publications Ltd
Designed by David Gibbons. Edited by Michael Boxall
Printed in Spain.

CONTENTS

LIST OF ILLUSTRATIONS

ACKNOWLEDGEMENTS

I would like to thank the following people for their help, their contributions, their knowledge and their patience:

My Aunt, Ethel Salter and her son Vick, for trusting me with Harry's war diary and approaching me with the project.

Jacques Morel, Director of the Canadian National Vimy Memorial and his Canadian students and staff, for backing the project, helping me to find Harry's way across the battlefields in Loos and Vimy Ridge and for Jacques' generosity with his time as well as his introductions to so many interested and varied experts in the field.

Keith D. Maxwell, OMH, CD, Colonel (retired), Canadian Forces, senior operations analyst at NATO for his involvement, enthusiasm and continuous support, finding Harry's path along the Western Front and writing introductions to the start of each chapter.

Isabelle Pilarowski of Sur Les Traces de La Grande Guerre at Loos-en-Gohelle for her interest, assistance and for sharing her fascinating work, researching the findings in tunnels under Loos and Vimy.

Curator Mme Prevost-Bault and technician Steve Macartney of the Historial de la Grande Guerre at Peronne.

Thanks to explosives expert Rob Lion for the use of his bombs; Geoff Beel, John Urch, Peter Mason, Michael Hills, Paul Copeman (Isle College, Wisbech), Deborah Partridge, Dave at the Arianne Hotel (Ypres); and Beverley Housden for her friendship and support, accompanying me on the battlefields of France and Flanders to locate the places in Harry's drawings.

Virginia Mayo 2002

A SING SONG.

For Harry

A general strategic guide to the principal places Harry mentions in his narrative, as depicted in the campaign map in the 47 (London) Division history. This shows all the actions in which the division participated during the war, both before and after Harry's service on the Western Front. The map has been reproduced in two sections for greater clarity.

INTRODUCTION

HARRY STINTON was born on 21 December 1891 in Bethnal Green, East London. Aged 23, he volunteered for service on 21 May 1915. His regiment was the 1/7th (City of London Battalion), The London Regiment, known as 'The Shiny Seventh', a Territorial Army unit forming part of the 4th Brigade of the 2nd London Division. At the time of Harry joining, the brigade and division were re-designated as the 140th Brigade of the 47th Division.

During his two years and 127 days of combat Harry remained a private soldier throughout. Soon after arriving in France, he volunteered to join 'The Suicide Club' (bombing platoon), serving with Lieutenant St. Chatterton, MC. Sent to Arras on the Western Front in October 1915, Harry arrived in the wake of the Battle of Loos and the Hohenzollern Redoubt, and took part in the fighting at Loos Towers. Moving on to Vimy Ridge in February 1916, he fought in 'Zouave' Valley near Souchez until May. For five months, he served as batman to Second Lieutenant Hope (June–October

1916). In July he was in training for the Somme and arrived in Albert on 14 September for the battle of Flers—Courcelette, seeing action at Delville Wood, High Wood, and Transloy making towards the Butte de Warlencourt. By the winter of 1916 he was at Ypres, tunnelling under Hill Sixty, and where, in 1917 he was wounded at the battle for Messines Ridge before the Third Battle of Ypres (known to the soldiers as Passchendaele) in August.

He made a record of his daily service life in the trenches in a diary, along with his drawings, describing experiences as profound as bomb-raiding in No Man's Land to things as trivial as the general British expression of horror at French ideas of decency! With Lieutenant Hope, Harry describes seeing the first British tank arrive at the Somme on the eve of the battle. He recalls going over the top with exhausted comrades still eating their sandwiches; trying to cook bacon in the ammunition store during a gas attack at Loos, and writes of the time when he saw his best friend killed.

His wounded right shoulder earned at Ypres put an end to Harry's soldiering and after hospitalisation and convalescence, he was discharged on 25 September 1917 aged 26, with a war pension of 11 shillings per week. He returned to his parents' home at 12 Wadeson Street, Cambridge Heath in Bethnal Green and promptly bought a notebook and set to write. This account of his experiences in The Great War is a combination of his own diaries with drawings done on the spot, and his later reminiscences. His unemotional, matter of fact tone, whether describing the mundane or the profound, never wavers – an outlook typical of hundreds of thousands of rank and file soldiers who never wrote of their experiences. Harry's is the authentic voice of Tommy Atkins.

Harry never married. After the War, he returned to his former trade of circular sawyer at the woodyard in Bethnal Green and died in the 1960s. When his sister, Ethel Goodchild, was clearing his house, a plain black hardback notebook was found, entitled: 'My Experiences in the Army during the Great War 1914–1918' and signed H. Stinton 23/5/15–25/10/17.

Researching Harry Stinton's book has taken five years. Because he wrote his diary as a continuous train of thought without paragraphs, dates, headings or chapters, it is clear that Harry put down his thoughts in a diary for his own cathartic reasons. In today's world we may no longer get his joke when he and Matthews are referred to as the 'Brothers Mac', or looking 'such a sketch' after being wounded at the Battle of Messines. It is difficult to imagine a situation when you can lose your friends, your health and your dignity and yet maintain a strong spirit. Sometimes, the memory and the detail became more important than grammatical correctness. Harry was a keen artist; no other work of his survives. This is the work of a young cockney lad embarking on the greatest adventure of his life. The challenge has been to present Harry and his experiences in his own words, but to extend them to the wider audience.

GETING
WATER
FROM PUMP LOO'S

'... The night was darker than usual and each side got the idea that it was an ideal night to make a bombing raid. We saw our men first. There were about twenty of them, creeping across towards the enemy lines. Then when they got within about a hundred yards of the enemy, out came a party of German bombers on their way to our lines. Evidently, our men saw the other bombers coming, for they all crouched down and waited for them to get nearer. Almost at the same moment, they started bombing each other. Several of the Germans went down with the rest working gradually back to their own lines, throwing bombs as they went. Our men followed them up until they had used all their bombs and then hurriedly made towards our lines. By this time, the German bombers had got back to their trench where, getting a fresh supply of bombs, started throwing them out front. Someone on the German side mistook the happening for something more serious and called upon the artillery, who began to send over hundreds of shells our way. Our artillery, seeing and hearing this bombardment going on and thinking it was a German attack, opened out for all they were worth on the German lines.

We poor blokes were stuck out in the middle of it! Gosh there was a din! For my part, I tried to make myself as small as possible while at the same time keeping a look out. We crouched there with great dobs of mud falling on top of us, shells and shrapnel screaming overhead and bullets buzzing in the top of our shell hole. It seemed like one continual bang. In the midst of it, I heard a thud just in front of me and the earth came up and spanked me on the nose and chin such a wallop it made my eyes water! A second or two afterwards, the man next to me gave a groan and fell like a dead weight on top of me. As he did so I felt a drip, drip of something on my neck.

"The chap must be wounded or killed," I thought. I rolled him off me and one of the other men helped me search as best we could for the injuries. We were unable to find any but the man still lay as if dead except that he was breathing. The bombardment only lasted perhaps a quarter of an hour and then died down as suddenly as it began. What a relief! We shook off us what mud and dirt we could and had another go at examining our man. While examining him, he came to with a groan and put his hand up to his head. We removed his helmet, which had a large dent in it and felt, very tenderly, a big bump on his head. His helmet had saved his life, without it his head would certainly have been crushed in ...'

Lone Tree Post, Anaught trenches, Ypres 1917

CHAPTER ONE
SUMMER OF 1914

Harry's experience of being recruited and his training in England is typical of many soldiers at this stage of the war. He was trained in only the most basic of skills – drill, trench-digging and some marksmanship. His attitudes about the war are shaped by the reports in the British press, much of it specifically intended as propaganda, regarding German atrocities and disregard of international agreements. He also reflects the fervent patriotism of the times and the unquestioning acceptance that he was going to fight for a just cause. This attitude did much to sustain the morale of British Empire troops throughout the war. Harry's initial rejection by the Engineers and the Artillery reflects the surge of volunteers joining the British Army at this time – they had more men than they could handle and, in the specialised corps, were very selective. It would be almost another year after Harry joined before manpower became more difficult to recruit, which eventually led to conscription.

HOW THE TROUBLES BEGAN IN EUROPE

It is well known how the trouble started in Europe, which eventually led us into the largest war that the world has ever witnessed, as far as history tells us. Germany, it has been proved, was preparing for a war for some years, and was on the alert for some excuse for starting it. The chance came on the 28th June 1914 when a Bosnian Serb, maddened by the annexation of his country, assassinated the Archduke Franz Ferdinand and his wife. The Foreign Minister, Count Forgach, notorious for forging documents against the Serbs in the Agram Trial, then stated that he had evidence to prove that the Archduke and his wife were murdered by the order of Serbian officials. On this charge, the Austrians tried to rob Serbia of her independence.

Britain, France, Russia and other countries tried their utmost to keep the peace of Europe as agreed and signed by the largest powers of Europe, Germany included. But, encouraged by Germany, the Austrians declared war on Serbia on July 28th 1914, and bombarded Belgrade. Russia, to protect the small state Serbia, declared war on Austria July 30th 1914. Next day, Germany declared war on Russia, and also France, for they were upholding the protection of Serbia, as in the agreement. An agreement had also been made between England and France to protect each other's interests. France undertook to mass her main Fleet for the protection of British and French interests in the Mediter-ranean while Britain looked after the interest of both countries in the Channel and the North Sea. Thus, when France entered into war, we were in honour bound to protect the shores of Northern France. A treaty had also been signed by us to protect the neutrality of Belgium and Holland. So on the 3rd August 1914 when German troops broke over the boundaries of Belgium, our Government sent an ultimatum to Germany, which was ignored. To act up to our promises signed in the Treaty we declared war on Germany to protect Belgium on the 4th August 1914.

MEANWHILE, IN ENGLAND …

SLEEPING UNDER THE STARS

About this time, the August holidays were in progress and my brother-in-law and I were set to spend our holidays taking a bicycle trip to visit some friends we had not seen for several years who were living in Norfolk. We commenced our journey on a bright Sunday morning around 7 a.m. Our road took us through Epping Forest, which was looking fine. The trees were in full leaf, blackberries were plentiful, so were the crab apples. There were plenty of people about in the forest, and quite a large number with bicycles. We rode steadily, stopping now and then for a snack, or a drink at a wayside inn. It was late in the afternoon when we stopped at a village called Haver-hill where we made a small meal out of ham and eggs with tea. The man who served us told us he was

Overleaf

Plate 1 (left)
Village church
at Northwold,
Norfolk

Plate 2 (right)
High Street
Epping

THE VILLAGE CHURCH
NORTH WALD

HIGH STREET
EPPING

expecting to be called up for war at any time, which meant losing his little business. We paid for the meal, which was very cheap, and taking some sandwiches with us we went on our way. At our next stopping place we intended staying for the night, but it happened that there was a fair on, and try as we might, we could not get lodgings. So that night we slept in a wood.

We were very cold when we woke up next morning, and were glad to get on our bikes to get exercise and warm ourselves. We soon got warm, and after a while we stopped at a stream and had a good wash. Getting on our journey we reached Northwold, our destination, after a ride of about twelve miles. The time was about 7 a.m. It was a very small village, but it had a pretty little church. We stopped at an inn called King George where we had breakfast. Then after writing home, we called on my brother-in-law's friends. Among them were two elderly ladies who were sisters, their ages being ninety-six and seventy. One was quite nimble while the other was an invalid. They were glad to see us, and made us welcome. In their garden were several fruit trees and a variety of flowers.

Leaving the cottage for a time, we strolled round the lanes returning to join the ladies to partake of tea. After tea, we sat chatting with our hosts for some time. Then giving them our thanks and wishing them 'goodnight' we went to the King George Inn where we arranged lodgings for the week. We spent a very comfortable time during our stay, and were sorry when it was time to start back on our homeward journey. It took much less time going home than it did coming. We rode hard all day arriving at Epping Forest dead-beat. It was now late at night, so we decided to sleep a few hours in the forest among the ferns. Arising next morning, we continued our journey.

HARRY JOINS UP

Passing the 10th London Territorial Head Quarters in Mare Street, Hackney, we noticed a sentry posted at the gates. On arriving home we had breakfast, and the general conversation was how the War was progressing. The following Monday we began work again. As the days passed, we read that the War was getting more serious. The Germans had over-run Belgium, plundering and burning as they advanced. They behaved generally like wild beasts, killing young and old if they in any way hampered their progress. In all parts of England, men were being called up in their thousands, these being reserves. Thousands more were eager to don khaki and get at the Germans. The Belgians had a small army that fought well, and bravely tried to check the German advance. The Kaiser and Germans in general sneered at the army of Britain saying: 'We will soon smash their contemptible small army'.

The German advance had been fast and furious and France had lost miles of ground to the enemy. The French troops never lost heart but fought all the more. Recruiting meetings were held all over England with good results, and soon we had a great army to fight the Hun. Leaving work one evening, I had the toothache very bad, so I went to have the tooth out. The first dentist I visited tried to remove it, but after pulling it about, failed to remove it. My face was painful, so I made my way to another dentist. On the way there, I met a recruiting meeting and was stopped and asked if I would join up. I thought more about having my tooth out, promising that I would do so later. Finding the other dentist, he extracted the decayed tooth with some difficulty.

Weeks passed, and recruits were still needed. Advertisements were pasted on walls appealing to all that are able to carry arms to join up at once. Thinking I would join up I went to the 'Royal Engineers', but after they had taken my particulars, I was refused. I tried again to get into the 'Artillery' but was again refused. I decided that the need for men was not so urgent after all. I tried to forget about it but never felt satisfied with myself. After a time I went to the quarters of the 7th London Territorial Regiment and here I succeeded in joining up on May 25th 1915.

THE 1/7TH BATTALION, THE LONDON REGIMENT, TERRITORIAL UNIT ASSIGNED TO THE 140TH BRIGADE

After being 'sworn-in', some more and I were kept waiting for an hour or so to be examined by the doctor. When he did arrive, he went through the pretence of examining us. One chap, for instance, had bad eyesight and could not read letters an inch big at six yards distance, but he was passed as fit. I returned home and informed my parents of what I had done, they were upset but thought it was better to go voluntarily than to be forced.

Next morning I started my drills with some more recruits in the hall of the barracks. Clothes and equipment were scarce and it was more than a week before we received our clothes, then some got only part of the uniform. Staying here for perhaps a month with occasional recruiting marches, and drills at Victoria Park, we were sent to Hammersmith to continue our drills in the grounds of Pute House. We drilled from 8 a.m. until about 4 p.m. From here, we were sent to Barnes Common, where we had all the rooms we required. After staying here for about three weeks, we all went to Orpington, Kent. Our barracks was a disused brewery, and when it had been altered it made a nice show. We soon settled down in our new quarters, and found them quite comfortable. Our beds were arranged in rows, in my room for instance, there were about fifty beds divided up into three rows. The beds consisted of straw mattresses which we had to fill ourselves, and a pillow. The mattress raised up off the floor by boards about six inches broad, with three blankets covered over us, made up our bed.

The rooms were cleaned out every morning, beds rolled up, blankets were folded in one particular way,

Overleaf

Plate 3
High Street
Epping (second
version)

Plate 4
Trench making
at Ongar, Essex

EPPING

TRENCH MAKEING
ONGAR ESSEX

YMCA

and everything was neat and tidy before we went on parade. The food we had here was good and plentiful. Our regiment was still recruiting men and it was advertised as the best-fed regiment in the Army. This may have been an exaggeration, but I know myself we had plenty and variety in the way of food. We used to rise at 6 a.m., tidy our beds, wash and shave, and then get a bowl of cocoa and biscuits. After this we went on parade for physical drill with just our trousers, shirt and slippers on. After doing about an hour of physical drill, we formed up in fours, and had a two or three-mile run around the lanes. On returning from our run we had breakfast. When breakfast was over we cleaned our boots, clothing and brass-work on our equipment, then on parade again until twelve o'clock, when we would go to dinner. About half an hour after dinner we would set out on a route march, and was accompanied by the Lord Mayor's 'Silver Band' which supplied us with music. These marches were short at first, but each day they were lengthened until we were doing about twelve miles. We would return hot and tired, well able to eat the tea that was already laid for us. After a short rest we would amuse ourselves in games. Then most of us would have a hot shower bath.

THE FALSE EYE

Once we went to a swimming bath, when something happened there, which I thought rather comical. The chaps were diving and swimming about when one of them shouted out: 'I've lost my eye!' We stared at him, wondering what he meant, until we came to the conclusion that the 'eye' was a false one. It caused roars of laughter and fun as different men dived in and tried to recover it. But unfortunately it was never found. We all had to be in bed by nine, and regulations were strict against making any noise after we retired. No lights were allowed on account of them attracting notice of enemy aircraft. We were sometimes sound asleep about one or two in the morning when we would be awakened and marched out of barracks into some adjoining field, taking with us a spade or a pick-axe to dig trenches for about two hours. These trenches were only for digging practice for when we should have to dig them in earnest. Strict silence was kept coming and going on these trench-digging parades. Every Sunday we had church parade, which was enjoyed both by the troops and visitors. We were granted leave to go home at weekends now and again. Those that were not granted leave used to have some nice walks round about the lanes.

HARRY MEETS MATTHEWS AND BRIDGE

During my stay at the barracks, some of us picked our particular chums. My chums were named Matthews and Bridge, and we were mostly together during our leisure time. We had not enough rifles to supply all of us, so we used to take it in turns to drill with those that we had. All of us travelled to

Rainham in Essex situated along side the Thames, where there were large rifle ranges, and each of us fired at targets, ranging from fifty to a thousand yards away. Most of us did fairly well, those that were poor shots had to return again for another course later on. We already had the 1st Battalion on active service in France. We used to get news of their actions, and rumours went around that they would soon need men from our battalion to make up their strength again. They had been in action in the battle of Loos round about a coal-mining village, and had given a good account of themselves. My chums and I enquired if we could go when the next draft went out to join the 1st Battalion. Several days later, a list of names of those that were going in the next draft was posted on the notice board. Reading down the list we were very disappointed to find our names were not there, despite the fact that they had promised we would be sent. Whilst waiting for the next draft to be called for, about fifty of us were told to parade very early one morning. We had no idea what it was all about, but were marched off to the railway station where we entrained.

TRAINING AT EPPING AND ONGAR

After travelling for a decent while, sometimes underground, turning ways we had no idea of, we came to some Docks where we stopped a while. Some of us thought that we were going aboard a ship to be sent abroad, but eventually the train started again and we finished our train journey at Epping. Getting out of the train, we marched about two miles to a place called Ongar, where there was a small camp of army bell-tents. We were each allotted a place in one of the tents. While we were here we dug trenches for the outer defence of London for a period of two or three weeks. We spent a pleasant time here, there being few restrictions. We passed the day by arising at seven o'clock, folding our blankets, tidying the camp, and by the time we had finished this, the bugle went for breakfast. Sometimes we had bacon, and sometimes rissoles, a form of mincemeat cooked in fat. Vegetables and bread were plentiful, and we all had plenty to eat. We cleaned ourselves up and went on parade, when we were marched off to do trench digging. We were kept busy here until dinner-time and then after dinner, we were back again until 4 o'clock, then the rest of the day was our own to do what we wished, except that we were kept within certain bounds of the camp.

Weekend leave was granted to some men, others took 'French leave'. Several struggles and fights occurred between the camp and railway station, when the Military Police challenged the men for their passes. I never required a pass to go on leave to London as a sister of mine was living at a small farm just a few miles from camp. My chum, Matthews and I went as often as we could and were always made welcome, and had a good time in general. Whilst we were there, my sister tried to ride a bicycle. Falling off several times in the road and running into a ditch full of nettles which stung her rather badly; she gave up the idea of riding a bicycle!

MEN OF THE 1/6TH LONDON REGIMENT

One day there was trouble at the camp. The men of the 6th London Regiment who were camping with us, made complaints about the stew they had for dinner, saying they could not eat it as it was too fatty. No notice being taken of their complaint, they all left camp until something was done regarding their grievance. Several men were put under arrest and handcuffed to the tent poles. Things were quiet until the night-time when the men made attempts to rescue their companions who were under arrest. Tents were pulled down and the YMCA tent raided and the men refused to go to bed until a promise was made to see into the complaint. Next morning enquiries were made regarding it, but what the results were I don't know as our men had to return to the barracks at Orpington, before the case was settled.

It was not long after returning that another draft of men was called for to join the Battalion in France. In time, the names of those that were picked to go were posted up. My chum and I were pleased to see our names among them. All those that were picked had special drills for a day or two; new clothes and equipment were issued, and we were all rather excited. A week's leave was granted to allow us to bid our rela-

tions and friends 'goodbye' before leaving for France. After our week's leave was at an end we returned to barracks, and then on the following Sunday, early in the morning, we entrained for Southampton with the good wishes of all those we were leaving behind.

We thought we were going straight over to France, but on arriving at Southampton we were surprised to be marched to a camp situated some distance from the town. It was rather a large camp, and all troops going to France stayed here for different periods. We had no drills to do, lectures were given to us by the camp's commander and no one was allowed to leave camp unless by permit or pass signed by the Commandant. We had very little to do whilst here. We had to keep our quarters neat and tidy but apart from this we could do practically as we pleased. Some of us played cards, others played football, whilst others just looked on. The weather turned cold, and we were glad of the coal fires that were in our huts. Each hut had so much coal allotted to it every morning, and after this was burnt, no more was to be had until next morning. The coal for our fire was burnt out quite early in the evening and we looked like having a cold time during the night. We applied for more coal but were refused. The coal dumps or bins were quite close to our huts, so when it was dark, some of the men sneaked by the guard over the bins, filled their haversacks with coal, and got back to the huts without being discovered.

Plate 5
The Barracks, formerly Fox's Brewery, Farnborough, Kent

THE BARRACKS
Formerly Fox's Brewery
Farnbough Kent.

There were fresh arrivals of troops every day, and also troops leaving for parts unknown. After about a week at the camp, we were marched down to the dockside along with men of other regiments. We entered one of the big sheds that were here, and each man was given a set of webbing equipment, a rifle and bayonet, several hundred rounds of ammunition, and afterwards marched on to a large transport ship. We strolled about talking, one with the other, smoked, and not a few filled in the time eating pork pies that were being sold by some men and women at the side of the ship.

It was quite late at night when at last we set sail, some of the troops had found a place to lay down on the decks or in the cabins, and were fast asleep. Others like myself prepared to keep awake on deck. It was not long before we were out over the Channel, escorted by several war ships. No lights were shown, except when the ships were signalling to one another, and these only appeared like pinpoints of light. The sea was fairly rough, and being at the fore part of the ship, most of us got a shower or two of spray over us. For my part I enjoyed the trip over, but there was a good many that didn't. Some men of the Scotch regiment were very bad with seasickness, and lay on the deck groaning quite helpless. The decks were awash with water at times, and these poor chaps rolled with the ship from side to side, their clothes and kilts being soaking wet. I guess there must have been a lot of chaps regretting having ever eaten pork pies before they'd crossed the Channel. The ship steered a zigzag course, and when we were about half way across, we passed a large hospital ship on its way to England with its load of sick and wounded. It was well lit up, and was easily recognised as a hospital ship, but on arriving at Le Havre next morning we heard that it had been sunk by German submarines.

CHAPTER TWO
BOMBING SCHOOL

Harry joined his battalion in France shortly after they had participated in the Battle of Loos, which was one of the first major offensive actions by the United Kingdom during the war. The battalion was in the process of recovering from the battle – training, carrying out reinforcement, reorganising the unit, work parties and conducting route marches to toughen up the soldiers. Harry's experiences at the Divisional Bombing School were also quite typical – soldiers were never as well looked after outside their own battalion as they were 'at home'. The training repeated that received in the unit, which was used as an informal screening process for those chosen for specialised work such as being a bomber.

FROM LE HAVRE TO OUR FIRST BATTALION IN LILLERS

After we arrived in France, we remained anchored in the harbour for quite a while. Those that were able to eat had breakfast on board, and then we landed and marched some miles to a camp, or a base, composed of tents. The ground was covered with snow, but not a lot, and it was very cold. Men of the different regiments were soon sorted out, and every ten or twelve men were allotted a tent. We were given plenty of blankets but did not relish the prospect of sleeping in the tents, thinking we were to spend a cold uncomfortable night but it was surprising how warm it turned out to be when we had all got settled down to sleep.

Next morning reveille sounded, and we all got up, and got busy clearing away the snow. Having washed, shaved and made ourselves tidy, we trooped into a large hut and had breakfast. There were pots of jam, biscuits, bread, tea or cocoa, all spread along the tables and we helped ourselves to what we fancied. We were left alone all the first day, except when we were called together, and the camp commandant made a speech to the effect that we were in for a stiff week's training. It was to include marching, firing, bomb throwing, trench digging, the making of wire entanglements and raiding. Next morning some of the men went route marching, but some others and I were put in the charge of a snappy Scotch officer, and marched off to the firing butts or range. There was quite a party of us and we were told in fives or sixes to take our turn firing at small targets. I must say, the officer was a grumpy old man and wanted a lot of pleasing, we didn't seem to do anything to his liking. One test of firing was to fire through loopholes at these small targets. We were supposed to fire fifteen rounds in a minute. We all got into our positions, the word or signal was given to start firing. We all blazed away but after I had fired about six shots, I'd blown my target to small pieces, so having no target to shoot at I stopped. The officer soon spotted me and, with a lot of shouting and swearing, came over to me and said:

'What the so-and-so have you stopped firing for?' Telling him I had no target to fire at, he danced about and shouted:

'Blaze at somebody else's then you so-and-so idiot!'

I soon got busy and potted my neighbour's target more than once before the signal came to cease-fire.

THREE-DAY TRAIN JOURNEY TO LILLERS

We were all kept busy for a week and then set off one morning to the railway station to join our First Battalion. They were in billets at a village by the name of Le Lairs [Lillers] and we were glad to get away from Le Havre base and the grumpy old officer. Before leaving for our journey, every man was issued with bread, biscuits, tea, sugar, cheese, jam and condensed milk to last us for a couple of days. We had quite a load to carry, as apart from these things, we had a complete change of underclothes, two pairs of socks, a rubber ground sheet, overcoat, ninety rounds of ammunition, rifle and an entrenching tool. We set off, and I thought at the time we were loaded up like donkeys instead of soldiers. The train pulled in and we found it was made up principally of covered-in trucks. There were a few carriages up in front, but those were taken over by the officers and NCO. I guess in our truck there were twenty or twenty-five men and when we got our equipment off and put it on the floor there was very little room to spare. We had to make the best of it, and we started off.

THE QUEST FOR A CUP OF TEA ON THE TRAIN
The train travelled very slowly, the sliding doors on each side of the truck were kept open all the time, and for a while we were quite interested looking at the scenery as we went along. Attached to our truck behind was a kind of a hut and at the first chance I got, I scrambled out and climbed up into it. It was only a small affair – just room enough for one to sit down in and built just above the level of the top of the truck. It had two side windows and a fine view could be had whilst sitting down. I thought it much better than sitting cramped up inside the truck, and I stopped up there for some hours. Time passed and soon we were getting hungry. We got on with our eatables and then someone said:

'What about making some tea?'
We all liked the idea but how were we to make it? We had tea, sugar, milk and water but we wanted to boil

the water. We all hunted round and someone found an empty biscuit tin, someone else found wood, and a few small pieces of coal were spotted in the corners of the truck. Some holes were made in the bottom and sides of the tin with an entrenching tool, the wood was split up and we were ready to light our fire. The fire was lit, and we got plenty of smoke. Soon we were all coughing with tears running down our faces. We tried blowing through the holes, swinging the tin from side to side and even putting it on the edge of the door in an effort to make the fire burn up, but it was all no use. The fire would simply not burn up but only gave off clouds of smoke. We stood it for some time then one of the men said:

'**** the fire' and kicked it out on to the lines and so that was that.

The speed the train travelled at was a surprise to us all. It would go for miles at a speed we could easily run along-side, some of us did this and we were able to run ahead and visit the other men in the forepart of the train. Standing and sitting about in a truck was a cold pastime and it was quite nice to be able to jump out and warm yourself up with a good run alongside the train. Of course the train went quick at times, and if you happened to be running and the train quickened its speed too much, you had to get back again quick. On our visits to some of the other trucks, we found that they had got hot water off the engine driver and were enjoying a drink of hot tea. The engine was too far ahead for us to do this, but it gave me an idea. I got my mess tin, put tea, sugar and milk into it and kept a sharp look out along the front. I had noticed that we generally went slower going through goods yards and sidings, and also there was generally an engine or two at a standstill with steam and hot water coming out of a pipe down by the back wheels. When the next siding came in sight, there was the engine, as hoped, with plenty of water hot from the pipe. I dashed across the lines, got my water, fixed the lid on and run back to my own train. I was not able to catch my own truck, but at the rear end of the train were some flat trucks loaded with wood. On one of these I scrambled and, after drinking my tea, which wasn't too good but better than none, I gradually made my way back to our truck.

The day passed and it began to get dark, there was now little to see, and so we sat about talking and listening to the talk of one or two men that had been out before, telling of their experiences. The weather turned colder, so we partly shut the doors and tried to sort ourselves into as comfortable positions as we could to try and get some sleep. A few were able to stretch out on the floor, but most of us sat huddled up together and dozed off that way. We passed the night somehow, and we were all pretty miserable and fed up with riding hour after hour.

About seven o'clock next morning we pulled into a goods yard and stopped. Here we all had to get out, and having collected our property, we were lined up and told we were to stop there until another train could be had to complete our journey. No one was to leave the yard, and arrangements were made so that we could have something hot for breakfast. This was good news, and we were soon hunting about to find out where the breakfast was coming from. We soon found in a corner of the yard, some men brewing some tea for us, also a nice lot of bacon and I must say it smelt rather good after having to put up with jam and biscuits, cold water and bread and cheese.

Breakfast soon over, next we hunted around for a place where we might have a wash. We found several big taps and one and all were not long before they were using them. We felt quite good after this and were more cheerful. Card games sprang up, also football, the ball being a bundle of paper tied up with string. Although the orders were that no-one was to leave the yard, a few men managed to get out and into a village near-by where they said they enjoyed themselves. I think (myself) these men must have been those that had been out before because none of us had had any pay. The majority of us would not have known what to do if we were suddenly dumped down in a French village with no money and unable to make ourselves understood.

FROM TRUCKS TO CARRIAGES
Time went on and dinnertime came round. Our friends, the cooks, had got a nice stew made and we all enjoyed it, there was plenty for all and some to spare. Games again, after dinner, until it became too

dark to play and we all sat round fires, made in old pails, chatting and singing until around seven o'clock in the evening, when our train pulled into take us on our journey. We all had hot cocoa with bread and cheese before going aboard the train. The train was carriages this time and we had very little room the way they packed us in. We put some of our equipment on the racks, the rest we had to put under the seats on the floor. It was now pitch dark and we fumbled about to find a place to seat ourselves. Chained to our luggage rack was an oil can lamp, fastened with a large padlock. We examined it and tried to light it but were not successful, as there was not a drain of oil in it. We sat there for some hours smoking and stamping our feet to try and keep them warm. Of course we all started grumbling and wished we were back in the trucks again where at least we could get a little sleep.

This train, like the last one, was ever so slow and stopped dozens of times during the journey to our destination. The weather was very cold and the windows of the carriage were broken, letting in gusts of wind and snow which now had begun to fall. To make room on the seats, one or two sat down on the equipment that was on the floor. This made us on the seats a bit more comfortable and we had a try to sleep. It was not much of a success, as just as you were nodding off the train would give a jerk, and you would find yourself on the floor mixed up with the equipment.

THE RUN-AWAY TRAIN AND EVERY-DAY LIFE IN FRANCE

It seemed a terribly long night, but at last daylight began to show itself, and we could look out at the scenery that we were passing through, and have something to occupy our minds. We found it had been snowing quite a bit during the night, and the fields and trees were all mantled in white. There were ever so many level crossings along the line, being guarded by a long pole, painted black and white, which was let down across the lanes or roads when a train was due to pass. The working of the level crossings was in the charge of a woman, in nearly every case. When the train had passed, the woman had to lift the pole so that it stood upright at the side of the road. There were more often than not some French people waiting at the crossings, and there was always a waving of hands and a smile for us as we passed. There was always something new to be seen, the way the people dressed, the build of the houses, the way the workpeople went about their business. A thing that claimed my attention was the way that the dogs were harnessed to small carts and made to pull them about, just like horses do in England. We called out Good morning to anyone we saw along the line, and they waved and said something in return, but most of us had no idea what they said, as we could not understand the French language.

We travelled hour after hour, sometimes fairly fast, but best part of the time it was a mere six to ten miles

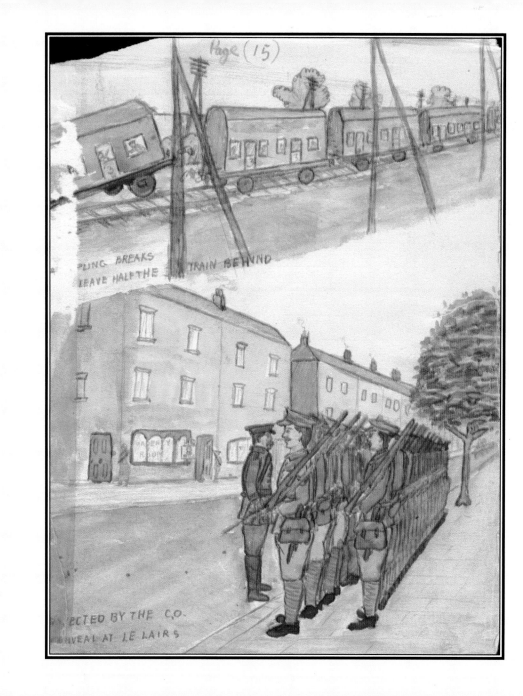

Plate 6
Coupling breaks leaving half the train behind, France; and
Inspected by the CO on arrival at Lillers

an hour. We had got a bit of a speed on and were talking together, when our carriage gave a jerk, the rear wheels left the rails and came down again with a bump. We all tumbled on the floor and wondered what could have happened. We came to the conclusion that we had run over something, but on looking out of the window, we found that a coupling had broken, and we had left part of the train behind. This caused some amusement, and we went on for some time when someone suggested we do something about it. We did! At every crossing we passed over, we shouted out to the woman that the train had broken in two. We might have known that she was unable to understand what we said, no more than we could understand her language. We did the same thing when we passed through a station goods yard, but all the railway-men did was to smile and wave to us. We had travelled some miles by this time, when a man in our carriage climbed out and went along the train on the top of the carriages until he came to the engine driver and made the driver understand that the train had broken. At the next siding the train pulled in and stopped. The engine was uncoupled and started back along the line to find and bring back our missing part of the train.

Quite near to where we had stopped was a village, and it was not long before we were out of the train and having a look around. Some of the men wanted to buy things at the village, but having no money they thought of the idea of swapping their new lot of underclothes for chocolate and things. The French people got some rare bargains off our men, as the men had no idea of the value of the money that was offered for the clothing. There was one coin that had the appearance of silver, about the size of a shilling, but was really only worth about five pence in English money. We spent quite a time in the village looking round. It was quite a novelty to us, as we had not got a chance to mix with the French people since we had landed in the country. I knew, or at least I thought I knew, a few words of French. I tried them out and got along rather well with them. The word went around that our engine was coming back with the missing half of the train, so off we scampered back to the railway and got back into our carriage. We all felt better for our visit to the village and we were rid of the cramp we'd got through travelling for so long and we'd got warm again. Away we went again, the village people waving us goodbye and very pleased, no doubt, that we had stopped with them for a long time.

Among the other things bought at the village were cigarettes and matches. The cigarettes were French-made and not worth smoking. They were made of shag and terribly strong and smelt like burnt rag. The matches also French, were sulphur matches. When struck on the box, they did not burst into flame, but just gave a splutter, and a little blue light. Then after a second or two, the stick caught fire and made a flame. It's usual when lighting a cigarette to strike a match and immediately put it to a cigarette and draw, but when you tried this with the French matches, all you got was a mouthful of sulphur! Or again, should one of the matches be struck in the sunlight, it would not appear to be lit at all, and you'd throw it away as a dud, when really it was quite all right. I have watched a man throw away half a box of matches like this, and had a good laugh over it.

WEEK 1 AT BATTALION HQ, LILLERS—COLONEL E. FAUX AND C COMPANY, 12 PLATOON

The snow had stopped and when the sun came out, fields and trees lost their covering of snow. All around was dripping wet. After a few more hours we arrived at our destination, the village of Lillers. The chaps at the village evidently knew when we were due to arrive as there were quite a number of them waiting at the station to greet their particular friends, who were amongst our number. We all bundled out on to the platform, and then there was a lot of hand-shaking and talking until the officer in-charge called us new arrivals to attention and marched us off to the high street of the village where the Battalion Head Quarters were situated. We were formed up in a double rank outside headquarters and stood there for a time when the CO came out and inspected us. His name was Colonel Falks (Faux) and he had come out with the regiment. He was fairly old, of average height, spoke a trifle through his nose, and had a long white moustache, which hung drooping from his mouth.

It did not take him long to inspect us, and when he was done, we were put in the charge of several NCOs. They split us up into parties of threes and fours, and we were distributed about in different houses in the village. Where it was possible, men of the new draft were put in the same billets as their friends. Asked if we would like to join any particular company, my friend and I said it did not matter much, so we went into C Company, number 12 Platoon. There were about twenty men in our party, and off we marched in the charge of an NCO. Every now and then, two or three of us would be told to take up our quarters in a house or cottage, along with some more men already billeted there.

BILLETED DIGS AND RATIONS

Matthews and I were the last to be billeted. Our billet was in one of three cottages down a lane, some distance from the high street, and the cottages were built on the edge of a ditch or small stream, which we crossed, by a small bridge of planks. There were already four or five men billeted here, and they soon introduced themselves to us and made us welcome. We were soon chatting together like old friends, and they gave us a general outline of what we had to do, now that we had joined the First Battalion. While we were talking together the bugle blew cookhouse for dinner. Two men at the billet had been detailed as orderlies for the day. Their job was to bring to the other men all their food from the cooking wagon some distance down the lane. After serving it out, they were to return the dixie (or boiler) in which the

Overleaf

Plate 7 Troop inspection at Lillers

Plate 8 Sleeping-quarters at Lillers

LIVEING
ROOM

SLEEPING
QUARTERS

food was cooked, cleaned and full of fresh water, back to the wagon. This had to be done at breakfast, dinner and tea. In the evening, before retiring to sleep, they had to get rations in the way of bread, biscuits, jam and cheese, and the men's letters and parcels if any. These rations were being issued for use the next day.

It was a puzzle at times to share the rations out equally, as they were never the same two days running. Perhaps there would be seven men in a billet and the rations would be the lot – say two loaves of bread, one tin of jam, about one and a half-pound of cheese, twenty biscuits, a half tin of butter, and perhaps a few figs. The orderlies would share it out as best they could, but there was always a squabble as to who would mind the jam, cheese and butter, and then one would say that another had taken more than his share, and so on. On other occasions, the jam would not be touched at all, nobody seemed to want it, and so with the cheese and butter. When this happened, we generally used to give this to the French people at the house where we were billeted, or sometimes we would put it in our pack against a time when we would be short of rations. I always kept a few biscuits and a tin of bully in my pack as I found they came in very handy on several occasions when we were short with rations.

On this particular day, Matthews and I went along with the men to draw rations, as we guessed we would have to be orderlies in our turn, and by going with them we should know where to go and what to do.

Having got back to the billet with the dinner, we all sat down together to enjoy it. Our quarters were upstairs, but the woman of the house allowed us to use her kitchen so that we could eat our meals and lent us plates. Nine times out of ten it was stew, and we would have had to use our mess tins. Plates were much nicer to eat from, and without the kitchen for our use, we would have had to just sit on the floor and eat our meals that way. There was always something over when we'd finished eating, and the French people were always glad to accept it.

The family at our billet was working class. The husband, if I remember right, worked in a coal mine some distance away – far enough that he was only able to come home about once a fortnight. The woman was middle aged and had a daughter of about ten years old, and a son of about fourteen who were at home all day except for the time they were away at school in the village. Then there was another daughter of about seventeen years that used to work at some farm not a great distance away. She used to go to work in the roughest of clothes, a bright handkerchief tied over her head, wooden clogs and no stockings. She was away all day, leaving home about six, and returning about five in the evening. After having a meal, she would wash, take off her working clothes and make herself up in really nice clothes with a pair of neat shoes, a hat, and make-up on her face, and the alteration was great – it was hard to recognise her as the same girl. The boy used to do odd jobs after school hours, sometimes selling newspapers in the village, the favourite paper being 'The Petite Parisienne'. All the vendors, or people selling things round the streets, used to use a small trumpet which they blew occasionally to attract attention. After dinner, we were shown our sleeping quarters upstairs, which was also the bedroom of the boy and girls. Only a canvas curtain divided them from us. Both the boy and the girls slept in the same bed, which was made up on the floor, and should their side be lit, and our side dark, we could see them quite plainly. To get to their sleeping place, the children had to pass through our part. We didn't like this arrangement but the people of the house were not worried about it at all, the custom seemed to be quite the usual thing. There was plenty of room for us. We were given about four blankets and made up our bed of these on the floor using our pack and boots as a pillow.

News from the Front on the Battle for Loos

We learned that the regiment had already stopped at the village for about a week and were expecting to stop for another three weeks for a rest after giving a good account of themselves in the battle of Loos. I believe they said that they had acted as support to 'the Scotch Guards' in one battle, and were doing so well that they asked if they might give their support again in a following battle the next day. The regiment made good on both occasions and it was interesting to listen to some of the tales that they told of their own and others' experiences during the time the battles were on. At this time, the Germans were better equipped than we were in every way. Guns were scarce, rifles were not of the best, and transport could have been a lot better. Hand grenades, or bombs, were hand-made by the troops and not always reliable.

A, B and D Companies

At about two o'clock the bugle blew calling us to parade. We all trooped out into a lane leading to the high street. All us new arrivals paraded separately from the regiment until we had a lecture from the CO and then we were placed with the others, being put in the different companies where we were told it would always be our place to parade in future. Orders were given and we formed fours and marched off to the high street where we joined the other three companies A, B and D. The regiment had a small drum and fife band, and with this striking up a marching tune, we all moved off at a smart walk, marching at attention. As soon as the village was left behind, the Colonel, riding a horse at the front, gave orders to march at ease – from now on we could talk, smoke, and sing if we wished, so long as we kept in step. Of course it wasn't long before we were introducing ourselves and chumming up with the men about us, there being a lot to tell each other and plenty of questions to ask. We walked some miles around the country lanes and returned back to the village somewhere about five

Plate 9
Carrying the dixie of stew

o'clock when we were dismissed and were free to go where we liked. We made our way back to our billet, took off our equipment, had a wash and brush up and by this time, the orderlies had brought the tea.

We all had a good meal and afterwards our new mates asked if we would like to be shown round the village. Of course Matthews and I said 'yes'. We spent a good while strolling round the village, looking in the shop windows which were not very big or very well stocked, but it was quite a novelty to us. There was also a market in one part of the village and we were amused to hear the French people haggling over bargains there. The wagons and carts were built differently to those in England. A good many of the carts had only three wheels, two behind and one in front. The horses drawing them looked very poorly and in most cases were driven with only one rein. The principal things sold were cows, pigs, potatoes, grain, green stuff and a little furniture. The French population was mostly women and children, a few men were about but these were elderly men that were sick or crippled. The young women, if not married, had moved to the bigger towns where, I suppose, more money was to be had as wages for the work they did. The same applied to the young men that were not yet wanted for the army or navy.

Seeing all we could, we returned back to our billet just in time to catch the orderlies with the rations and post. There were a couple of parcels sent to our billet and several letters. The parcels were opened and were shared around. Some of the contents were cigarettes and matches and those offered to Matthews and myself came very acceptable, as we had none and had not had any pay since landing in France to enable us to buy any. Afterwards, we sat round the fire talking about different things until the boy living in the house came in and we tried to understand each other's language. This caused some fun and laughter for each of us and went on for some time. Then cards were brought out and we all had a game of pontoon, the French playing with us. About nine o'clock, the orderly corporal came round and read out the orders for the following day.

JOINING BOMBING PLATOON

Things in general stayed much the same for several days when one morning, volunteers were asked to join the bombing platoon. Matthews and I hadn't a very clear idea of what was meant and so we of course started asking questions. A corporal or sergeant passing by overheard us and said that he would be glad to explain if we would go along with him to his billet. We explained that we couldn't do that, as we were to go on parade very shortly with the battalion. He said we would soon get over that difficulty and straight away went and asked permission for us to miss parade, which was readily granted.

Away we went with our guide, who proved to be a bomber himself and, with grins from the other men which we didn't understand at the time, we soon arrived at the bombers' billet. After introducing us to the others, the sergeant gave us an outline of the duties bombers had to do. It all sounded fine the way he put it and, in particular he pointed out, that when we were with the bombers, we were a party all on our own which did its own duties and no guards, fatigue parties (etc.) as the men in the ranks did. Not only this, but we would have our own mess, take orders only from our own officer and NCO and could always be sure of our pay, extra clothing and boots if we needed them. Altogether we were to have a soft time. If, after we had been tried out in bomb throwing and were found good enough to pass, we could decide whether to join the bombing platoon.

Snow had been falling on and off for a couple of days and because it was so cold, it had settled. We watched the battalion march away on its usual route march to perform its drills out of the village. As soon as they were gone, the sergeant formed up the bombing platoon, numbering about twenty men and away we marched in a different direction to the rest of the regiment. The bombers were a lively and jolly lot of chaps and made us very welcome. We marched along the lanes for half an hour or more when we entered a field and tried our hand at bomb throwing. Several bombs had been brought along for the very purpose. They were all duds and quite harmless until a detonator was put into them and a spring adjusted. Lots of times we lost the bombs in the six inches of snow and then we stopped throwing the bombs about

and had a snowball fight instead. We picked sides and had a fine time pelting each other. The other side managed to take shelter round a haystack until we pelted them away from it. This was all practice for bombing and I enjoyed it very much.

NEW ORDERS FROM LIEUTENANT ST. CHATTERTON

Back again on the road and returning by another way, we got back to the village and were dismissed until the afternoon, long before the regiment got back from their drills and route march. Being back early, Matthews and I drew dinner for the rest of our billet and the orderlies thanked us, as they were rather tired after the march and drills they had done. We noticed they gave us some strange looks, winked at each other and grinned a good deal, but we didn't pay much attention to it, as we didn't know what it was all about. After dinner, the regiment went for another route march and Matthews and I went to report at the bombers' billet. The other men were all there and were waiting orders from the officer, his name was St. Chatterton and the men liked him very much. He came after a time and Matthews and I were introduced and asked what we thought of joining the bombing platoon. The sergeant gave details of what we did during the morning and said he thought we would be suitable as bombers with practice if we would care to volunteer. So far as we had seen, the bombing platoon was all right and we both volunteered and were signed on.

The officer asked for suggestions as to what should be done during the afternoon and the sergeant asked if we might all go and have a bath.

'An excellent idea! You may take the men as soon as you like,' the officer said.

'Now that you are both one of us, you had better bring your belongings to this billet,' suggested the sergeant.

So Matthews and I carried our things from down the lane and took up our quarters with the bombers. There were quite a number of us at this new place, not only us bombers but also several men from the ordinary ranks and some cooks. The cooks were based here because the mess cart, or cooking wagon, was stationed in front of the billet and it was handy for them as they had to be up and on their job hours before the rest of the men.

REFUGEE FAMILY'S ESCAPE FROM GERMAN-HELD TOWN

This house, or rather shop, was larger than the last place we had been using and there was plenty of room. The lower part was used as an estaminet, or wine shop and we were only allowed down there during business hours. The people owning the place were refugees from another town in France now in the hands of the Germans. For a time, they had stopped at their old house after the Germans had captured the place. The woman told us that the house became occupied by German officers who demanded this, that and the other, ordering her and others of her family to do different work for them. They used her belongings as they pleased and only allowed them a small room for the family to use. All the men and youths had fled as soon as it was known that the Germans were going to occupy the place, so that it was mostly females that were left when the Germans entered. This particular family stopped a week or more then planned to escape.

A close watch was kept on all the people in the village or town. They were not allowed to gather in numbers at any time and all had to be indoors after a certain time at night. Anyone found out after this time was liable to be shot by German patrols. On the night that these people escaped, it was very dark and raining. There was the mother, two daughters and a small boy. They of course knew the lay of the land and the best places to go in order to get away. They said that they took as much of value as they could easily carry and started off. Everything was going well until they were almost out of the area controlled by the Germans when they had to get over a wall. They managed it, but when, some distance away a voice challenged them to stop in German, they gave a look behind and seeing no one, ran for all they were worth. Rifles crackled and bullets buzzed about but none of them were hit. They ran until they could run no further and then walked, expecting every minute to be overtaken but nothing happened. Later on, they

Overleaf

Plate 10
The bombers' billet over the Estaminet in Lillers

Plate 11
Bath-house at Lillers (some of us feel uncomfortable)

ESTAMIVET

BOMBERS BILLET. Le Lairs

ran into a scouting party of French soldiers who conducted them safely into the nearest town. Here, after enquiries, they got in touch with their men folk who had charge of their money and eventually they had taken on this estaminet until such a time that the war was over when they intended to return to their own home, if there was anything left of it. The mother and daughters ran the estaminet. The father was in the French army.

MAKESHIFT BATHS C/O RAMC AT LILLERS' BREWERY

Getting our things tidy in the places allotted to us, we left the billet and joined the others that were waiting for us outside, each of us carrying soap and towel and some had clean underwear to put on after they had bathed. We marched down the high street and turning right, we went some distance into the village until we came to a large gateway. Through here we marched into a building which was a brewery. The owners had lent one part of the building to troops happening to be in or around the village and allowed them to bathe there. It was only a makeshift baths, for all kinds of things were used for a bath. There were barrels sawn in half, metal tanks of different sizes and one large tank, half sank into the ground, in which a dozen or more men could bathe at the same time. To get into this, one had to descend down a ladder into the hot water, which was about two feet deep. Then at the back, raised above the ground level was a place in the

charge of the R.A.M.C. (Royal Army Medical Corps), who had the underclothes you took off and after bathing, issued another set that had been washed. One man was busy with a hot flat iron, ironing the seams of coats and trousers when I went in for my clean change. When I asked what was he doing that for, I was told he was trying to kill the vermin that had got into the clothes. Seeing my surprised look, the man said:

'Just wait until you've been out here a week or two and you'll soon know all about it!'

We all undressed where the clean clothes were issued and coming out, we went down about four steps to the ground level, taking with us the soap. I went with several more into the large tank and we were soon splashing about having a fine time. The water was hot and there was plenty of it. I just happened to look up over the top of our bath or tank when I spotted several women passing by. I think I must have stared in surprise for another man in the bath with me burst into laughter while I ducked as much of myself as I could, under the soapy water.

'That's quite the usual thing here!' he explained. 'The village people are allowed to come here when ever they like to get hot water – and to get it they have to pass between us lot enjoying a bath. But don't worry, for you see, they don't!'

He was right – the women passed us in and out and for all the notice they took, we might just as well not have been there at all. None the more for that, most of us waited our opportunity when there was no women in sight and made a dash quickly to the dressing room. We must have spent a good time in the baths, as it was somewhere about ten when we came out again, feeling much better than when we entered.

JOINING THE SUICIDE CLUB

The weather was still very cold but nice and bright, so our sergeant decided to take us for a route march until dinner time. We all enjoyed our march and returned quite ready to tuck into our dinner. In the lane, we met a couple of the men from our old billet who, on sighting us gave a grin again, so we asked them what was the joke.

'The joke's on you!' they said. 'For you have joined what we call the 'suicide club'!'

With that, they walked off laughing, leaving us to puzzle it all out. We couldn't make head or tail of it, so that evening we paid a visit to our old billet and asked the chaps there to explain what they meant by 'suicide club'. They explained that when in the line or trenches, the bombers got most of the risky jobs and were exposed to much more danger than the ordinary man of the regiment. At times a bomber had to depend on his own resources to get himself out of any trouble that might crop up. Altogether these chaps made out that we would be in for a very unhealthy time when the regiment moved up to the line again. We could only listen to them as they of course had been in the front line and could say what

went on from experience, but at the same time we believed they were sketching it a bit.

We played a game of cards. Having no money, since we still hadn't received any pay so far, we played for cigarettes. There were plenty of these, for besides the cigarettes that came in parcels, there was a big issue given when we drew rations. Matthew's and my luck must have been in this evening, for we came away with our pockets crammed with cigarettes, with more than a hundred each. We got back to billet just before roll call. We made our beds and sat about talking amongst ourselves, whilst others were writing home. One man of the ranks stood up among us and read a chapter from the Bible. It was rather a plucky thing to do as most of us were a rough and ready kind of crowd and we chipped him unmercifully whilst he was reading and some went so far as to throw caps, empty jam tins and other people's boots at him. He took it all in good part and some how always managed to finish the chapter he had chosen. This happened every night until we got tired of trying to interrupt him and we used to let him have his way.

MAKING BATTY BOMBS AT BOMBING SCHOOL

Next day, us bombers had orders to parade and go to a bombing school. The school was situated about a mile out of the village in a small field. Here, short trenches had been dug for men to throw from, and out in front were other trenches with barbed wire in front that represented the enemy line. First of all we were taken into a barn where the officer gave us a lecture on bombing tactics and how bombs were made. He had several makes and sizes of bombs, some as used by the British and some we had captured from the enemy. It was explained in detail how they worked and the time the bomb took to explode after the time fuse had been lit. Next we were all given a job to make some bombs. These bombs were named the 'Batty' bombs. We were given a cast-iron kind of cylinder weighing about a half pound, one end of which was open. The cylinders had to be nearly filled with some stuff called ammonal, which looked and felt like grey sand. This stuff was used in most of our explosives such as bombs, shells and mines. It was quite harmless until another explosion took place amongst it. For instance, a handful could be thrown on to an open fire and very little would happen. But should the same quantity be put into a closed receptacle along with formulate [fulminate] of mercury and the fuse lit, there would be a tremendous explosion enough to wreck an ordinary house. This formulate of mercury was very dangerous stuff to handle. It used to come to us in small copper tubes about two inches long and not quite as thick as a lead pencil. Attached to them were a seven-second fuse and a percussion cap. Being detonators, they had been know to explode with a scratch of the fingernail, or by being pressed between the fingers. Several men had been known to

lose their hand this way.

After having nearly filled the cylinder with the ammonal, we had to press the detonator into the centre. Over this, a wooden plug was fixed, the fuse passing through a small hole in the centre. This made the bomb practically watertight, but to make more certain, we smeared clay into the crevices. To complete the bomb, we added the fuse-lighter which was worked like an ordinary match on a match box, this being also enclosed in a small cardboard box, with a safety-pin piercing it. We made several dozen each of these and took them down to the practice trench. The officer explained and demonstrated how to throw the bombs, then each of us was given a few. A target was chosen and we had to try and get as near to it as possible. We had no complaints so guessed we had not done so badly in our first real bomb throwing. After packing up the things connected with the bombing, we returned to our billets. For several days after this, we went out practising bomb throwing with the dummy bombs, more for throwing accurately and lengthening the distance of our throw. On the test we had found there was only one man who could throw further than me.

EVENING RECREATION AT THE ESTAMINET
In the evenings, we used to have some good concerts amongst ourselves and any French people that may have come into the estaminet to drink wines or beer sold at the place. It was very cosy and was warmed by

Plate 12
A sing-song at
the Estaminet

A SING SONG.

a large fire. The fires were not as we have in England, but were placed almost in the centre of the room. They were made of cast-iron, shaped like an ordinary pail, resting on a box also made of iron. The box acted as a receptacle for dust and ashes falling from the fire, it having a kind of drawer, which could be pulled out and emptied. The pail or top part was indeed like a pail except it had a small hole about half an inch in diameter where one poked the fire. Covering the top was a thin sheet of iron that could be removed when pots were placed upon it for cooking purposes. From the top edge, the flue passed to the chimney. Fixed underneath the flue was the oven. These fires would burn almost anything for fuel and would sometimes be white hot. The woman and the girls sang at our little concerts and enjoyed them as much as we did. One of their songs I remember was sung to the tune of one of our well-known hymns and they were surprised that we could hum the tune whilst they were singing, in French of course. These concerts generally lasted up until about 9.30 as at this time 'lights out' was sounded on the bugle and we were all supposed to be in bed.

WEEK 2 AT LILLERS HQ – PAY DAY, FRENCH DECENCY AND BOMBING COURSE

We had now been with the first battalion for over a week and at last, orders came to parade for pay. We were paid out at the officers' quarters, a little distance past our billet. The officers' quarters were in a fine looking house called a chateau and covered a lot of ground with large gardens attached. We all waited about in the lane outside the chateau for our turn to draw pay. There were perhaps two or three hundred of us and we made a large crowd.

Whilst standing about, a French courting couple came down the lane arm in arm. They were talking one with the other and walked past us on their way to the village. When they had got about fifty yards past us, the chap stopped and passed water in the gutter, his girl still having her arm through his and quite unconcerned, was chatting away to him. This, of course, the men could not help noticing and they acted in different ways. Some turned away their heads, others roared with laughter, whilst others called out to the couple that they ought to be ashamed of themselves. The couple, who took not much notice of any of it, perhaps wondered what it was all about for the French sense of decency was far different from our own.

Nearly all the public latrines were in full view of the public, and both male and female used them at the same time. Then again, there were hundreds of photos and pictures in shop windows showing men, women and children in the nude and seemed quite popular. The females thought nothing of pulling their skirts right up in public to fix part of their clothing that had come undone. In the larger towns, the authorities allowed women of a certain class to hire themselves out to any male that cared to pay them a certain sum in money. There were regular houses used for this kind of thing and were well patronised. The house or hotel generally had a red lamp outside denoting what kind of house it was. I have seen men lined up outside these places just like people do in England who are waiting to enter a Music Hall or picture show.

Having got our pay, most of us were not long in spending part of it in different ways. I drew 10 Francs, a Franc being about 10 pence in English money. After tea a few others and I strolled to the village to see what we could buy. In particular I wanted a writing pad because so far, I hadn't written a letter home yet. All they had received was a card via the regiment on which a soldier could say whether he was well, sick or wounded and nothing else. As most of the letter writing was done in our sleeping quarters at night, we did our writing by candlelight so that was another thing I wanted – candles and of course, a pencil. No stamps were necessary to send a letter home, but the orderly officer censored every letter before it was sent. Should he consider something written was not in order, he would erase it or return it back to you with a reprimand not to write such stuff again.

I had had a few lessons in French whilst I was at school, but it was very little. One of the bombers, who was one of our party, talked French like a native, so I asked him to tell me what to say in French for things that I wanted. Having told me, I entered a shop where something of all sorts was sold. The shop was pretty full with customers and it was some time before I could get to the counter. Madame at the counter asked what I wanted and for the life of me I couldn't say in French what I did want. I felt a fool with all eyes turned upon me, but managed by signs and attempts at speaking French to make known my requirements. The other chaps who were waiting for me outside asked where I had been for such a long time. When I told them about what had gone on inside the shop they had a good laugh at my expense.

After walking around a bit, we returned to our billet and had our tea and then went out again to visit a Music Hall that was giving a show in the village. The hall was not very big and it had a gallery. The artists and performers were all from the ranks of the army and some quite good turns were given by some of them. Of course, the rank and file of the army was composed of men from all stations of life, so why not some from the stage. Anyway I think all of us voted it a good evening well spent and we enjoyed it immensely.

Having money now, we were able, when we returned to our billets, to treat ourselves to a supper of fried eggs and potatoes with a bowl of coffee. This dish was a favourite at all times of the day and coffee was in great demand also. If we were out walking, we could knock at any cottage door and ask for egg and chips with coffee and would get it – the people being delighted to serve us and always made us welcome if we should call on them. After supper, we returned to our sleeping quarters and got busy with pencil and paper writing home to friends and relations in England. This finished, we chatted together, played cards and otherwise spent our time until it was bed time.

DIVISIONAL BOMBING SCHOOL

The orderly corporal came round with orders for the next day and read out that Matthews and I were to report at 10 o'clock at Orderly Room to proceed to Divisional Bombing School to undergo a course of instruction. Before reporting we decided to have another bath in the village. Just before ten, we reported to the Orderly Room, our names were taken and we were told to wait outside for further orders. The orders came that we were to get all our belongings together, full marching order and report at a bombing school about seven miles away. Directions were given to us and off we set. Eventually, after one or two rests we arrived about dinnertime. The village proved to be not as large as Lillers. Finding the bombing officer, we reported to him and he sent a guide with us to our quarters where we were to stay whilst undergoing our course of instruction. The guide led us to the opposite side of the village into a kind of farmyard. At the end of the yard was a ramshackle old barn with holes in the walls, tiles all loose, doors hanging off their hinges and the woodwork rotting. We were very surprised

to learn that this place was to be our living quarters whilst on our course. Going into an Army stores, we drew five blankets each and on returning found a crowd of other men from different regiments who, like ourselves, were about to embark on the course. The barn was divided into two sections by two low walls about 3 feet 6 inches high, which left a kind of path in the centre wide enough for a wagon to pass right through the barn. On the inner side of each wall, the floor was covered to a depth of a foot with straw that was none too clean. Matthews and I chose a place for ourselves on the straw and pitched our blankets. We joined the other men and there was a general air of grumbling amongst us about these quarters that we were to live in.

Orders came to draw dinner for the whole crowd, the numbers of which were about forty. A small dixie of stew was brought back to the barn for us and when shared out it was a very small portion indeed that each man received, about half the amount we had been used to getting with our regiment. We had nothing to do that afternoon and we stood about feeling miserable and cold until someone made a ball of old sacking and picked sides – we had a football match in a field at the rear of the barn. The game warmed us, despite the fact that it was now snowing hard and in a very short time there was several inches of it. It became too bad to play any longer, so we filled in our time before tea by pelting each other with snow.

Plate 13
Bombing practice at Lillers

BOMBING
PRACTICE
\ LE LAIRS \

A and B were mostly used in the early part of the war, and were partly made by the men using them

C then came into notice, and A and B were then only used for practice

D and E are rifle grenades fired from a rifle by means of a blank cartridge

CRICKET BALL

BATTY

MILLS

PIPPIN

HAILES

G shows the arangement used when firing the bomb C when converted into a rifle grenade

this was done by screwing a rod on to its base

F is a bomb much used by the germans.

We had tea, but like the dinner the quantity was smaller than what we had been used to. Snow was still falling and it was not much use going for walks as there were no special attractions to spend one's time in the village. We prepared for sleep very early that evening with the snow blowing through the tiles and holes in the walls whilst we made our beds. Matthews and I decided to sleep together for warmth, as it was now terribly cold and freezing hard. Considering the conditions, we had a comfortable night's sleep. We arose about seven and found snow still falling with long icicles hanging from the edge of the roof of our barn. No water was to be had for washing purposes that morning so we all washed in the snow. After washing and drying ourselves, our faces were all aglow. Breakfast was drawn from the cookhouse, consisting of the small dixie of tea with a small rasher of bacon per man. Matthews and I had brought along with us a loaf of bread, some cheese and half a tin of jam, which helped to satisfy our hunger.

THROWING AND CONSTRUCTING BRITISH AND GERMAN DUMMY BOMBS

After breakfast we all paraded and trudged through the snow to the bombing school about half a mile away. The place was much the same as the other school we had been to and the lectures we received that day were much about the same also. We threw dummy bombs of both British and German make and had some difficulty in finding them again when we wanted to use them. We were frozen with the cold and could hardly feel our fingers. When dismissed, most of us ran back to our quarters to get some warmth into ourselves. The dinner, which was stew again, was very welcome, so also was the currant pudding that was issued as extras. This day, we felt our hunger was more satisfied than the day before. In the afternoon, we each had to explain in our turn the name and construction of the bombs and make them up ready for use. We spent about two hours at this, until we were dismissed again to return to our quarters at the barn.

Next day we had nothing to do until after dinner. It was snowing again and the straw and our blankets were getting very damp. I awoke that morning with pains in my stomach and had diarrhoea and sickness. I enquired if there was a medical officer in the village and finding him I asked for treatment for my complaint. The latrines were situated at the further side of the green from the barn and they had no cover whatever overhead. I think I must have travelled a dozen times backwards and forwards that morning and by dinner time, my clothes and shirt tail was decidedly damp and chilly through undressing and dressing in the snow, which was still falling heavily.

AN INCIDENT WHILE THROWING THE 10 SECOND FUSE BOMB

After dinner, we went again to the bombing school for the purpose of throwing live bombs. There were dozens of these thrown by the men and they were of all makes and sizes. I was given a bomb that was slightly larger than a cricket ball, it had a smooth surface with a ten-second fuse attached. This bomb was not used much in actual warfare. Generally, bombs were in segments, or casts, so that when they exploded they flew into hundreds of pieces. When throwing the bombs, only the man throwing and the bombing sergeant were allowed in that particular part of the trench. The other men were perhaps ten yards away round a bend in the trench a-waiting their turn to throw, or else watching the others throw. I grasped the bomb given me, drew the safety pin, set the fuse going and swung back my arm, intending throwing it extra hard. In swinging my hand back with the bomb in it, I struck it on the side of the trench, which was frozen hard. I hurt my hand rather badly making a small cut on the knuckles. The bomb rolled away under some trench boards that were a fixture in the bottom of the trench. I stooped down to try and get it out, but finding I was unable to do so, I shouted a warning and scrambled out on to the top of the trench and lay flat in the snow. The sergeant bolted along the trench warning the other men as he passed them. Hardly had I got down in the snow when the bomb went off. It went off with a loud 'bang', dirt, stones and wood went flying in the air leaving a large hole in the bottom of the trench. There was nobody hurt but the officer and other men were almost certain that I was, as they did not notice me scramble out of the trench. I got back again in the trench and the officer questioned me as to how the accident had happened. I explained to him showing my cut hand and he was rather decent about it. He asked me if I was quite certain I was not nervous of handling bombs but I told him I was not and asked permission to throw again. This seemed to satisfy him and I threw several more of various makes and was complimented by the officer for the accuracy and distance I threw the bombs.

We returned to the barn once more and was pleased that I was feeling much better than I did during the morning, although I had to run across the village several times and it had now ceased snowing. Our course of instruction was now completed and we were to return next morning to our particular regiments, not sorry to leave the draughty old barn! We spent another chilly and uncomfortable night, washed as before in the snow, then after having breakfast, we returned the blankets to the stores and put on our great-coats and equipment, ready to leave. Most of us had to travel in the same direction, so we formed up into fours and marched away in step, whistling or singing a lively tune.

Getting back to Lillers, we reported ourselves at the Orderly room and afterwards went back to our old billets. There was nobody about when we arrived, so Matthews and I went for a walk returning just before dinner. By this time, the other bombers had returned and we gave them an outline of what we had

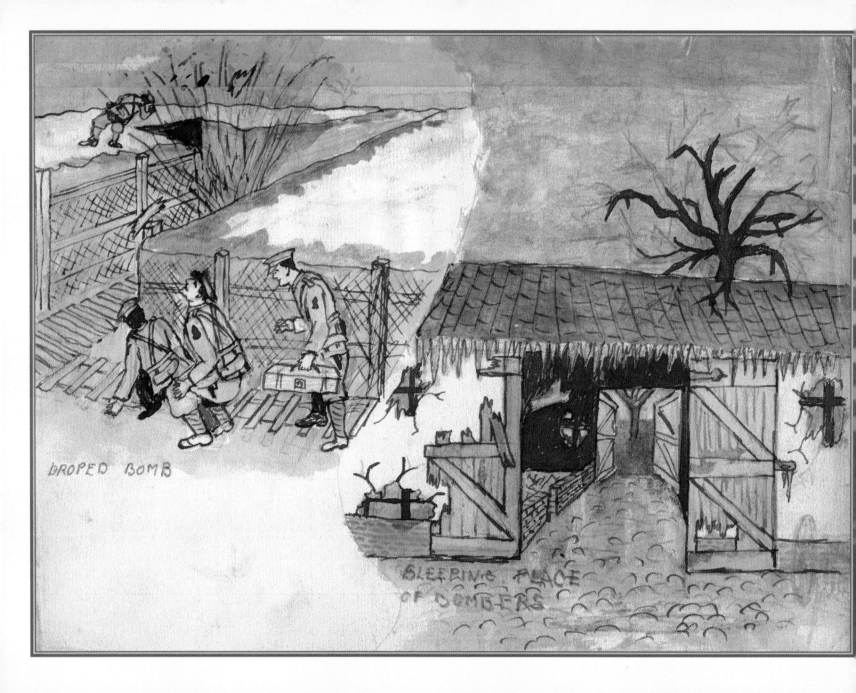

done at the Divisional bombing school. They were pleased that I had not got hurt by the slip I had with the bomb and hoped that I would soon be feeling better and free from the attack of diarrhoea – contracted whilst at the school.

We had dinner with our old comrades and we once again had a proper fill. After dinner, we went out route marching and bomb throwing and had several snow-fights on the way. We returned, had tea and finished the day off with a singsong down in the estaminet. Orders given that night were for us bombers to parade with the regiment as extra long route-marches were planned for several days ahead to get the men fit for the front line again. Matthews and I were issued with a red cloth badge, which we had to sew on to the upper part of the left arm of our sleeve or tunic. We put this on so that we would be recognised as bombers, entitling us to extra pay.

ROUTE-MARCHING

We paraded next morning with the regiment, each of us in our own platoon. The colonel led us on our march on horseback and it was quite strange to be marching with the other men of the regiment. It was a bright day and all were in high spirits. After the orders to 'march at ease' had been passed down the line, it seemed to be a signal for the men in our platoon to chip my chum and I about the 'suicide club' as they called it, to which we now belonged. They made up the most horrid yarns they could

about what happened to bombers when they were in the line. We defended ourselves, telling them that at least we never had to do guards or working-parties all times of the day and night and that we had a much easier time than they did.

We marched along, the band playing most of the time and covered quite a distance. We marched perhaps for an hour and a half and then had a quarter-of-an-hour rest, all men having to take off their equipment whilst doing so. On these marches, we had the mess carts with us, which cooked the food for the men while they went along. At dinnertime, 12.30, we all fell out at the side of the road for one hour while we had dinner. Some of the roads we marched along were in a very bad state of repair, the holes with cobbles sticking up, twisted our ankles this way and that. We passed through one village street where the cobbles stuck up like so many half balls, as smooth as glass. My chum, Matthews, slipped on one of them and ricked his ankle rather badly so that it was painful for him to continue marching. At the next halt, he complained to the officer in charge of our platoon and asked permission to ride on one of the wagons. He was refused and completed the march, which must have been very painful for him.

When, about an hour's march from our billet, I had another attack of diarrhoea and asked permission to go into a field to relieve myself, this was also refused by the officer. I had to continue to the end of the march suffering agonies that made me sweat. Getting

Plate 14
Dropped bomb and the sleeping-place of Bombers

outside our billet, we were dismissed feeling rather tired and foot-sore and I made a dash towards the latrines, which was in the rear of the estaminet garden. Getting in sight of it, I found it was already occupied, so breaking the buttons of all my trousers in my haste to relieve myself, I stooped down with a big sigh behind some bushes in the garden. What a relief! I was all of a sweat. It was now dusk and, after relieving myself, I looked up and found I was relieving myself right in front of the living room window of the estaminet, which was filled with several persons, staring at me. I didn't stop to count them but hurriedly adjusted my clothes and bolted inside. Evidently, the people did not recognise me and no one else saw me enter the garden, for the people made complaints to the orderly officer, and he sent out orders for the man to confess his guilt. Of course, seeing that they did not know who it was, I didn't volunteer the information – had I done so, I no doubt would have got into serious trouble. For my own part, I thought I had had enough trouble during the last week.

The route marches continued every day, going in a different direction each time, the journey getting longer and us more fit. Another pay day came round, which would be the last for some time and, on the advice of the men of the regiment, we got in a supply of cigarettes, matches and candles. All the men did not spend their money as we did, some made their way to the estaminet in the village. There were a variety of drinks, mostly wines, these were several colours – red, green and white: Vinrouche, Vermithe and Vin-Blanche [vin rouge, Vermouth, vin blanc]. Then there was beer. I had sampled all these at different times and found the wines a sickly sweet drink and the beer was beer in name only for it was only like so much coloured water. The men drinking these wines must have drunk quite a lot for some of them got drunk and quarrelsome. In one estaminet, a fight started between the men of our regiment and some other. Chairs and tables were over-turned, one or two windows broken and the proprietor had to call in the help of the Military Police. There were one or two arrests, but none of our men were caught, although several of them were under suspicion for taking part in the riot. Next day, all estaminets in the village were put out of bounds. Some men visiting the village from another regiment and wanting a drink were refused admission and wanted to know why. Not knowing of the trouble the day before, they forced their way into the estaminet and under threats, the proprietor served them. He spoke of having them arrested, at which point they lost their tempers and started another riot. Considerable damage was done to the property. The bill for the damage was sent into our regiment and so much per-man was stopped from his wages to make good the damage. That night, the orders were read out that we were to move up to the Line.

CHAPTER THREE
LOOS

Harry's Division manned the trenches in the area around Loos throughout the winter of 1915/1916. Harry's experience would have been typical, rotating through a week in the front-line trenches, a week in the support trenches, and a week behind the lines, with some periods out of the battle area altogether. This section of the line was quite an active area, where both sides carried out trench raids, mining, shelling at any sign of life and generally aggressive occupation of the sector. While no major offensive took place by either side in this period, life was still difficult and very dangerous.

On the way up the Line to Loos

The Line was some distance from the village, but on quiet days, with the wind in the right direction, we could sometimes hear the rumble of the guns. Next morning, everyone was busy packing up, and by about ten o'clock we set out on our march. We marched all that day, passing on our way the bombing school, where we had spent such an uncomfortable time. Early in the evening we arrived at a village, where we stayed the night. Packing up again next morning, we continued our march. All that day we marched and the signs of warfare became plainer every mile we went. French civilians became scarce and more troops became noticeable. Of the French and British guns we noticed here and there, we could see that they had been camouflaged in an effort to prevent them from being spotted from the air. Guns could be heard firing now quite plainly, and by dusk we entered a ruined village. Here, we had to find what shelter we could, no lights were to be shown and strict orders given not to wander about. All next day, we hid ourselves in among the ruins, and as soon as it was dark, we were marched off to some trenches on the left of the village of Loos.

The Brothers Mack on double sentry

The troops we relieved were of a regular regiment. The night was quiet, as things go in the Line, there was very little gunfire and not much machine-gun and rifle-fire. The trenches were rather knocked about and with plenty of water, in some places knee-deep. The soil was clay with chalk mixed and it was not long before we were covered in sloshy mud. Matthews and I kept together, although we were on friendly terms with all the chaps by now. We were so much together that the others nicknamed us 'the Brothers Mack'. Our first sentry was done together, double sentries being the custom whilst in the line. It's a strange kind of experience, doing it the first time, with it being pitch dark, the ground in front of you all churned up by shell-fire, and only a tangle of wire and posts to gaze through. Every now and then, a white glare went skywards caused by a 'Very Light' being fired into the air. These 'Very Lights' were a form of firework similar to the Roman candle used on Guy Fawkes Nights. They lit up the ground quite brightly for perhaps a minute and were used by both sides to discover if anyone was prowling about in no-man's-land. No-man's-land was the name given to the space dividing the enemy's line and ours. Matthews and I stood on the firing step, looking out in front and from side to side, pointing out different objects that came to view when the Very Lights lit the ground up. The Germans were continually throwing their lights into the air, five or six to our one, and the same applied to the shells. If our guns about a mile away to the rear sent one shell into enemy lines, we could always reckon on getting at least six in return. Our sentry duty was for one hour and we were visited by some of the other men, including our bombing sergeant. These visitors explained different things to us and warned us not to expose ourselves too much above the top of the trench. They also told us that if we should see a movement out in front, we were to fire at once and ask no questions. If it was our men out there, word would have been sent along about it and we would have been told when they returned again to our trenches. We' had got our feet and part of our legs wet coming up the line and before our hour's duty was up, we were numb and shivering with the cold.

Being relieved by two more men, we went into a small dugout, where there were four or five other men already sleeping.

'Find yourself some room mates and get some sleep if you can, for you go on sentry again in four hours time.'

The dugout was lit by a single candle and the entrance was covered with half of an old blanket so the light would not be seen from outside. The men's packs were used as pillows, and their haversacks were hung on wooden pegs, driven into the chalky sides of the dugout. It was surprising how dry the dugout was, considering the amount of water that was in the trenches round about. The rest of the men's equipment was not allowed to be taken off so everyone had to lie down with it on, the rifle was always kept close at hand. We had a smoke for a few minutes and then lay down on the floor beside the others and tried to sleep. We slept all right until somebody trod on us,

either on their way out to do sentry duty or it was the late sentries coming back. It didn't seem as if we had slept half an hour, when we were woke up and told it was our turn for sentry again. So, out we went again, very sleepy-eyed. This soon wore off and we were soon talking together and keeping a sharp look out. This kind of thing went on all through the night, until about half an hour before dawn, when every man had to be out in the trench ready for anything that might come along. Dawn was a favourite time for attacks. If nothing happened by full daylight, men were allowed to do as they wished for the rest of the day but they had to remain in the trench where they could be found if needed.

NIGHTLY ORDERLY DUTIES

There were orderly duties in the line at night, and they were carried out in much the same way as before we came to the front line, except that all food had to be cooked by the men themselves as best they could. When the orderlies went for rations, they had to tramp along the trenches until they got to a ruined village, or perhaps a certain lane, which might be a mile or so away from the front line. If the enemy's shelling allowed there would be an army cart with food and post for the whole regiment. It was all packed in sandbags, marked with the letter of a particular company. The orderlies grabbed hold of them and got back to the trenches to safety as soon as they could. These ruined villages and roads near by were shelled heavily at times after dark, and there was very little shelter to be found in them. When the rations and post arrived, they were shared out and then it was up to the men to cook it. We got beef, mutton, bacon, cheese, butter, jam, bread and an extra issue of biscuits. Cigarettes were also issued in the line.

As a rule, the men using a dugout all mucked in together sharing the food, cooking it and another tiresome job – getting water. This sometimes had to be carried from a mile away in petrol tins. On these journeys, the men got sniped at or shelled, for the enemy realised that these trenches were being continually used by men, going and returning from the front line. Sometimes we would be lucky enough to possess a brazier or an old tin to make a fire in. One had to be very careful making any smoke during the day or letting the glow of the fire show at night, as it would be sure to attract the enemy's notice and whizz, over would come several shells, round about where the smoke, or fire glare, was showing. Those without a brazier managed with a small tin or made a hole in the fire step and filled it with a mixture of candle, paper, rag or a bit of sacking. Lighting that would get you a nice blaze for your cooking. One candle, broken into small pieces, would just about boil a pint or more of tea, or fry a couple of rashers of bacon. If a piece of meat were to be cooked, more candles would be needed. Some coke was used on the braziers, which was brought up the line by the ration

orderlies, but charcoal was the principal fuel used as this, besides being lighter to carry, gave off very little smoke when lit.

The doctor of the regiment always came into the line with us, and under his orders there were about twenty stretcher-bearers or sick-orderlies. These men, when out of the line, acted as bandsmen and sanitary men. All men taken in the line were supposed to be washed and shaved by 9 o'clock, they were the orders, but as a rule we had completed this much earlier in the morning. As soon as the order was passed along 'Stand down', most of us used to get busy cleaning our rifle and afterwards, shave and wash. There was an inspection of trenches and dugouts nearly every morning, after we had been inspected ourselves. Should a part of the trench have been blown in by shellfire, or collapsed through the frost or rain, it was noted and when night came, men were told to repair it. The same applied to the barbed wire out in front. When these working parties were needed, instead of going to sleep when your hour's sentry was done, you had to join one of these parties for an hour, and then go to sleep. There have been times that I have done an hour's sentry, go on a working party, and then back again as sentry, all through the night, but this did not often happen.

The second morning we were in the line, quite a lot of us reported sick with sore feet. This bad feet business was caused through continually standing about in the wet and getting the feet almost frozen. Nothing

much could be done about it, the doctor could only advise us to try and dry our socks, boots and puttees when possible and gave us some whale oil to rub on our feet and legs. Every morning, during the cold weather, an issue of rum was brought round to the men, but not everyone drank it. We were allowed about three tablespoons full per man. Those that didn't drink used to take it and pass their issue on to somebody that did. I didn't used to drink my rum at this time, but gave it to my chum Matthews. At a later time, I drank my own and could help out with somebody else's too.

To Grenay for 4 or 5 days

We stayed in the front line for perhaps a week and then we moved back to a ruined village about a mile away and another regiment took our place. These changes always took place whilst it was dark. The walk to the village was rather painful, our feet were cold when we started, and numbed, but as we got a move on and our feet began to get warm, so we began to feel the pain. It was a mining village, and although so near the line, I believe some men still worked down below. The houses, rather newly built, were knocked about but not so bad as others we had seen. The roofs and upper parts had suffered the most damage, but down below wasn't so bad. The troops were billeted in the lower rooms and should the enemy start shelling the village, which they did at all times during the day and night, we would make our way in a hurry

to the cellars. It was safer than being up above, but if a shell happened to fall right overhead there was the chance of getting buried and having to dig yourselves out. Our first job, when we got settled in one of the houses, was to get a fire going to dry our clothes. We got wood by pulling down the doors and rafters, and going up the village, we were able to get as much coal as we needed. Soon we had a good fire going and we all dried our clothes. Washing our feet and rubbing some oil on them, we then changed our socks and were feeling much better.

Gas attack preparations

It was early morning before we got down to sleep. Sentries were posted here and there about the village, both day and night principally to give the alarm in case of poisonous gases being sent over by the enemy. Should gas be used, the Sentries beat on a gong, and gave a warning to everyone round about. The gongs were empty shell cases, hung up by a string or piece of wire, and made quite a din when struck with a stick or stone. Each man was supplied with two gas masks and a pair of goggles, the goggles were for covering the eyes when tear shell gas was used against us. When in the fighting area, these masks were always to be carried on one's person, whether awake or asleep and woe betides any man found without one. The masks were made of a double thickness of flannelette, saturated in some kind of chemical and were always damp. The cloth was made into a kind of bag, with goggles fixed on to it. To use it, the bag was pulled over the head and the lower part tucked under the coat collar, and we breathed through the cloth. The masks were carried about in a small waterproof satchel, hung by tapes from the shoulder. The tear shell gas was often used against us. A shell would be sent over, and when it exploded would, apart from the ordinary damage, give off a thick cloud of chemical gas, which caused the eyes to smart and run with water. If there were no goggles to put on, it was difficult to see and painful to the eyes.

CARRYING SUPPLIES UP THE LINE

Whilst at the village, we were in reserve to those men on the front line and, should they need us, we were rushed up to help them and give them our support. There were working parties every night. Men were told to do different jobs. Some would repair roads damaged by shellfire while others would go up the front line and fix up barbed wire. Then there were the men who would carry materials of different kinds from the village or nearby to the support lines, just behind the front lines or trenches. On about the third night, I was picked out with about forty others to go on a working party. We had to carry barbed wire, ammunition, bombs, trench boards, picks and shovels, and some large sheets of corrugated iron to support lines. It was on this working party that I witnessed our first casualty. It was a very dark night with a drizzle of rain coming down, no moon showing or stars. Having picked up our loads we were to carry, we got on our way. Had the night been fine and a moon shining we would have had to go part of the way at least by trench. But this way of travelling would have taken a lot longer with our loads and would have been very awkward and trying on the nerves. We would have been continually stopping to let other parties squeeze by us. No doubt one or the other of us would have managed to fall down some of the holes that were in the trenches and as they were sometimes over a foot deep and full of water, it would have been very trying indeed! However, as it was dark, the officer in charge of the party decided to go by road all the way instead, risking his and our chances of getting hit by machine-gun or shell fire. We went along in single file at a fairly fast walk, dodging round the plentiful shell holes and now and again, having to leave the road because of barbed wire entanglements. Some of us were able to carry our loads fairly comfortably. For instance those having boxes of bombs to carry or rifle ammunition may have had a decent weight to carry but the boxes had rope handles on them, making them much easier to hold. Barbed wire on the other hand was not so easy, apart from it being heavy it was awkward to carry and the barbs were continually sticking into different parts of your clothes or other's, which caused not a few swear words! Then there were the sheets of corrugated iron. These were very awkward to carry as you could not get a proper grip on them and the sharp edges cut into the fingers. Whatever position they were carried in, the wind used to catch them, making the arms and wrists ache trying to prevent them twisting out of your hands.

SHUT UP WOLFE!

A man by the name of Wolfe was carrying a couple of sheets of iron, he was one of the men that came to France with our party. He was noted for grumbling at every opportunity he got, and he had a very loud voice. We could hear him swearing and carrying on all the time we were walking. More than once someone dropped the iron with a clatter in the road and then there were swear words from most of us as, should the enemy hear the noise, they might think it worth while to sweep the road with machine-guns. We were almost sure to be hit for there was no cover whatsoever. Having arrived at the place to dump our loads, we placed them as much out of sight as we could and waited for the rest of the party to arrive. The last of them were some time in coming they having dropped behind in the dark. Among them was our friend Wolfe. We could hear his voice long before he arrived and also other voices telling him to shut-up. We were quite near the front trenches now and could see quite plainly the flash of the rifles and machine-guns when they were fired. When a Very light went up both ours and the enemy lines could be seen plainly. Occasionally a bullet buzzed in our direction and a shell or two burst a good distance away but near enough for some of the shrapnel to fall nearby us. We crouched down in the many shell holes that were about and waited for the last of our party to come up with us. Matthews and I were together as usual in a shell hole chuckling to ourselves at swear words some of the men were using when *buzz* a stray bullet buried itself in the ground right between us. We were about to make some remark about it when Wolfe arrived with his sheets of iron. He didn't stop to place them on the ground quietly like the others but threw them down. Of course, they made a clatter and all of us got as low into the shell holes as possible expecting a rain of bullets to come our way. The men called Wolfe a good number of different names and the officer wanted to know what man had made all that noise. He wasn't told, but Wolfe instead of taking cover like the rest of us stood up there in his usual way swearing and grumbling at everybody and everything in general, calling us a lot of windy so and so's for crouching down in the shell holes. There was a general chorus of shut-up and get down you fool. He got down and hardly had he done so when machine-guns opened out and the whole place round about was swept with bullets and one or two shrapnel shells burst above the road. This went on in relays for about half an hour and then Wolfe started grumbling again and wanted to know why we couldn't have come by trench instead of being exposed to the bullets out in the open and how were we going to get back. Again the general chorus was shut up from the rest of us.

At last the machine-guns seemed to have stopped for a time and we were ordered to get on to the road for our return journey. All was fairly quiet again, the roll was called to see if all the men were there and we moved off. Hardly had we gone a hundred yards when a machine-gun opened fire again. We all made a dash for the side of the road and dropped down into a ditch or gully that was there. Because the road was built a couple of feet or more above the surrounding ground, in the ditch we were well protected from the bullets hitting the road and making sparks fly. Everyone, so we thought, had managed to find cover when someone gave a loud yell and fell to the ground groaning. Someone darted back, grabbed the fallen man and dragged him into the gully. The man hit was Wolfe. A bullet had hit him in the back, passed right through and come out of his stomach. He was moaning quite a lot, but in a short time he had his wounds dressed by stretcher-bearers that had come along with us. They placed him on a wheeled stretcher and we were on our way back again to the village.

I for one was glad when we got back without more men getting hit by bullets, for they came so near us on several occasions before we got out of range. We had a nice fire and some cocoa waiting for us when we returned, also rum if any cared for it. We recounted our experiences to the other chaps that had stopped behind and got down on the floor to sleep until morning. Next day we were pulling down some rafters for firing when a Frenchman in uniform came to us in an excited kind of way, throwing his arms this way and that and he got quite red in the face. We came to the conclusion that he did not like us pulling the house down so we made ourselves scarce as soon as possible before he could recognise us and report us to the CO. There was an enquiry made but we weren't discovered. After this we were careful when we went wood hunting.

Happy Christmas, 1915

It was getting near Christmas and the men were in receipt of an extra lot of parcels, not to mention letters and Christmas Greetings cards. We had cigarettes galore both from friends and via different Newspapers. We also had mince pies and Christmas puddings sent to us. The puddings were in tins weighing four or five pounds each and every man got a large piece for himself. We got shelled once or twice and had to duck down to the cellars but nobody got hurt that I knew of. Several houses got hit and these collapsed making a cloud of dust. After four or five days at the village we moved to the support lines.

Flooded front trenches at the support lines

Here we had a fairly comfortable time but it rained every day and the trenches got flooded with water. At nights we got working parties and during the day we tried in different ways to get rid of the water in

Plate 15
Shut up Wolfe!

the trench. We dug deep holes in the bottom of the trench to collect the water and then got pumps to pump the water out. We worked for hours at this but didn't seem to make much headway in lowering the depth of the water. There was one good thing about it, the job kept you warm and we pumped the water from our trench in the direction of the enemy's line. We hoped he was as uncomfortable as we were and that the water from our trench would find its way into his. We stopped a few days in support and then on Christmas Eve we moved to front line trenches again. They were flooded worse than the support lines and we had no dugout to take shelter in. There was not a dry spot anywhere. If we sat down it was in mud, our clothes were wet through for it rained continually and there was enough water in the trench to float a row boat. The water was above our knees. During the day my chum and I hunted round for material to make a shelter for our selves. We got several lengths of wood, some wire and about fifty empty sandbags. With these we made a small shelter in the corner of the fire step. The trench just here was very narrow and there was only room for one person to walk along. The step on which we built our shelter was only about two feet wide so we had very little room. My chum and I had just about enough room to sit down and get our feet and legs out of the water. Later on we found a small brazier and we made a fire. This we placed between us and it gave us some comfort and warmth. A ground sheet was spread for us to sit on, so now we could go in our shelter when not on duty and try to get some sleep. All day long, one or the other of us was at the pumps and at night, after doing a turn of sentry, we were at it again.

NIGHT-TIME BOMBING RAID

To liven things up a bit, the enemy started shelling the trenches that made them begin to crumple up all around the place. Some nights we had to repair them. Having no dry dirt with which to fill the sandbags, we filled them with semi-liquid mud and quite a job we had to make them stop in place! The rations that came to us were wet and sometimes all muddy. There was mud everywhere and it was only by covering up our rifles in sandbags that we were able to keep these free from it and in a workable condition. Even under these conditions, we somehow kept cheerful and jokes were made about the water business. Men would pass us paddling through the water and ask:

'Anymore for the Skylark?'

Or if you happened to be working the pumps:

'Ain't you got rid of the water yet? My, you are slow!'

On about the third night that we were in the line, the bombing officer got together a party of bombers and went out over to the enemy lines. They bombed them good and plenty. Machine-guns were what we were after principally but we managed to bomb a few dugouts besides. Our bombers had it all their own way for a time and then the enemy started throwing his, which is when our men got out as quick as they could. The enemy bombers followed ours out into no man's land and here a stand was made each bombing the other. They kept it up till they had no more bombs to throw and then each side made a dash towards his own lines. I believe the bombing officer enjoyed these raids and the men would go anywhere with him, he was well liked. Coming back, a German bomb fell quite near the officer and exploded knocking him over. He scrambled up again very quickly and laughing aloud said he was all right when the bombers asked if he was hurt. The whole party got back without harm but they were all smothered in thick mud. The bombs the Germans used were not like ours made of cast iron that flew about when exploded. Theirs were like a tin canister fixed on a stick. They gave a loud noise when they exploded but did little damage compared to ours. We got shelled a bit over this raid, but things were a little quieter when Matthews and I went on sentry.

Early Christmas morning – Swearing at the Padre

Christmas early morning, and what a Christmas! Here we were covered from head to foot with mud, gazing out on to heaps of more mud, nearly frozen with cold with the prospect of spending another week like it. We talked of home and pictured to ourselves what our friends were doing, hoping they were enjoying themselves. The water in the trench seemed to get higher each time we looked at it. We could no longer feel our feet. Part way up the legs and all the rest of the body were aches and pains. Some of the men going sick were taken out of the line, which made the duties of those left behind last a bit longer and harder. My chum and I were doing one hour's sentry; one hour's pumping or repairing trenches and then one hour's rest, right through the night. We had got our little fire going this night and was sitting one each side, with our feet dangling in the water. Every now and then, somebody came along and kicked into them. Then there were swear words from us:

'Can't you mind where you're walking!'

And from the men wading along the trench:

'Take your so-and-so feet out of the so-and-so way!'

We were dozing off to sleep when somebody else bumped into us. Of course we let the usual swear words fly about, but the man out in the trench didn't return our compliments as usual. This being strange, we took a closer look at him and found it was the padre. He apologised for nearly falling over our feet, hoped we were not suffering too badly and that we'd soon be out of it all. He felt very sorry for us and asked if we'd like a Christmas card. We answered in some way or other, taking the card he offered, also a cigarette. Our own cigarettes of which we'd had quite a lot, were now a sodden mass in the bottom of our pocket or haversack. We enjoyed that smoke,

A MERRY CHRISTMAS 1915

managed to screw ourselves up with our feet inside and dozed off again.

CHRISTMAS DAY, 1915

Morning came and it was still drizzling with rain. The usual custom was carried out, stand to and stand down, then along came the NCO with the rum ration. He was carrying the rum bottle, but this time he issued the rum in an enamel mug instead of the customary spoon. As usual, I shook my head and said 'No thanks' when some was offered to me but this morning, no refusal was taken. The doctor's orders were that each man was to take the rum as medicine because of the conditions we were living under, refusing to drink would amount to disobeying orders. I drank my issue, having to take one or two goes to get it down. It was strong stuff and made me choke a bit, besides making my eyes water. I could feel it in my inside and it certainly warmed me up. Next came round the Christmas cards, chocolates and cigarettes – we were doing well this Christmas morning. By now, I was feeling the effects of the rum, all the things around seemed different and appeared to move about. Some sweets from a box were offered to me. At first, I could see one, but as I looked it changed into two or three. I guessed I was drunk and wondered which box was the right one. I thought my legs were going to give way and I felt kind of contented and sleepy, so I made my way to the shelter we had made and went fast off to sleep. How long I slept I can't say, but when I woke up the top was off our little shanty and I was sitting in a puddle of rainwater. Getting up, I drank the tea I had left from breakfast, ate some bread and felt much better. Chatting to the men afterwards, I learnt that while I'd been asleep we had been bombarded with shells. I could see the damage they had done round about me. The strange part of it was that I'd been asleep through it all. We got some good news, we learnt that we were to be relieved a day or two earlier and then inspected, because of the conditions.

GUMBOOT ISSUE FOR HALF A DAY

Another thing was that it had at least stopped raining and gumboots were being issued out to the men. There had been a few about before, but the officers and a lucky few men had used these. When we finally got the gumboots, we had difficulty taking off our ordinary boots and putting the others on. These gumboots reached to the hips and were fairly watertight. Why we couldn't have had them before I don't know. After we had worn them for a time, we could gradually feel the use coming back into our feet. They began to swell and feel very painful. The pumps were still being worked and gradually the water got lower until the bottom of the trench could be seen. In the afternoon, the rumour went around that we were to be relieved after dark. And so it turned out that before going we had to give up the gumboots. They were a bit of a job to get off but not half so troublesome as

Plate 16
A Merry
Christmas, 1915

getting the ordinary ones back on. I got mine on after a struggle but could not do the laces up. My feet felt as if they were in a vice and I could only hobble along. Everyone was having the same trouble and it was a slow and painful journey getting out of the line after we were relieved.

TRENCH FOOT

When we were well away from the line, we found some motor lorries pulled up at the side of the lane, waiting for us. Gladly we got into these and rode some distance (about eight to ten miles) to a small village. It had been painful to walk on the soft mud back at the trenches, but it was even worse on the hard cobbles at the village. We were allotted our quarters and painfully made our way to them. Our billet proved to be a kind of loft over a cow shed. To get to it we walked by the cows tied up side by side, went up a ladder and through an opening in the ceiling. The floor of the loft was paved with stone and we were able to have a fire in an old pail. Blankets were given and the men whose feet were all right brought food and cocoa to us. It was not long before we all had our boots and clothes off, and they were hung up about the place to dry. An extra drink of rum was given to each of us and we were all soon asleep. Waking up late next morning, most of us found that our feet were in such a bad way we couldn't stand on them. Some feet and legs were very swollen, and all were terribly sore. When the orderly corporal came round we told him

we wished to go sick but that we were unable to walk to the doctor. He told us all to stop as we were, in the blankets. Later he came back with the doctor, who examined all our feet. The worst of the cases were sent to hospital. The rest of us were told to rub our feet with the whale oil and put on clean socks. We could not get our boots on for two or three days and when we finally managed it we could only hobble about for a short distance. In time, our feet got better and we were able to carry on as usual. We spent several weeks here and then packed up ready for the line again.

GUARDING THE FRONT LINE BLOCKADE AT FOSSE SEVEN

This time my chum and I went into the line as bombers. The sector we took over was known to be a rough spot and not at all quiet like the last sector we were in. The place was named Fosse Seven. We got shelled going in, snipers tried to pick us off going along the trenches and as we went to relieve the other men. They left very hurriedly, leaving some of their property behind. We had wanted to ask them what the place was like and how they had been carrying on but they were all for getting away from the place. They did inform us that four men had been killed just here only that morning by a trench mortar and showed us the stains of blood round about. This didn't sound very cheerful but we would have to make the best of it.

MILLS BOMBS

There were five of us bombers in our little party and we had to hold this trench which was well in front of the front line and reached within twenty yards of the German line. Our trench came to a dead end, that is, it was blocked up, otherwise it led right into the German lines and we could hear them talking and walking about when things were quiet. We took up our positions at the dead end of the trench where there was a lot of shelter – just a few pieces of wood stretched across the trench with a layer of sandbags on top. This would give us shelter should it rain and would stop small pieces of shrapnel. If a shell were to have exploded anywhere near, the whole lot would have collapsed and fallen on top of us. We then decided this was unlikely as we were too near the enemy line. It would be our own shells, if any came, and there were very few being used at this time. Our position was well guarded with a tangle of barbed wire out on top, but it was still possible for the enemy to blow down the blockade or remove it in some other way to make a clear passage into our lines. This, our little party had to prevent! The enemy had a party in place on his side of the blockade for the same reason. We had taken in a good supply of bombs some of them being Mills bombs – a great improvement on the old style of bomb. We distributed them about so that they would be handy to catch up at any time we might need them. Dawn came and so did the shells that the enemy continued to fire into our lines all day.

We couldn't see what damage they had done or know how many casualties they caused as we were not to leave our post unless in extreme necessity. The shells passed over our heads to land into our front lines and only seemed to skim our trench. We got some of the dirt and stones when the shells exploded, but nothing to speak of.

BOMBER DEFENCE

What we were on the look out for were bombs, rifle grenades and trench mortars. We kept as quiet as we could, if we spoke it was in whispers and we all listened carefully to make sure that the enemy did not tamper with the blockade. Once or twice we heard somebody moving about and threw over a couple of bombs. These seemed to keep them at a distance but it didn't prevent them from firing rifle grenades at us. We could see these as they came over and dodged this way and that accordingly to get out of their way before they exploded. They did not explode until they struck the ground – very few fell right into the trench. We felt sorry for the men holding the line they were having a rough time of it. Besides the shells they were getting rifle grenades and trench mortar bombs which not only did a lot of damage but made a lot of noise.

One of us used to go back to our lines once a day for rations, post and water, otherwise we never left our post. We slept when we could and seldom got anything hot to eat or drink whilst we were here. One day, there was a quiet spell in the bombardment and most of us took the opportunity to sit down under our shelter and try to get some sleep. All of a sudden the shelling started again and roused us up. We didn't get up immediately – and a good job for us that we didn't! Over came several rifle grenades round about where we generally stood and one fell right on top of a couple of our own bombs. Our bombs had been lying on a ledge roughly six yards away from us, round a bend in the trench. There was an extra large explosion, dirt and stuff flew about all about us and when the air had cleared a little, we scanned the area to see what damage had been done. Part of the trench was down, two rifles were blown useless to matchwood, a haversack was missing, and shrapnel had ripped through my pack that I'd been sitting on at the time.

SHRAPNEL INJURIES

One of the chaps had either a small piece of shrapnel or possibly a stone hit him on the cheek. His face was bleeding and when we thought it safe, he went back to the line and had it dressed. It was not long before he was back again, accompanied by the bombing officer. Later in the day I got out a half-loaf of bread from my pack and was eating it up when my knife rubbed on to something hard. Examining the bread I found a piece of shrapnel approximately an inch square embedded in it. We all considered ourselves lucky we had not been hit. We learned later that,

considering all the stuff the enemy had put into our lines, the casualties were few. The weather was not so cold as it had been and we got little rain while we were here. After perhaps a week we were relieved and went back to our cowshed billet.

BOMBER DEFENCE AT LOOS TOWERS

The men of the regiment got working parties every night mostly to go up the line and repair the damage to trenches and barbed wire. When we were out of the line, my chum and I were excused these parties and also doing guards. This caused a bit of grumbling from the men going on these working parties but they didn't care to join the bombers and so enjoy our privilege. Sometimes, we bombers were sent to different places to detonate bombs but this was always during the day and we never had to go into the front line to do it. We spent only a few days here and then we were off to take over some trenches outside Loos.

We were short of NCOs and capable men were needed to become corporals. Some men, when asked to take a stripe refused it but there were others who were anxious to become corporals, four of them being men who came over with me. I heard them arguing together one day, putting their views as to why they should be selected. Their age, strength of voice and length of service were some of the arguments brought forward but I believe none of them got a stripe. This part of the line we had taken over was fairly quiet and the trenches were none too

Plate 17
Foot inspection after being in the trenches, Christmas week 1915, above the knees in water

FEET INSPECTION AFTER
BEING IN THE TRENCHES CHRISTMAS WEEK 1915
ABOVE THE KNEES IN WATER

strong. Each trench was given the name of some well-known London street. There was Oxford Street, Piccadilly, King's Cross and others and it sounded strange to be told to go to these places when being directed or directing someone to a certain place in the line. Our trenches were on a slight hill and were some of those our regiment had helped to capture before we joined them. With care, we got a fine view of the country round about and could trace the trenches for miles. A short distance to our left was some ironwork structures built in the form of towers. They were known as Loos' Towers and were part of a coal mine. The enemy was continually shelling them while we were in these trenches but the shells appeared to do them very little harm. The party of bombers we were with had a fine dugout for our use. It went underground to quite a depth and had some twenty steps leading down to it. It had two entrances. The line hereabouts was supposed to be easy to attack and we bombers were put here to beat off an attack should it come. We roamed about this part of the line, looking over to the enemy by means of a periscope every once in a while. No men of the line came here so we bombers had it all to ourselves. We had a good time, very few shells came our way but if one did hit the top of the trench it went right through, the sides were so thin.

Some enemy snipers were worrying our men further up the line and a corporal of ours wandered up to our part because he thought he could get the snipers better from here. He picked a spot to fire from and waited. When the snipers fired our way the corporal fixed on the snipers. This went on for a time until the corporal got a bullet through his shoulder. He dropped to the bottom of the trench moaning and we had difficulty picking him up because his equipment had got entangled in some splintered woodwork. Getting some stretcher-bearers, they soon dressed his wounds and took him out of the line. Our men to the same extent as the enemy did not do sniping, a reason being that we did not have the gadgets. Our men sometimes went out at night after snipers. If they captured one or bowled him over they used to bring back his rifle and other things he might have had. In nearly every case, the rifle was fitted with a telescopic sight that brought the object aimed at right close to the one firing the rifle. Then there was a periscope arrangement so fitted to the snipers' rifle that he could be at the bottom of the trench, well out of harm's way, but could see all that passed in front of his rifle. He would press a trigger, connected to the trigger of his rifle lying on the top of the trench and fire away until the magazine was empty. I saw very few of these things used on our side.

OBSERVING ENEMY TRENCH REPAIRS

After our man had been taken out of the line, two or three of us bombers kept a look out to see if we could get our own back. The enemy lines seemed to be in the same condition as ours and we could see them occasionally throwing up shovel-fulls of dirt in their efforts to make their line stronger. We saw little of the men themselves until around dusk when gradually they showed more and more of themselves. Then little working parties dared to get out on top with a machine-gun, protecting them. The gun continually swept the top of our trenches to prevent our men firing at them. Our men did take pot shots at the working parties but it was risky on account of the machine-gun as well as the thinness of our trench. The machine-gun didn't sweep our part of the line as much as they did further up so we were able to watch and wait our opportunity. One particular working party claimed our attention. There were about a dozen very busy men over there, only two hundred yards away that appeared to be making a gun emplacement or a dugout. They were carrying timber about with some sheets of iron, with the rest digging with picks and shovels. We planned amongst ourselves to let the party work until they got bunched together and then on the signal, all of us were to fire on them as fast as we could and then clear off to some other part of the line. The signal came and we fired off about five rounds each. There was such a scamper over there that most of them fell down, dropping the iron with a clatter. Shouts arose and other working parties made a dive for their trench. What damage we did we were unable to tell since it was getting dark. We cleared off back near our dugout and waited. A second or two later, the enemy's machine-gun swept the top of the trench where we'd been standing, tearing holes in the sandbags. For good measure they sent some small shells as well.

DODGING THE WHIZZ-BANGS

All night long, the enemy and we were digging and making our trenches stronger, both sides trying to hit each other's working parties. We bombers had to take it in turns to crawl out over the top with bombs and watch to see that Fritz didn't try to enter our lines. We were backed up with a machine-gun though this was only to be used in the event of an attack by the enemy. We lay out there a good way from our lines and hid ourselves as well as we could in shell holes. Shells came over but not near us. The most dangerous part was going out or returning to the trench with machine-guns that were constantly sweeping the ground round about, not to mention German riflemen fixed on us. After a time, we got used to the machine-guns and could tell by the sound if they were sweeping in our direction. Then we would duck into a shell hole and wait until the sweep had passed us by. The small shells they were using against us gave us a lot of trouble. They were known as Whizz-bangs and were fired over to us at all times of the day and night. The period between gun firing and shell exploding was so short that there was just a rushing noise – whizz through the air and the shell would explode bang! The whole action took perhaps only a few seconds, little more. One day I was sitting down

Overleaf

Plate 18
Trench at Loos
Towers

Plate 19
The cellars
beneath Loos

TRENCH AT
LOOS TOWERS

213

CELLERS
UNDER LOOS

on the top step of our dugout when I heard one of these whizz-bangs explode just round the corner from where I was. I got some dirt over me and that was all. I waited a minute or two and then got up to go and have a look at the damage. When I got round the corner I saw a lump taken off the top of the trench and found one of our men with his head practically blown off. He was covered up with sandbags, placed on a stretcher, taken out of the line and buried. The parson attached to the regiment always read a burial service and was present when the man was buried. When a man was killed he was buried in all his clothes, only articles found in his pockets and his identity disk were saved. Sometimes knickknacks found in their pack were collected also. These were sent home to relations with a letter of sympathy from the War Office. I learned afterwards that this particular man was one of the four who had wanted to take a stripe. It appears that he had been looking through a periscope when the shell came right through the trench, just where he was standing. The periscope was never found. Some said that they thought he might have moved the periscope about and that it had been this catching the sun's rays and reflecting them towards the enemy lines that had caused him to be sighted directly by the enemy. It was after this that men using periscopes were careful not to wriggle them about, only allowed just enough periscope to stick up above the trench and camouflaged them to look like a lump of dirt or sandbags.

GERMAN SURPRISE ATTACK

After we'd been here perhaps a week, we were standing to, just before dusk like we always did when Fritz opened up a heavy bombardment on our lines. 'This is it,' we thought. 'He's going to attack.'

We all ran to our stations and were ready and on the look out for what might happen. Our guns behind let go at the enemy lines, and some good work they did! It was the heaviest firing that I had heard or seen so far and I was very excited. We had several narrow squeaks with bursting shells. The bombardment only lasted about ten minutes on our part of the line. Then it stopped as suddenly as it had started. Looking to our right we could see shells and dozens of bombs still bursting along trenches belonging to us almost half a mile away. We had a good view from our position. Gradually the shelling stopped and then there was only the bombing and machine-gun fire. We listened and watched for two hours until the bombing quietened down and then we got busy on our own jobs. Next day we learned that the enemy had tried to capture a particular piece of our line by bombing our men out but our side appeared to have given Fritz more than he wanted in the way of bombs. He had had to go back to his own lines without getting the ground that he had wanted.

A PEACEFUL FORTNIGHT

After this bombing attack, things went on in the normal way. The trenches were getting more tidy and stronger. Gangs of our men were busy every night, filling sandbags and strengthening the side nearest the enemy. Now his shells didn't penetrate so easily. Other men from the back areas came up and worked, putting up barbed wire out in front. We bombers went out in front of the working parties to give them some protection in case an enemy patrol or bombing party should come over and attack them unawares. Nothing extraordinary happened on those turnouts and for the whole fortnight we had good bright weather.

VISIT TO MAROC

Being relieved, we marched out to a village that was really in the lines. Trenches ran across the streets and under the houses and were used as support to the front line, two or three hundred yards away. The name of this village was Maroc and it was the neatest planned village I had seen whilst in France. The cottages were newly built and arranged all in a line in rows. They were all of the same pattern, except for the odd one that was larger and more solidly built. Surrounding the village was a red brick wall, broken now and again by an iron gateway. Every cottage had a nice garden that had been well cared for. We learned that the inhabitants had only evacuated the place a few weeks before and had had to get out in a hurry. The cottages were not so badly knocked about considering how close they were to the enemy. Most of the houses still had items of furniture in them, no doubt prized by their late owners and here they were lying about, covered with brick dust and spoiled. From time to time, people came and claimed some of the furniture but I suppose most of them thought that their homes were past being used again and so they didn't bother. We had orders not to show ourselves in the streets and gardens of the village but most of us did do some exploring in the different houses. We saw some sad sights and could imagine the happy families that used to live in them. In plenty of cases pictures still hung upon the walls, dresses lay about the floors, cupboards still had crockery and the remains of food in them and more than one cradle was seen amongst the other furniture. The men's quarters were in the cellars and a lot of the furniture, by way of tables and chairs, was being used by them to make their quarters more comfortable.

FIELD KITCHENS

Our field kitchens were brought up and hidden between some houses, well back from the trenches so that we were able to get our meals cooked for us. The cooks had to be careful about the smoke, but as most of us had a fire going in the trenches at the rear of the houses where we lived, the enemy couldn't tell which fire was which. There were lots of things left growing in the gardens such as potatoes and onions to which the men helped themselves. Whilst we were here the regiment acted as support to the front line and parties of men went up front every night on some work or other. Our trenches were patrolled at all times by a few men, and gas guards were stationed here and there. As usual, we bombers were excused these excursions but we had to hold ourselves in readiness to rush up front with our bombs in case we were needed.

GAS ATTACK ON BRITISH EIGHTEEN-POUND GUNS – BREAKFAST IN THE BOMB STORE

Matthews and I got a job looking after a bomb store. It was in the cellar of one of the larger houses and I suppose there were thousands of bombs packed away all in boxes. Each box held a dozen Mills bombs. All we had to do was to give out boxes of bombs to working parties going up to the line and then stock away any more that came along. Quite a good time we had. Shells came over occasionally but not that frequently. At night, the enemy fired his machine-

guns into the village and so it became very unhealthy to walk about in the gardens, streets or even the houses at night. We had several machine-guns in the village that we used to fire on to the enemy lines during the night and several batteries of eighteen-pounders were dotted about. These had some good results. One battery was quite near to our bomb store and we used to watch them firing the guns and see where the shells landed. The guns were placed in shallow pits and covered over with some light material, coloured to match the surrounding parts of the ground. One morning at about eight o'clock, my chum and I were frying some bacon on a fire we had in the bomb store and making some tea when an extra lot of enemy shells began to come over. They all appeared to be exploding in the village and one or two burst somewhere at the back of our house. We didn't pay much attention to them as we were busy with our cooking and it would have to have been a direct hit to hurt us. Our fire was smoking a bit which made our eyes water and both of us started coughing. The air seemed extra cloudy and we were making our way to open the door to let some of it out when someone knocked loudly on the outside. Opening the door, we saw a man with his gas mask on and it was then that we realised that the shells coming over were gas shells. The man made signs for us to don our masks, which we did in quick time, noting that the gas gongs were ringing round about us. We all went into the store and waited for the shelling to cease. I've often wondered since, what an awful mess there would have been if one of those shells had found our bomb store. An hour or so after the shelling had stopped we went outside and had a look around. It appeared that the shelling had been for the benefit of our eighteen-pounders. The enemy had tried to smash the guns while at the same time gas the gun crews. They'd been unsuccessful since not one gun had been hit, with only a few men slightly injured. The clouds of gas must have been strong because parts of the ground had been discoloured. Tree trunks and bushes were all filmed with green coloured stuff and anything metal seemed to have got an extra dose! As far as we could find out, the gas had seriously harmed no one.

WRITING HOME, AL FRESCO

A day or two later, three or four of us went into a front room of one of the houses to write some letters. It being a bright sunny day, the sun shone well into our room especially where shells had blown the best part of the wall away some time back. We had a table and chairs and were really quite comfortable. There was very little shelling going on and we were all busy with our writing. Then suddenly we heard an extra large shell screaming towards us. The thought occurred to the other chaps as well as me that it was going to go right over us, as they generally did, to somewhere beyond the village. None of us even attempted to move. In the next second there was a big explosion sending us toppling to the floor with plaster, brick dust and dirt on top of us. We weren't really hurt very much and we were all able to make a quick dive for the cellar steps. We waited below for some time, expecting more shells to come our way but they never came. Hurriedly, we collected our unfinished letters and took them below to complete them. We knew it had been a lucky escape. The shell had exploded right in front of our room. Another five yards forward and it would have burst in the middle of us. I suppose observation men in enemy lines had seen us moving about and thought it worth while to send a shell over. After this, I, for one, didn't go writing in front rooms any more!

German raids on civilians

The regiment dodged about in this part of the line for some months. First, in the line and then out again but never far away. We could find plenty to do but we were always in the range of the enemy guns. Sometimes we would go a mile or more back to a village where the French still lived and carried on with their business. Most of them traded with us Tommies, selling post cards, writing material, chocolate, eggs, chips and coffee. There were one or two Estaminets, or Wine shops and the men patronised them well. Now and again these villages would get shelled, sending their inhabitants hurrying down to the dugouts they'd made for themselves under the houses. We had been billeted in the village and had a room in the house of a woman with four young children. One day while we were upstairs in the house I looked out at around noon and remarked how all was peaceful and quiet. The villagers were working and their children playing in the street made war seem miles away. Without warning, a volley of perhaps a dozen shells came over, exploding in different parts of the village. In an instant, the place was in panic, children screaming for mothers and mothers their children, then all of them running for shelter in the dugouts. We went downstairs to see if any one was hurt and found the woman and her family kneeling round a crucifix, praying. Out in the street we learned that several people had narrowly escaped death or injury but that no body had been hurt except for one of our men who was hoping his wound was bad enough to get him back to Blighty.

'Dignity' and 'Impudence' at Loos village

Our next turn in the line was on the borders of the village of Loos. We had had several hours' march to get there and we could see the serious shell damage to roads and houses en route. Thankfully the night was fairly bright otherwise there would have been more of us tumbling into shell holes. All the time as we were walking along, warnings passed from front to rear:

'Shell hole on the right… Shell hole left…' Or 'Mind the wire!'

Shrapnel shells burst overhead the closer we got to the village. Some men were hit and immediately taken to a hollow or broken-down wall at the side of the road to have their wounds attended. Later an ambulance came along and carted them away. Halted outside the remains of what was left of the village, we noticed two shells stood up on end by the roadside. One that was four feet high had written on it in chalk the word: 'Dignity'. The other, a little aircraft shell approximately eight inches high was marked: 'Impudence'. They attracted everyone's attention and caused some smiles. We recognised the large shell as the type used by the enemy during the last battle in this region. Some of our men who had been in the battle, recounted knowledge of the damage these shells had done. Sure enough, when we got right into the village I could then understand how there was not one house, or even a wall, left standing. The village was one big heap of bricks, tiles and mortar and it was all that the regiment had to shield itself with. We clambered over bricks and rubble to access stairs leading down into cellars. Some of the cellars linked up underground with a dozen or more entrances and were large affairs, sheltering quite a number of men. But we bombers found a cosy little cellar acquired an old fire pail to do the cooking on, making a hole in the roof for the smoke, and we made ourselves comfortable.

We had to be careful moving about. Bullets and shells were being pitched among the ruins at all times and every one of us was in full enemy view by day. At dusk, Matthews and I went out hunting for firewood, now made scarce by the number of fires burning since troops had been hidden there. We dodged about until we found something to suit us on the edge of the village. Clambering over what was once part of a windowsill, we discovered floorboards and broken rafters and got busy. It was now dark and we relied on the Very Lights fired in the lines to show us what we wanted. The wood must have been covering a large unexploded shell because when my chum went to climb out he trod on it and it rolled from under him. When he saw what he'd done, he didn't stop for his firewood but hurried away from that shell as fast as he could. The shell was like the one we'd seen at the roadside and would have weighed half a ton.

Water was also dangerous to get. There were only two pumps still working that we, as well as the enemy knew of. Machine-guns were trained on them with bullets flying every now and again to catch a number of our chaps going or returning for water. After waiting for an hour to get them filled it was very annoying to have a bullet hole knocked through them! We carried

GETING
WATER
FROM PUMP LOO'S

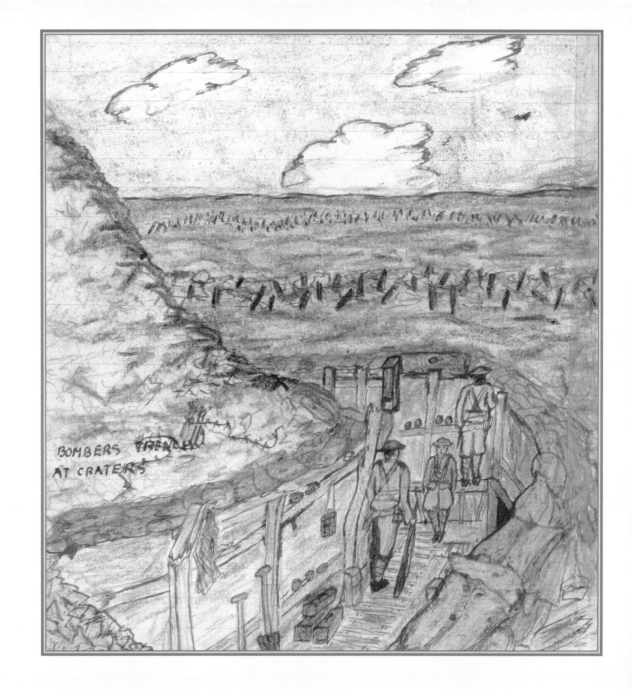

BOMBERS TRENCH AT CRATERS

Plate 20 (left)
Getting water from the pump at Loos,
Dignity and Impudence

Plate 21 (right)
Bombers' trench at the craters, Loos

the water in petrol tins and tossed coins for who was sent. It was a job we could only do after dark; a man wouldn't have stood half a chance moving about during the day. We stayed for only a few more days then moved to the front line.

COMMUNICATION ALONG TRENCHES LEADING TO THE FRONT LINE

The part we took over was that sector that the enemy bombarded so heavily a few weeks back and then attempted to capture. The trenches were in a bad way and not even deep enough by half to give protection to men passing along. In order to reach the front line we had to go along a communication trench so heavily shelled that in places it was nearly filled up with dirt with every exposed place having a machine-gun trained on it. When we got to these points, half a dozen of us at a time would make a dash and clamber over as soon as the bullets stopped only to get along to the next point, where the same business had to be done again. Sometimes the trench was so narrow that we had to force our way through. Our packs would get jammed and those men behind would have to give their help by pushing the man until he got free. Now and again another trench would adjoin our one at right angles or we come to a place where the trenches forked. The trouble was to know which trench to go along when it was pitch dark, one man following the other in front and so on, from the leading man right back to the last in the regiment. It was only possible to go in single file so that whenever we were held up by enemy fire, we would lose touch with the man in front. The grumbling and swearing that would go on when that happened!

'Get along in front! What the so-and-so's the matter with you? Get on!'

If a man going along were to find that the one behind had dropped back and couldn't be heard or seen, he would send a message forward:

'Lost touch in the rear.'

This or any other message, for that matter, would be passed from man to man until it got to the front leading man who was generally an officer in command. Then he would stop and wait for the lost men to catch up or send a message back for the last man to wait and act as guide. Another common occurrence to hold us up would be when a man's rifle would get entangled in some overhead wires (generally telephone wires). Lord, the cursing and swearing while trying to disentangle the wire, especially if the men behind him happened to be in an exposed position, not knowing any second if a gun might open up and mow them down! Some would take a chance, climb out of the trench and walk along the top. As we got nearer the front line so we began to get shells and trench mortar bombs flying around. The trench mortars were the worst of the two and when they dropped anywhere near the trench, the whole lot would cave in. The concussion from the explosion would knock you over and almost deafen you.

THE BRITISH FRONT LINE AND FIVE MINE CRATERS

At last we got to the front line, or what was left of it. The enemy must have wanted it badly or was trying very hard to keep us out of it. There were five mine craters at intervals and no great distance apart along our front line. It had been the intention of the enemy to own these craters after he had made them but not one did he get! These mines were used by both sides and entailed a lot of hard work sometimes taking months to complete. If either side decided to mine their opponent's position, they would have to dig a small tunnel from their own lines to lead underneath the enemy's. Then at the end a large quantity of explosive would be packed in. When this went off, the ground overhead would be blown sky high and guns, men or anything else went with it. As a rule, the part of the line where these mines were let off would become disorganised so that during the excitement, the side that exploded the mine can attempt to capture the position. Our duties when we arrived were to guard these craters and prevent the enemy capturing them.

The craters were high mounds of earth between twenty and thirty feet high and hollow in the middle. We had to take up our positions in the hollow on that side which was nearest the enemy. Our positions had to be taken over during dark and once we were there, we could not leave until the next night. Food, water, bombs and ammunition had to be taken to last you till that time arrived. There were two or three of us bombers to each crater and we used a periscope during the day for observation purposes. During daylight, we hid ourselves as well as we could from aeroplanes. If the enemy knew we were in the crater, he could bomb us quite easily from his trenches and we would have no chance of getting away. That night and the following day passed off all right for us in the crater but it was not so in the other parts of the line. We could hear the shells, bombs and trench mortars exploding continuously. Night came again and some more bombers relieved us. The bombers had made their Headquarters at the foot of the next crater. By some lucky chance, a dugout had escaped damage by the exploding mine and it was here that we went to when we were relieved. We gave our report of what we had seen and got on with some bread and cheese and hot cocoa. Not having slept for more than twenty-four hours, we got on the floor and were soon fast asleep.

PROVIDING BOMB COVER TO A WORKING PARTY IN NO MAN'S LAND

We were not disturbed for some hours then we were woken up and had to go on duty. I was told to go out in No man's land with a bag of bombs to protect a working party making a new trench in place of the one that had got minced. It was pouring with rain and I didn't care much for my job. Matthews, my chum, was placed in a part to the right of the working party

UNDER THE
ENIMYES WIRE

where some of our trenches had caved in. I was ordered to get as near to the enemy's position as possible and, in the event of a party getting out of their trenches to attack, I was to throw my bombs and get back to our lines as best I could. For my protection, a rifleman was placed between the working party and me and it was his job to come and tell me when to come back.

The ground I had to crawl over was strewn with lumps of chalk blown there by the mine and I knocked them together, going along, they tinkled like china causing enemy sentries to take pot shots at where the sound was coming from. Before I had crawled far I was wringing wet and the front of me was smothered with mud. Eventually, I got right up to the barbed wire in front of the enemy's line. I found a shell hole and waited here hoping that the attack would not come off and that I wouldn't need to use my ten bombs. I had my rifle with me but it wouldn't have been much use to me at such close quarters and it hampered my movements when crawling along the ground. It got in an awful mess, at least the covering of canvas that I had over it did. Having hidden myself, getting as comfortable as I could, I kept a sharp look out both for my own sake and the working party behind which I could now hear digging. I was glad in a way that the rain was coming down as hard as ever, for I guess it drove most of the Germans to shelter. Had it been fine, some of them were likely to have looked over the top and seen me.

Then what a poor chance I would have stood!

I hadn't been in my position long before I found out where the German sentries and a machine-gun emplacement were sited. There was not much movement in the German trench. Now and again I may have heard men passing along or talking when the sentry was relieved, but apart from this it was fairly quiet. The sentries fired a Very Light into the air about every ten minutes, but these went well behind me. They showed up the ground as bright as day near where they fell. Our working party worked fairly quietly for a time but when they got down deeper they were not so careful. They made enough noise to set the machine-gun going and didn't I bless them! I looked round several times to see if I could spot the rifleman who was covering me. He must have hid up well for I never discovered him. Our line was getting its share of shells and our shells seemed to skim just above my head before they landed with a crash into the German trenches. I was thankful that none dropped near me because I was feeling not one bit cheerful. What with being wet to the skin and having to keep very still, I got cold and cramp through staying in one position and my shell hole was collecting quite a lot of water.

Glancing along to my right I saw about a dozen men get out of our trenches about two hundred yards away and wander about in No-man's-land. They were out there for quite a while, what for I couldn't guess, as they didn't seem to have any

Plate 22
Under the enemy's wire, Loos

objective in view, they simply wandered around. They were not men of our regiment but the one next to us in the line. The German sentries must have heard them moving about out there because Very Lights were put up one after the other and shots fired several times. Like black shadows, I saw the men duck down and gradually move off towards their own lines. Before they all got back, a machine-gun started firing and bowled one of them over. He started to yell for help and called to the others to help him. This aroused other enemy soldiers who not only fired their rifles but started throwing bombs on the chance that there were some more of our men out there still. As far as I could see they all got back except for this one man. For hours, it seemed to me, this wounded man begged for someone to help him, calling out: 'Oh my poor wife and kiddies! What will they do without me? I'm bleeding to death … won't some of you come and help me!' All this time, the Germans kept up their bombing and firing in case anyone should try and go to the man's aid. Gradually the wounded man's cries got fainter and fainter until I could hear him no more. Then the firing died down. I looked out but I didn't see anyone go out to find the man.

Our working party was making quite a lot of noise now and I could hear the mumble of their voices as they talked to one another. The machine-gun near me had kept firing over that way every now and again but now that the working party had made itself some cover, I guess that they must have thought the gun was not much use. Not to be outdone, several Germans then got some rifle grenades and fired them at the working party. These were more effective, causing the working party to seek safer quarters and finish working for the night.

I knew nothing of this at the time and still hung on to my job. The hours I must have spent there and still no one came to let me know I could get back! When dawn was not far off, just when I'd began to think they had forgotten me and was about to go back on my own account, I heard a faint voice behind me. Someone tugged at my foot and looking round I saw a man making signals for me to return to our line. He didn't stop for me but wriggled away as fast as he could. I got ready to follow him only to find that my gas mask had somehow got entangled in the barbed wire. I tried to release it but my fingers were numbed with the cold. I didn't dare make a noise pulling it out so I slipped under the wire and left the thing hanging there. Now to get back! I was so stiff I could hardly move my limbs but progressing with them to get further and further along, the use came back into them. I got within a few yards of the trench they had made when that machine-gun started again. I got into a shell hole, as low as I could with the bullets buzzing around me, too close for my liking. I waited in there for the gun to stop and then made a dash, throwing myself over the parapet and falling into the trench, safe from bullets at last.

RETURN TO BASE AND MY CHUM

Making my way to our dugout where they had a nice fire going, my chum and the sergeant greeted me. They helped me to a good drink of hot cocoa and something to eat, followed by a tot of rum. Afterwards, we sat round the fire talking and tried to dry some of my clothes. My chum hadn't got wet when he was out on his job because he'd been able to stand up and had worn his ground sheet over his shoulders. One thing that I was glad about was that I hadn't been wearing my greatcoat, so it was quite dry. While we were chatting an order came that one bomber, or two if they could be had, were to go and join some others in a piece of trench at the foot of one of the craters. Another bomber was to go on duty round the side of it. Whoever was picked for the trench job had to go there before daylight to avoid being seen. Matthews and I were the only two available so I got picked for the trench job and my chum had the other one. A rifleman was to go with me and when we set out we were to take the day's rations of water and post with us for the whole party. First the sergeant showed us the way and gave some orders to the bombers already there. Then we went back and collected our loads. I carried the water and post and the other chap carried the rations. We had to do things in a hurry as daylight was breaking. On the way to the trench we passed my chum's post and we spoke a few words to each other. I believe this was the first time that we had not shared the same duty. Where we had to go was only a short distance away from him, perhaps forty yards. Before we could get there the enemy started shelling and we had to run for it.

A SHARED DUTY WITHOUT MATTHEWS

We got there safely, went down the dugout and went to sleep for a few hours. Altogether there were eight of us bombers, five belonging to our regiment and three from another. We didn't have much to do during the day apart from at least two men being on duty in the trench. But at night we had to keep very alert because this very trench we were holding was the one the Germans had bombed and attempted to capture a little while back. Both regiments had a good supply of bombs. The other bombing regiment was stationed ten yards further along at the foot of the mine crater. During the night when we were posted on double sentries, I was put with the rifleman. He didn't like being with us at all and was ever so nervous. He was afraid to look out over the top because of the rifle grenades that kept coming our way and I was forever trying to make him keep a proper look out. He fair got on my nerves and was no help to me at all! All the time it would be:

'Hark! What's that? Somebody's coming! Throw a bomb!'

Or he would be asking the time every ten minutes:

'How much longer before we're relieved?'

At last I gave him the watch to hold and did the looking-out on my own!

THE HIDDEN MINE AND THE DEATH OF A FRIEND

On the second day, things were quieter than usual but I fancied I had heard a thumping noise coming along the ground sounding like posts were being driven in. When the bombing officer visited us I mentioned the fact. He answered:

'Probably they're making a dugout or something over there and that's what you can hear ...'

He considered the idea that another mine was being prepared under us, out of the question. He thought a bombing raid was more likely and warned us to be prepared for it. Next morning, before daylight, the rifleman and I were sent for the rations and post with the warning to get back before light. We carried the rations and post in a large mailbag and the water in two petrol tins. The chap with me asked if someone else could be put in his place but was refused. On our way back I stopped to have a chat with Matthews who was on duty at the time. I continued on, taking the lead and carrying the water with the other chap close behind me carrying the mailbag. To cover the distance between Matthews' post to ours took no more than a minute but hardly had we dropped into the trench when a mine was exploded virtually under us. Around us the earth quivered and heaved and at the same moment a huge sheet of flame shot out of the ground to a great height. With it came volumes of smoke and tons of earth, chalk and barbed wire entanglements. The centre of the explosion was where I had just left my chum, Matthews.

FULL ENEMY ATTACK

Our trench crumpled down on top of us and we were buried to above the waist. I struggled out of the dirt somehow and crouched under a ledge in the side of the trench that was less damaged. I stayed long enough to allow the stuff flying up in the air to come down and then rushed along the few yards of trench to our store of bombs. The rest of our bombing regiment was in the dugout which through a miracle was hardly hurt. The stairs leading down into the bottom of the dugout were lop-sided and a little chalk had fallen but that was all. The men came running up as I arrived and we all grabbed a couple of bombs apiece and waited. We fully expected the enemy to come and attack us. Our bombing officer came over the top to join us. Hell broke loose, hundreds of explosions were happening around us. Something of all sorts were being fired at us; shells, bombs, rifle grenades, mini 'werfers' (trench mortars), machine-guns and rifles. The air was filled with smoke, shrapnel and flying dirt. The noise made you dizzy.

BURIED IN THE EXPLOSION

The enemy attack on our position never came because men in our trenches behind us fired volleys of bullets over the enemy lines, preventing them from getting out. Round the back of one of the craters, a party of German bombers made an attempt to enter our lines but were all shot down by our machine-gunner. Like us, the gunner had had the trench cave in around him but had got free, remounted his gun and stopped the raiding party. He and his company officer were duly awarded the Military Medal. *(Note: only private soldiers and NCOs were awarded the Military Medal (MM). Junior officers were normally awarded the Military Cross (MC) for similar actions. On this day Lieutenant St Chatterton was awarded the MC.)* It was considered that the raiders had been trying to capture the crater left by the exploded mine and already some of our men were climbing up the sides of the crater before the dust had settled. One

man got half way up and was beckoning to the others to follow when he was riddled with bullets and rolled back down to the bottom, dead. The three bombers belonging to the other regiment all got buried alive under the tons of dirt thrown up by the mine. We got shovels and tried to get to them but the enemy saw us and kept us away with gunfire. Later on we had to build over the spot creating a barrier of earth and sandbags for our own protection. The chap that had been with me could not be found and it was supposed that he had got buried under the fallen trench. We couldn't get there to investigate, as it would force us to be fully exposed to the enemy. Finally, we learned that he had been only partially buried and getting free had run in a panic towards our front line. He was seen by an officer who threatened him with his revolver and told him to return to us. The chap fainted and was dragged into the trench. He was eventually given a court martial and pleaded for his defence that he was under age for military service. This was found to be correct but to look at him you would think he was a lot older than seventeen years old. He was a tall well-built chap and looked at least nineteen. What happened to him after that I don't know but I am almost sure I saw him from a distance in Gravesend, Kent, whilst I was riding on a tram car. He was then in uniform and I had just been discharged from the army.

EXPLOSION AFTERMATH

The time following the mine explosion was rather bad for all of us in the line. The enemy continually bombarded us with all sorts during daylight and at night, raiding parties tried us with bombs. To make the craters more difficult to capture, some of us were sent out to run barbed wire around them and up the side nearest the enemy. We were unable to put much down as the enemy, expecting us to do something of the sort, was on the look out for us. A number of Germans surprised one of our men in the crater one night and got the better of him. There was a scuffle and our man called out for help. Before anyone could get to him, we heard him cry 'Oh! several times and then he started shouting: 'Murder! Murder!' Then everything went quiet. When some of our men finally got to him, he was dead. He had either been bayoneted or stabbed with a knife. Bombs were thrown at where the Germans were thought to be but I think they got away safely.

'MINI WERFERS' [OR 'MINNIES', FROM A TYPE OF GERMAN TRENCH MORTAR CALLED *Minenwerfer*]

I was on the front line for the whole day and we were never at ease for more than five minutes. Sleep or rest was impossible and we managed on snacks. Throughout, the enemy fired large trench mortars over at us. We could hear the guns being fired in the enemy line and watched the bomb coming across, towards us. It would be fired high into the air and then drop down somewhere in our lines. Although few fell accurately, it was sufficient if they fell four yards away to make the trench cave in at that spot. Dugouts were no more when one of these mini werfers near enough dropped on top! One or two men, usually NCOs, were stationed along the trench to give warning when the mini werfers were coming. They had a whistle so they could blow loudly and shout: 'Bomb right!' or 'Bomb left!' according to where they thought the thing would fall. Then all the men would scamper along the trench out of harm's way. This kind of thing went on all day long and was very tiring. I heard one man, puffing and blowing through running up and down saying: 'So-and-so on the so-and-so bombs! I ain't going to run no more!' He sat down on the fire step but when the whistle blew again, I saw him running with the rest as usual.

LIKE RATS IN A CAGE

Another time, two men were asleep on a fire step where the sides of the trench had been kept up by thick wire mesh held in place by struts of wood. When a mini werfer came over and landed a few yards from the trench, the explosion caused the sides of the trench where they had been sleeping to bulge out. Slowly the wire mesh bent over with the weight of dirt behind it until it had enfolded the men and trapped them like rats in a cage. They woke up, of course, but not in time to get out so they started to shout for help. Men came to find the root of the trouble and realising what had happened could only laugh at their predicament. In the end they released them, unharmed and unscathed!

SIX MILE WALK TO A VILLAGE AFTER RELIEF

Trench digging and repairs went on both day and night. With little sleep and scarce food, the men became exhausted. The weather turned colder and once again, I was back in the bit of trench out in front. Positioned here, we could at least get a few hours sleep and were thankful for the fire in the dugout. Short-handed for bombers, we now all had to do extra hours on duty. The regiment was relieved the following night at around 9 o'clock, but bombers were not relieved until several hours later. Our remaining party of twenty had some narrow escapes from small shells and sniper bullets before we could get to a road and begin a steady march to a village, five or six miles away. I was not feeling so good by the time we got marching and as we walked I began to feel really ill and tired out. Six miles to walk did not sound a lot but after five I felt as if I'd walked fifty and collapsed in the road. The party stopped and I was helped to the side. After waiting a few minutes I tried to get going again but it was no use, my legs wouldn't support me. I was given a drink of water, then the party gave me directions to the next village and went off and left me.

ASSISTANCE FROM THE GUNNERS

I lay down and must have slept, for when I awoke I felt cold and ill. My clothes were caked with mud and my boots and puttees were coated in a layer of clay a half an inch thick. Realising I was doing myself no good lying here, with an effort I got to my feet and started to walk towards the village. I felt as if I was drunk as I proceeded, stumbling along from one side of the road to the other. A little way along I came to a battery of heavy guns where a man saw me passing and stepped out in front of me. He flashed a torch in my face:

'What's the matter chum, are you hurt or something?'

I told him where I had been for the last week or more and how I was feeling ill and tired out. While I was speaking my legs gave way again and I would have fallen if he hadn't caught me and held me up.

'Where are you making for?' he asked.

When I named the village he grew concerned.

'Come on with me,' he said. 'You are not fit to go there just now. Come over to our billet and have a rest first.'

He half-carried me to his billet, a small cottage. Inside it was very comfortable with a nice fire burning, lying on the floor beside the fire slept several men. This Good Samaritan gave me a hot cup of something to drink, it may have been tea, coffee or cocoa, I felt dazed I hardly knew what I was doing. All I wanted to do was sleep. One of the sleeping men was roused up and I took his place. I fell asleep almost immediately. By morning I found that my mud-drenched clothes had dried on me. My puttees were encased in a solid piece that had cracked as I moved and fallen on the floor in pieces. My friend was there when I woke and hoped I felt better. He explained that he knew we had been through it because his guns had been amongst those that had covered our sector and that he had been up there as an observer, correcting the aim of the guns. He was preparing breakfast and asked if I would join him. I was anxious to reach the village where my regiment was boarding a train to other parts and I told him I didn't wish to be left behind.

'Come on,' he said. 'It won't take long to have a cup of tea and a bite of something!'

I thanked him and stayed to enjoy a breakfast of eggs and bacon, tea and as much bread and butter as I wanted. He told me that one of the lorries was going my way soon and offered me a lift but I declined. I thanked him and explained that I wouldn't wait. He directed me to the village and I set out.

I felt weak about the knees and was glad of a ride from a wagon going my way. Arriving at the village, I could not see a sign of the regiment. There were very few people about as it was still early morning. Puzzled, I thought I might be in the wrong village. I had been staying at this particular village before so I went to a café I remembered and asked the French woman if she knew of the regiment's whereabouts.

'Yes they're here in this village," she assured me. 'But they haven't got up yet. They're all so tired and worn out!'

On hearing this I felt relieved and had another breakfast while I waited for the others to surface. I didn't have long to wait. Quite soon some of our chaps were dodging about so I asked them to direct me to the bombers' billet. I found my mates and reported myself present. They were pleased to know I was feeling better and glad to hear about the help I had received from the gunners. They told me that people here had stayed up all night with hot coffee and eatables to greet the men when they arrived because they knew what they'd been through. The bursting shells had been heard quite plainly from the village.

Soon, we were all busy scraping and brushing the mud off our clothes. Water taps lined the street at intervals and soon everyone was making use of them. Soapy water was running along the gutters and one and all had a good wash. Before midday we were looking more tidy and feeling heaps better. Again, we had our dinners cooked for us and were able to eat in peace. A rumour went around that we were moving off at 2 o'clock, which proved to be right. When the time arrived, we marched up to the railway station to the tune of a lively march. The villagers came out in force to see us off and soon we were on a train bound for a coal-mining centre by the name of Bethune.

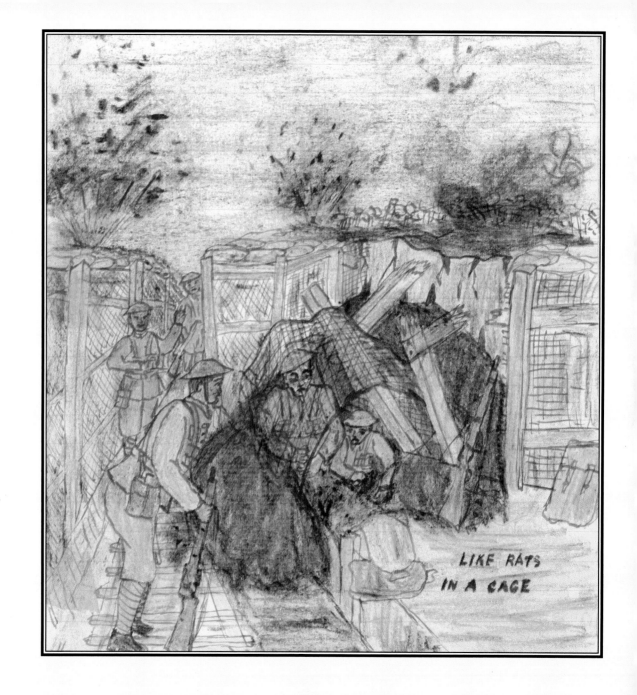

Plate 23 Like rats in a cage!

CHAPTER FOUR
VIMY RIDGE

Harry's memories of his experience in the Vimy Ridge sector are particularly poignant. The sector had a particularly bad reputation for the British troops. Trenches were all sited downhill from the Germans, and the whole area could be seen from the various German vantage-points near the top of the ridge. The French had held this section of front prior to the arrival of British troops in early 1916. They had attempted to take the Ridge after the capture of Lorette Heights in early 1915; however, they were unable to overcome the strong German defences, and Vimy Ridge remained in German hands. The Ridge was of particular importance to the Germans – it dominated the Allied approaches to the front for miles around and protected the Douai Plain behind the Ridge, which was a major area of industrial production for the Germans. Accordingly, the German line was particularly well defended and fortified in this area.

TWO WEEKS ON THE ROAD FROM BÉTHUNE TO VIMY VIA EXTRA COOTIE [ESTRÉE-CAUCHY, NEAR VILLERS-AU-BOIS]

Arriving in Bethune we were distributed around the village into different people's houses. I was billeted with four or five others with a family where the father and son both worked at the nearby coal mine. This was not their hometown. They had fled from their own village and for a time had been cared for in England. They spoke very highly of the treatment they had received whilst there and hoped to visit England again when the war was over. It was strange not to hear shells flying about; everything seemed so peaceful. Bethune was a fair-sized place with a number of good shops where something of everything was for sale. It also had a theatre that we visited several times. We were allowed to make use of the baths at the coal mine. About thirty or forty of us at a time would go to a large 40 x 100 foot building that had a glass roof. Within, a hundred sprinkler baths were arranged at regular intervals. Everything was neat, clean and tidy and we enjoyed the baths here very much. Those who wished to swim could go to a canal not far from the village.

CINEMATIC FILM TAKEN OF LORD MAJOR OF LONDON VISIT

On the third day at Bethune we had a surprise visit from the Lord Mayor of London who arrived just as the day's rations were being given out. A cinematograph camera was taking the whole incident.

The son who lived in our billet having reached the age of eighteen was called up for service. He and some others, who had all been called to the French colours, made the occasion a day of jollification. They all wore rosettes of red, white and blue ribbon on their caps or coats and linked arms as they went through the streets, singing. They frequently ventured into the wine shops and cafes and altogether appeared to be enjoying themselves. We remained for perhaps two or three weeks more and then we had to be on the move again, sorry to leave the place.

THE VILLAGE OF 'EXTRA COOTIE'

As we passed through some lovely scenery on our several days' march, the weather was good and the countryside looked fine. The place we were making for was Vimy Ridge. The nearer we got, the more the scenery changed. From bright fields and woods, comfortable looking farms and villages we came to shelled places and other signs of warfare. The people here even continued to till the land although a shell would sometimes explode in the field while they were ploughing. As a little girl watched over them, cows would browse along the lanes eating the grass at the side of the road. We came to a village named Estre Cooshy and we stopped for a few days. We had got ourselves free of body vermin at our last stop but after staying here only one night, we collected some more and renamed the place Extra Cootie! Our quarters were a large barn-like place that had been used as a warehouse or stores in peacetime. The words: 'International Stores' were on the stonework over the gateway. There was a thin layer of straw on the floor for us to lie on but we cleared it all out because we thought it was that that was harbouring the vermin. There had been some heavy fighting around here at one time and our billet had been used as a hospital. It held the whole company of men and room to spare.

DIGGING THE NEW TRENCH

At Estre Cooshy, we went up in working parties ten miles to the line every night and bombers were not excused. Large motor lorries drove us to within a mile of the line. It would be dusk when we set out and we arrived back at around five the next morning. Going along, we used to have a singsong but this would have to stop before we got too near the line. Each of us carrying a pickaxe and a shovel, we would arrive at a place called Larrett [Lorette] Heights. This was high ground lately captured from the Germans by the French and cost a great loss of lives. Our front line was some three hundred yards away and the enemy lines about another fifty. We could overlook them from where we were and some miles beyond. The lorries were left concealed in a wood and we walked across until the hill came to an abrupt end, the sides being nearly perpendicular and about forty feet high. We had to dig the new trench along this edge. On our way across we had to dodge round shell holes

by the hundred and now and again we had to crouch down in them when shells came over or a machine-gun fired our way. Strewn about all over the place were equipment, caps, helmets and rifles all of them damaged. It looked like a proper battlefield.

WAITING FOR THE ATTACK TO SUBSIDE

One night we were working on our trench and it rained all the time. It being clay ground, the stuff stuck to our shovels and picks and we couldn't get on at all. As we worked on new stretches they collected rain until it was over our boot tops and to make things even worse, the rain caused the sides of the trench we had already dug to fall in. Most of us had ground sheets over our shoulders so we kept fairly dry but I'm afraid there was little work done that night. With care, we were able to smoke and most of us did. An hour before we were to return, the enemy bombarded our front lines down below and we all watched it, a few of the shells coming our way but no harm was done. Then in the midst of it the Germans exploded a mine and we felt the ground rock. From both sides, we could see the guns now firing hundreds of bursting shells. They lit up the whole place – it looked like a firework display. With our own experiences of mines still fresh in our minds, we all felt sorry for the men down there. The mine crater came into our possession but there were a good many casualties. We stayed until the firing quietened down and then made our way back to the lorries.

Plate 24
The huts at
Villers-au-Bois

VILLA
RO BRAVE
NUTS

A petty inspection

The rain had turned the ground into an awful mess and we slipped and slid all the way back, getting covered head to toe in mud. We arrived rather late back at the billet and had our breakfast before the other men were up and prepared our selves for a few hours sleep. We hadn't been down long before we were woken up and told there was to be an inspection by the company commander at nine o'clock. A general moan went up from us men who had just returned:

'It's not fair! We've just come off a working party! Our clothes are all wet! We're smothered in mud! We ought to be excused! Etc. Etc.'

But it was no use, orders were that we were to parade and we would have to make as good a show as we could. We had a good try to make ourselves look tidy. We cleaned rifles, bayonets, buttons and brasswork on our equipment; removed as much mud as we could from boots puttees and clothes, shaved and washed all in about an hour. It was a scramble to get so much done at such short notice but we paraded on time. The officer inspected us and of course, noticed the condition of us men that had been out the night before. He reprimanded us, which I think was unfair and several of us as punishment were sent on another working party the following night.

On this occasion we had to dig a narrow trench about a foot wide in which was buried a thick cable of telephone wires. So many wires were getting cut with shrapnel and bullets that this idea was to be tried as an alternative. The ground we needed to dig was chalk and rather hard work going down four or five feet. Being so narrow it was also awkward. We got our job completed sooner than expected and were able to return early, somewhere around two o'clock in the morning. This kind of thing went on for roughly two weeks and then we moved to a front line trench.

Fortnight at Lorette Heights to make a new trench

The trenches in the front line were all dug out of chalk and so very few repairs had to be made. I think they may have previously been German trenches, they had quite a number of good deep dugouts. There was a scarcity of water here so it used to be rationed out at two pints to a man per day. It was stored in some large tanks in one of the back trenches or communication trench and each man had to get his own issue. One had to be careful as sniping was carried out a lot along these channels. Several of our men got hit including an officer who was killed. One day, I had just got my water and was returning along the trench when a sniper tried to get me. I ducked down quickly and in doing so, spilt all my water. I went back to get some more but I couldn't have any, so I went all day with hardly a drink. I said something to myself about Germans and snipers in particular!

We had to have places of convenience, or sanitary arrangements, in all the trenches. Usually a short bit of trench was dug out from the main one with the

W.C. screened off at the end with a piece of canvas. Unless it was well hidden, the enemy would notice the comings and goings in this area and would take pains to catch the men there. Sniper bullets or rifle grenades would fly around. One day a Whizz bang shell came over whilst a man was using the place. He wasn't hit but the explosion so near caused him to fall and he was not a nice sight to see! Poor chap; everyone shunned him until a means was found to get him a fresh suit of clothes. It rained part of the time while we were in the line but it drained off quickly as our trenches were dug on the slope of the hill. A stream ran across one of the trenches and although the water looked bright and clear, it was unsafe to drink under any conditions on account of the W.C. being near by.

Our next move was to man some trenches at the base of Larette Heights where we were reserves to men on the front line. The weather was fine and sunny and we had plenty of dugouts, deep down with room for all. We seldom got any shells and there were no bullets at all (as I remember). Altogether, we had a quiet time considering the distance we were from the front. There were working parties every night making a new trench to join on to a front line. Getting to and from the work was not healthy with us having to scramble into shell holes now and again to dodge the bullets. However once we got there and kept low we were fairly safe. There were no casualties on this job except for one, caused by one man accidentally hitting another on the head with a pickaxe in the dark.

SOUVENIR HUNTING

We had to cook our own food but this was very little trouble and we had plenty of braziers and charcoal. Some of us went souvenir hunting on the field up ahead but we found little worth saving. There were German helmets and other things but they were so riddled with shrapnel and bullets that they were not worth picking up. One party was supposed to have forced their way down an almost shattered dugout and found several dead Germans in sitting positions round a table. We queried the yarn and were invited to go and see for ourselves. We didn't go.

FRONTLINE WATER PROVISION

Every night, we took it in turns to go across country to a village (or the remains of one) to carry rations and some exciting times were had! We got shelled every time we went and were thankful when we got back. Often some of the rations would get spoilt when we jumped to avoid exploding shells. There was not time to pick or choose, accompanied by the rations you just threw yourself into the nearest shell hole even if it was half-full of water. Then it would always be best to stay in there until the shelling eased but this was no good for the rations especially if you happened to be carrying bread! Another job we would get would be to carry water from a spring situated a hundred yards from the trenches. We would toss up to choose which one of us would have to go and we'd cheer the hero if a shell came over just as he was filling the can. Then more of us would creep out slowly, hoping to go unnoticed and arrive at the small spring where we would try to fill up the petrol can as quickly as possible. Without success, eventually others would come on the errand until there were perhaps half a dozen of us. Then over would come some shells and we'd all have to run for it, leaving our partly filled tin behind! Waiting a while, we would creep out again and so on, until we got enough for our needs.

A 'COSY, QUIET TIME OF IT'

Letters and parcels from home were always welcome. If a parcel came for a man who had been killed, or was in hospital and unlikely to return, it was shared amongst his closest chums and a letter would be sent out to the people who had sent it explaining the circumstances. In nearly every parcel there was some stuff or other to use against the vermin that had got on our bodies and clothes. At times we were in a terrible way and we tried all kinds of means to rid ourselves of these horrid pests. We rubbed different salves and ointments on our bodies that were supposed to keep them away and we dusted our clothes with powders for the same reason but they still clung to us in their thousands. The best thing that I found was to light a candle, remove my clothes and draw the affected parts over the flame and burn them. This gave relief for a time but constantly doing this did the clothes no good! At every opportunity we

had a bath but sometimes months would go before we got the chance of another one.

Hair cutting was done by one of the men, and a nice bit of money he must have made out of it with half a franc being the general fee! This turn in the trenches was the cosiest and quietest time we had for months and in a way we enjoyed ourselves. Getting on the move again, we went to a village some three miles back. It was partly inhabited by French people but there were not many there. The place got shelled occasionally and very little glass was left in the windows. Linen was used in place of glass and although it let the light through you couldn't see through it. The weather was sunny and bright and whilst staying here most of us worked all day making a new line of trenches complete with barbed wire entanglements just outside the village. Enemy planes were continually coming overhead. Whether our work attracted them or they were trying to spot some guns placed about here, I don't know but our planes were always on guard and dozens of fights took place in the air every day. They were exciting to watch and I think our planes used to get the best of the duels. Quite a number of enemy planes crashed and some of ours as well. We had several pay days whilst we were here and we spent them in different ways. Some went to estaminets drinking wines and so-called beer or gambled with cards whilst others spent money on chocolate, tinned fruit, picture post cards and smokes, not forgetting candles. This was too good to last so after a few weeks we were off again to man the front line. We stayed here for perhaps a fortnight or more with nothing much out of the ordinary happening.

To Villers-au-Bois – bomb detonation, working parties and gas guards

After being relieved, we marched to a place called Ville a Bois some miles away. There was a camp of wooden huts hidden in a wood at the edge of a ruined village. We had our kitchens along with us but every care had to be taken with the smoke as the line was only about a half mile away and we could see the shells bursting quite plainly from where we were. There were cornfields between the line and us and no one was allowed to go in this part. We were free to go anywhere to the back of the wood and along the lanes but not in large numbers, the same applied to the ruins of the village. There were about three families living among the ruins. One man and sometimes his wife, tilled fields near by and also kept a shop where useful things could be bought such as cigarettes, matches, chocolate, writing material and candles. One or two children were here as well but I seldom saw them.

Showers set up in a large house

In one of the larger houses a bathing arrangement had been rigged up. A tank was kept filled up with water with a fire under it. The water was run off by pipes at the end of each was a spray situated above every tub. Four men would go into bathe at a time, each one to a tub. A signal would be given and the water would be allowed to spray over the men for half a minute and then turned of again. The bathers would lather themselves with soap as quick and best as they could when the water would be turned on again for another half minute to rinse the soap off. This done, another four men would take their place. This arrangement went on until the whole party had been bathed. It wasn't a good bath but it was better than none! It was surprising how quickly a number of men could bathe in such a short time. Having bathed and dried yourself, you passed to another room where clean changes of underclothes were given in exchange for those you took off and only the same number of articles. Some fun was caused by the fit of the clothes the men sometimes got. No notice was taken of your size, a parcel of shirts and pants would be given you and it would only be when they were unfolded that you found out whether they would fit or not. Sometimes they were too small, sometimes too large! Then exchanges with the clothes took place until everyone had got something that near enough suited him.

Letter to Matthews' wife

We had a good amount of time to ourselves for the first few days. I missed my late chum Matthews and went about generally by myself. I had some long rambles through the woods and enjoyed them. There were ever so many wild flowers growing and I picked a few of each to send home in my next letter. I was a long while writing to my chum's people to let them know of his death. I started to write more than once only to tear the letter up. I didn't like the job at all but at last I managed it. I addressed the letter to my chum's wife and received a reply from a clergyman who wrote on behalf of the lady. I was very sorry for her and hoped my letter helped to soften her grief.

SWIMMING IN THE QUARRY

By chance I had carried a swimming costume about with me in my pack ever since I had been in France. One day on my rambles I came across a pool of water, deep enough to swim in. Next day, having a few hours to myself, I took my costume to the pool and enjoyed a swim. The place was a quarry where stones and sand had been dug out. The quarry was twenty or thirty feet deep with the bottom filled with water to about eight feet in depth at the deepest part. It was cut out roughly in a square, each side being about forty yards long. Three sides were almost perpendicular from the top down to the water but the remaining side sloped down gradually. I swam up and down the centre. At the sides, dozens of tadpoles and frogs were doing the same. I got out and was just dressing when some artillerymen led about two dozen horses down to the pool to drink. I walked back to camp with my costume over my shoulder and was asked by some of our chaps where I had been swimming. Next day, several more men went with me and a fine time we

had! None of the others had any covering on whilst swimming, not that it mattered as we were miles from anywhere.

There was one place in the village where drinks were sold and a good number of the chaps used to spend the evening there. Others used to play cards. At dusk, some others and I armed with sticks, used to go rat hunting around the ponds and ruins of the village. There were scores and scores of rats all over the place. Shells occasionally dropped in the village during the evening but there were not many. At different times we would have inspections of clothes, boots, gas masks, equipment and rifles. Then there were lectures given on first aid, firing, gas masks and bombing. In the intervals, games of football were played under the trees.

BACK ON THE WORKING PARTIES

This kind of thing went on for about a week when working parties were formed for both day and night. These parties went up to the lines doing different jobs. Some parties would go after breakfast and return at about midday, others would go from midday until about six in the evening and then some more would start out at about nine pm and return at midnight. Guards were posted every day and also gas guards. Bombers on this occasion did no guards or working parties but we did get a job to detonate hundreds of bombs that were stored in a large dugout in the support lines.

RUINED CHURCH AT VILLERS-AU-BOIS

In places, the houses in the village were complete wrecks while others, by some chance, were nearly whole. The church had been partly destroyed, having large shell holes in the walls and through its tower or belfry. Some of us had a look around it one day. Some of the stones in the graveyards were blown to smithereens and graves had been uncovered by shell-fire. Inside, the church was all in disorder. The chairs and pews were covered in dust and tiles that had fallen from the roof. The altar wasn't very damaged and still had its bunches of flowers in vases, that were now all faded and covered in dust, still in place on tables. At the rear end of the church wall was a life sized figure of Christ on the cross and even though shells had burst through the walls within a foot or two of it, it still hung there undamaged.

There were several wells in the village but we were unable to use them as they were so deep and the ropes were missing. The only one in use was the one that supplied the baths with water and this was in the charge of the engineers. They had a small petrol motor that drew the water up as it was needed. There were one or two large barns in fair condition and in the evenings we sometimes used them as concert halls. These concerts were enjoyed by all of us of the regiment but men from other regiments used to come to them too, not only as part of the audience but to sing as well. The lighting was candlelight and had to be well screened so it shouldn't be seen from the outside. The artists, all men from the regiment, sang and we all joined in the chorus. Other men gave recitations, others dressed as females and kept us in roars of laughter with their antics and gags. One evening, a concert was held in one of the huts and the officers attending included the commanding officer. One officer gave a turn, which was very well done. He went through the actions of a lady dressing her hair in front of a mirror with combs, brushes, hairpins, mirror and hair all being imaginary. It was laughable to watch the expressions on his face and the twiddling about of the hands as he fixed imaginary hair with imaginary combs and hairpins. Refreshments were had in the way of tea and biscuits on this occasion and the final turn was a speech by the CO. The National Anthem being sung, we all went to our own huts well pleased with the evening spent.

DETONATION BY CANDLE-LIGHT

Next day, half a dozen of we bombers had to go to support lines to detonate about two or three thousand bombs. It took us all day and it was rather a dangerous job. We didn't have much room to move about in and the light was bad, having only one candle to work by that went out every time a shell exploded near by. The detonators we were handling had been known to explode with the scratch of a fingernail. Should one bomb be exploded accidentally it could set all the others off, so we were jolly careful. Altogether, though, we spent a comfortable time at Ville a Bois.

A SWIM IN A GRAVEL PIT

FOUR DAYS AT SOUCHEZ THEN TWO WEEKS IN THE VALLEY OF DEATH

Our next move was to a place called Souchez. We only stayed for four days, having renewals of different things such as rifles, equipment and gas masks. I believe it was here that we were issued with shrapnel helmets for the first time, we called them tin helmets. There was not enough to supply every man and none of us bombers got one. Starting out at about midnight, we marched to the trenches at Vimy Ridge, passing through Ville a Bois on our way, arriving in the trenches about daylight. Between the village and the trenches we had to cross open country and were kept on the jump by shells exploding around us. Some shells came fairly near but I believe we all got through safely. Just before we got to the trenches, situated on a hill or ridge, we had to cross a deep, narrow valley. The sides of the valley were very steep, almost upright and steps had to be dug out to go up or down. This valley was known as the Valley of Death on account of the number of men being killed there. It was frequently heavily shelled and no cover or protection could be had except along the edge nearest the enemy where hundreds of dugouts of different sizes were built.

DEEP DUGOUTS, SPRING WATER AND A NARROW-GAUGE RAILWAY

Keeping near the dugouts, it was fairly safe and it was possible to walk about for a mile or more without fear of a bullet hitting you. But shells came over at all times, also trench mortar bombs, and you had to be ready to bolt into a dugout at the first sign of a shell coming over. It was quite a novelty to us to be able to walk about so near the lines. They were only about two hundred yards away in places. Another thing here was a narrow gauge railway used a lot between dusk and daylight. Four to a dozen small trucks were coupled together and pulled along by one or two mules to and from the valley. The track was two or three miles long and went well out of the line. Ammunition, wood, barbed wire and other things were carried in and on the outward journey would be the dead and wounded men from the line. Good spring water was plentiful in the valley and several large tanks were always kept full under the charge of the men of the Royal Army Medical Corps, who gave it out as it was needed. More of the spring water was led into a roughly made bath built in the ground, about 18 feet long, 10 foot wide and to a depth of about four feet. Quite a number of the men used it and occasionally a man would get killed or wounded by shrapnel whilst bathing. Observation balloons were dotted about and the enemy was always on the look out for men crossing the valley. Should a good number try to cross at one time, a volley of different sized shells would be almost sure to burst over them and seldom did the party get across without leaving one or more killed behind.

Plate 25
A swim in a gravel pit, Villers-au-Bois

COMMUNICATION TRENCHES AND A SAP FOR BOMBERS

Leading out of the valley were communication trenches with a number of deep dugouts going to the depth of thirty feet or more and all cut out of chalk. Two companies held the front line, and two were in support lines, the two lines only being roughly fifty yards apart. Both lines got shelled frequently but not much damage was done and there were few casualties. Bombers took over the weakest part of the lines supported by machine-guns. Five others and I, in the charge of a corporal, took over a small trench, or sap, which ran out towards the enemy lines and was fairly close. The sap was in bad condition and gave little protection. We had to walk about in a crouching position in order to keep our heads below the top and we used a periscope to observe enemy movements. The top was well covered with barbed wire and a raiding party would have had difficulty getting into our trench.

PERISCOPE CASUALTY

During the day we simply went on duty and most of the time we observed through the periscope. When not on duty, we retired to a dugout a short distance away from the sap from where we could see our sentry. The shells came near our sap but Fritz had some tries to drop bombs and rifle grenades. Most of them fell short and no damage was done. We threw some back and when ours didn't drop into his trenches, after some time we both let each other alone to have a fairly quiet time. There was one mishap to a chap in our party who was on duty and all of us, including himself, reckoned he was fortunate. He was looking through the periscope when a shell came over and just hit the top of the periscope. The mirror inside was smashed and the wooden box affair was broken. The only other damage, apart from shock was that when the glass splintered it tore several holes in the man's cap and filled his hair with powdered glass. It was a near thing for him and made him feel bad for a time. As it was my turn to relieve the sentry, I didn't feel so good myself! I thought that shelling our sap was only the beginning and expected more to follow. It proved to be the only incident however and I rigged up another glass in a different position.

A SENTRY CALLED HAVENAL

It was a lovely day, the sun was shining and it was quite warm. Another man who didn't seem to realise when he was in danger relieved me from my post. I showed this chap where the glass was and how to use it and made my way to the dugout. A little later, happening to glance towards the post, we saw Havenal, the sentry, lying full-length along the top of the trench gazing at the enemy lines. Why he wasn't shot a hundred times over I can't explain! The corporal ran to him as quick as he could and pulled him down, calling him all the fouls that he could think of. But he only laughed and said:

'That's all right! I've been up there all the time and nobody has noticed me! Besides, I could see better that way!'

He was a likeable chap and very seldom did you hear him grumble. He was forever in hot water through losing parts of his equipment and going about in a slovenly manner. He did get a new pair of trousers when we were out last time after we got on to him about his appearance, promising to take more care. It seemed that he was trying to keep his promise for all the time he was brushing dirt off his trousers and trying to keep the crease in them. We chipped him a bit about them but he didn't mind.

One day we ran out of water and as usual we tossed up to see who should go for it. It was a two-man job as we had four petrol tins to fill and bring back. We had some distance to go and the trenches we had to go along were continually being shelled or having big trench mortars used on them. Men were always getting killed or wounded along here but if you wanted to get to the valley where the water was, there was no other way. Havenal and another man were picked for the job and off they started. We could see them as they went along and watched them ducking and dodging when the shells came over. The other man seemed to wish to get the job over quickly and soon left Havenal behind. Several trench mortars came over and exploded near them whilst they were going along. We watched Havenal with his two cans taking his time when a mortar exploded some

distance in front of him. He was unable to see exactly where it fell from his position so putting his tins down, he climbed to the top of the trench to get a better view. He had hardly got up there when another mortar dropped nearer than the first. The explosion caused Havenal to fall back into the trench right into a puddle of sloppy mud and his nice trousers were nice no longer! He and the other chap got back all right and we did have some fun with Havenal and his trousers! They soon got dry and we tried to get back the smart appearance and crease in them but it was no use. So, Havenal went back to his old ways and paid no more attention to his appearance. 'What's the use!' he said.

INTRODUCTION OF TINNED MEAT RATION

We all had to cook our own food whilst in the line, but as we got a good supply of charcoal, and water being plentiful, we did not mind so much. About this time, we had a fresh kind of food issue. This was what you might call a tinned Irish stew and it was not so bad if prepared right. The tin held roughly about a pound of meat and vegetables. These had been cooked before being tinned so that all we had to do was to make a small hole in the tin to allow the steam to escape and place the tin in hot water until the food was hot enough to suit. Some men could eat the food cold. I tried it but didn't like it that way. Usually I used to turn the contents of the tin out into my mess tin, add water to it to thin it out and then bring it to

THE VALLEY
VIMEY RIDGE

the boil. To make it more tasty, I added some small oval biscuits. I found that prepared this way, it made a satisfying meal and about all I could manage to eat.

Orders were strict about leaving food over lying about in the trenches. All waste food, paper, empty tins, etc. had to be placed in sand bags which were collected at night by a man appointed for the job who placed them in a shell hole and buried them. The shell hole was usually between the front and support lines and the man ran the risk of getting shot or caught by a bursting shell all the time he was up on top.

RETURN FORTNIGHT AT VILLERS-AU-BOIS

After a week or two spent here we were relieved and took over the huts again at Villers au Bois. We moved out in small parties quite early in the evening and had our tea at the huts when we arrived. The cooking wagons, or mess carts, were again here to cook our food and it was all prepared for us. Besides the tea, the cooks had cold ham or bacon for us and everyone enjoyed the surprise item at the time.

A MAN CALLED LEGG

It was still fairly early and those that had money and were that way inclined went to the estaminet to finish the day out. Amongst them was a man by the name of Legg who was quite a comic in his way. He had quite a store of funny sayings, jokes and stories and he kept us amused for hours. He was neither an old nor a young man but I should say older than most of us. I remember whilst on the march one day, he showed me a letter that had been sent to him from his wife. The news was to say that a child born to him had died, the child being only a month or two old. I gave him my sympathy.

'It's strange,' he said. 'But this is the first time I knew I had an increase in the family.'

Months after, he received another letter to say his wife was confined and he was the father of a baby girl. He had got the news of the death before the news of the birth of his child.

Legg came over to France with my party and shortly afterwards was sent to the base to be fitted with false teeth. Some others and I had been for a walk and on returning to camp we saw Legg staggering along the worse for drink, singing at the top of his voice. He was likely to get into trouble if found like this by an officer so we grabbed hold of him and got him to the hut as quickly as we could. In the huts we had roughly made beds, built about a foot off the ground. There was a framework of wood and stretched across it was hen-house wire mesh with a covering of canvas. This made quite a comfortable bed and we slept cosily with two blankets and our overcoats for covering. Having got Legg onto his bed, he lay there singing song after song after lights out until we persuaded him to stop or he would get a punishment. For a time, he lay quiet in the darkness and then started telling funny stories. He kept us awake for hours. Next morning,

Plate 26
'Zouave' Valley, Vimy Ridge

however there was a kit and hut inspection directly after breakfast.

Most of us were up and busy next morning tidying up but Legg and a few others were content to lie in bed as long as possible, not feeling so good after the drinking bout the night before. Each hut had two orderlies whose duty it was to draw rations for the rest of us and to return the dixie or boiler clean and full of water after meals. Another thing they did was to be responsible for the tidiness of the hut and take all rubbish that had been swept up to an incinerator to be burnt. The only brooms available were makeshift, sometimes a bundle of twigs had to serve but more often it was a sandbag rolled up and held in the hand. We were all more or less ready to go on parade when we noticed Legg hunting around on the floor and on his bed.

'What have you lost?' We enquired.

'I've lost my teeth!' Legg replied.

Of course a general laugh went up and we all helped to hunt for the missing teeth. Time for parade came and we left Legg in the hut still hunting for his teeth. On parade, roll was called and Legg wasn't there to answer to his name. The officer was about to send for him when he turned up still minus his teeth.

'What's the meaning of this Legg? Where have you been, didn't you know you had to parade?' asked the officer abruptly.

Legg was flustered and tried to tell the officer he had been looking for his lost teeth. The officer could not understand what Legg said and asked him again to explain. Without his teeth, poor Legg's speech got worse and the officer listened to the spluttering of him, gazing at Legg's face that was getting quite red in his attempts to make himself understood. We on parade had to laugh and the officer turned from Legg to us and ordered us to stop laughing. Then he asked one of the men:

'What's the joke?'

The man explained Legg's predicament and the officer had to smile himself.

'All right Legg! You had better hurry over to the incinerator and find your teeth before they get burnt!'

After hunting for a time, Legg found his teeth undamaged and returned to us with them in his pocket. When we were free to talk we chipped Legg about his teeth and got a laugh from his attempts to answer us back.

A LITTLE WAR OF THEIR OWN IN NO MAN'S LAND

We stayed at the huts for about a fortnight doing much the same kind of things that we did when we were here on the last occasion. There was some excitement caused one evening by the enemy bombarding our lines up front and also the villages and roads round about. Most of us were amusing ourselves in different ways and were rather scattered about although none of us were far from the huts. Some others and I were having some fine sport hunting rats near the wood when the guns opened up. From where we were we could look right over the front lines and the sight of shells bursting with dozens of Very Lights of different colours going up into the air looked like a firework display. Of course the alarm was sent out and we were all called back and paraded, ready to go to the assistance of the men up front if they needed us. We stood about waiting for the expected call for about an hour but we were not needed. Gradually the shelling died down to normal and we were dismissed. I believe the trouble started over bombers from both opposing sides meeting each other unexpectedly out in no man's land. They apparently had a little war of their own for a few minutes and then others joined in until it was quite a big affair.

RETURN TO THE FRONT LINES AND 24 HOURS OF FIGHTING

They came for us to go up to the front lines again but not the same line as we held last time. We took over some lines adjoining our last position and they were awkwardly placed and rather knocked about a bit. When we took over it was not too bad in the way of shelling but enough to keep you on the move and near enough to smother you in dirt and mud occasionally. The front line had been shelled until a long piece of it no longer existed. The remaining part was also very much knocked about and was taken over by one company of men numbering about eighty. The barbed wire entanglements in front were not very thick and altogether our position was not very strong against a determined attack. The distance between the enemy lines and ours was about fifty yards and with an effort we could reach them with our bombs. The first day in we exchanged rifle fire and bombs with the enemy but nothing out of the ordinary happened.

Our support line was about 25 to 30 yards behind the front with a piece of trench connecting the two. This piece of trench was taken over by the bombers, as in the event of an attack the enemy could be entering it to get between our front and support lines cutting off those in the front line from all assistance. The position was explained to us and we were told to hold our position at all costs. We had a good supply of bombs and rifle grenades and we used them at intervals all day. The enemy threw a good many at us but we managed to dodge them without one of us getting hurt. The enemy was not so fortunate. Every now and again we knew our bombs found somebody over there because we could hear it and our shells did some damage as well. This seemed to rouse their anger for they started to shell us with whizz bangs and trench mortars. We had next to no protection in the trench but we had plenty of room to dodge about in! And we dodged! Time after time we thought we were going to get killed or wounded but somehow we managed to get out of it, throwing another couple of bombs over for their trouble.

BUSY
TROWING
BOMBS
NIGHT AND DAY
VIMY RIDGE

A DECISION AT DAWN

During the night we were extra alert and kept up our bomb throwing. If we heard the least noise over the other side we threw a bomb. We didn't intend to let them get started on any business if we could help it. Our regular bombing officer was not with us on this occasion but in his place was an officer taken from the regiment. He was all over the place, dodging here and there and was quite interested in his job! He got so hot running about and throwing bombs that he took his coat off. The night wore on and at about an hour before dawn, the enemy seemed to be extra busy, judging by the noise he made, and we made a guess that he was being relieved. This seemed a good opportunity for our bombs and rifle grenades and we let them have some, with good effects. Then, talking the thing over amongst ourselves, we wondered if the enemy was up to something for our discomfort. It seemed a strange time to relieve, when we thought of it, and we came to the conclusion that he would attack at dawn. Everyone was warned and we were prepared to beat him off. Gradually it became lighter and we kept a good look out for him to start something. Half an hour went by, then an hour and still nothing happened. By this time the light was strong and we could see that there were more men in the enemy trenches than usual. We also noticed that two or three extra observation balloons were up. We didn't know whether they were our own or the enemy's but one of them was situated in line with our

trench and not all that far away. We waited for perhaps a couple of hours more and still nothing happened except that the firing from the enemy gradually increased in volume. Most of it was going on the support lines and into the valley, and in our trench we were getting whizz bangs and extra-large trench mortars thrown at us.

We didn't get a minute's rest, all the time we were running up and down, dodging the trench mortars as they came over or throwing bombs at the enemy trench. We had been on duty now for 24 hours and feeling tired, wishing we could have a rest and something to eat and drink. About midday, the firing slackened a bit and we curled ourselves up in the bottom of the trench and tried to get some sleep. But it was no use! Hardly had we got settled then a whizz bang would come somewhere near us, smother us in dirt and then we'd have to get out quick to another place in the trench. This kind of thing kept up until we deduced that the balloon was directing the shots towards us. There was a little of the trench unobserved by the observation balloon, we thought, so getting down on the bottom, we crawled along until we got to this part and got a little peace. A kind of recess had been dug into the sides of the trench here and there, so we squeezed as much of ourselves into them as we could and dozed off to sleep.

Every few minutes, we woke up with a start when shells burst near, but we were getting a rest of sorts. We had an hour or more like this when whizz bangs

Plate 27
Busy throwing bombs night and day, Vimy Ridge

started exploding along our bit of trench. They started at one end and gradually worked along, each shell exploding, getting a little nearer to us. We hung on to the last moment before we bolted out of danger. I had been carrying a bag of bombs about with me wherever I went … about twenty of them! These I placed at my side whilst dozing and the shell that caused me to move broke a chunk of the trench off and buried them. I got them out later, whilst dodging shells at other places.

The enemy fire gradually increased in volume again and we had a warm time! The officer came on a visit to us and ordered us to throw several volleys of bombs and rifle grenades over. We did, and I guess the enemy trench was crammed with men, for yells and screams went up every time our missiles dropped in. The officer was highly delighted with the results obtained but he, and the other bombers had to run for it when the enemy started to return our compliments with bombs, shells and trench mortars! Another man and I had to stay as it was our turn for sentry duty. I don't know how we managed to exist! There were explosions all around us and the air was full of smoke, dirt and flying shrapnel. The mini werfers they were now sending over made a hole about ten feet across and five feet deep. The noise of the explosions nearly deafened us and knocked us over. The trench was falling in all over the place, and in places, ceased to exist. Our front and support lines were getting it hot, also, and stretcher-bearers were busy picking up the casualties. My mate and I threw bombs till our arms ached! The shelling continued on and on. More bombers were rushed up; fresh supplies of bombs were given to us and with things now beginning to get serious, our artillery opened out in full strength on to the enemy lines.

RELIEVED TO THE DUGOUTS THROUGH FOG AND TEAR GAS

We, who had been on duty since we entered the trenches, were feeling tired out, so we were relieved by some other bombers. We made our way towards the dugouts in the valley with orders to hold ourselves in readiness to return back again at a moment's notice. We ran, crawled and scrambled through the thick smoke and bursting shells till we got to the valley. Here, it was as bad! There was a thick fog of smoke with dull red splashes of bursting shells showing through. We stumbled over men lying dead or injured, climbed in and out of shell holes, passing on our way stretchers carrying the wounded and others that were wounded but were able to walk. It was difficult to see our way but at last we found a dugout and got inside. Among the shells the enemy was putting over were some of the tear gas variety which made our eyes smart and throats dry. It made us feel as if we had had a bad attack of the flu.

We cleared our dugout of gas fumes by lighting about a dozen candles at one time. The candles warmed the air and kept the gas out. We could hardly hear ourselves speak. Sitting down, we had something to eat and drink. It was difficult to keep our eyes open and not fall off to sleep. Whilst sitting here, we heard cries for help not far away so putting on our gas masks, we went to investigate. A few yards away, we saw the ruins of a dugout from which the cries of help were coming. We got picks and shovels and dug away to clear the way for who ever was inside. It proved to be a man who had been wounded and placed in the dug-out until it was quieter, when he could then be removed from the line to the hospital. A shell had exploded near by and the dugout had collapsed on him. We got him out all right and took him to our dugout. He had been wounded in several places and was helpless to move.

ATTACK ON VIMY RIDGE

The shelling kept up when, at about dusk, it seemed to increase. The valley was filled with bursting shells. Dead and wounded were all over the place. Parties of men were going up the front line to help keep back the enemy who we were now sure, was going to attack. Rockets of different colours sent up signals of distress. The telephone wires had been cut by flung shrapnel and so runners and messengers had to cross the valley with verbal and written messages for help. It took some pluck to make this journey and not a few got killed whilst making the attempt. Some got through all right and in a short time, there were thousands of troops on their way to our help. They came from all around, some marched, whilst others travelled by motors and all had to get to us under heavy shellfire causing casualties among them. Things went from bad to worse. Our men fired their rifles until they were too hot to hold. The front line was getting flattened out but the men still remaining, held on. A few gas shells came over in the valley and then the enemy launched his attack.

We were called out to go up again, taking with us a load of bombs. I had got two boxes of bombs and was stumbling along with them when I came over dizzy and was very sick. I leant against the trench, hardly able to stand. I guess I had swallowed the gas fumes and, not only this but the strain of the last day or two had got me down. I was feeling, what the boys called, windy. I wished I could be well out of the present hell upon earth, it wasn't nice at all. Whilst standing here undecided what to do, a man of ours came staggering along holding his stomach mumbling:

'They have shot me! I am shot … Look! I've got a hole right through me! I can see daylight.'

The man was half-crazy, poor chap, and was certainly wounded. I helped him down to the valley and gave him over to some stretcher-bearers then this seemed about all I could manage. I was sick again so I made my way to the dugout and flopped down on the floor, not caring about anything further. The enemy attacked our position with a strong force of men, their numbers being more than ours but they didn't have it all their own way, by any means.

BRITISH FORCED TO SURRENDER

The trench that the others and I had manned had practically disappeared and so had all the bombers who had relieved us. Having demolished this trench, the enemy came over in swarms. Some attacked from the front whilst others worked their way to the back of the front line. Our men had to face both ways and put up a good fight. They held out until they were forced to surrender, with over half their number being killed or wounded. Those that were able to walk were taken prisoner and escorted over to the enemy lines. One who was taken was our officer in command but he refused to leave our trench until he had given first aid to one of his men who had been wounded. At the last moment, some of our men from the front line attempted to get back to our support line and continue the fight but not many succeeded. They were between two fires and had small hope of getting through. Among those who tried was a chum of mine, by the name of Bridge. He got about half way back when a splinter of shell ripped his leg open from hip to knee. He told me his experiences when I met up with him about a year later. He said he was 'given up for dead'. After getting wounded, he managed to crawl into a shell hole where he laid for two days before being found unconscious.

LOST AND REGAINED GROUND

Having captured our detached post or front line, the enemy now attempted to take the support line. I managed to get up there at the same time and it was touch and go if we could keep them off. Other men were set to work, digging another trench nearly on the edge of the valley in case we were forced to give up the one we were holding. Some of these men were getting hit by our own shells on account of the guns not having the proper range. The only way to rectify the problem was to send messages back (on foot) since the telephone lines had been cut. Extra artillery came up and poured shells into the trench that we had lately held. We kept up rapid fire all through the night and beat off the enemy time after time when he tried to gain our trench until he gave it up as a bad job. Things quietened down a bit and everyone that could be spared either helped with the wounded or gave a hand, digging the nearby trench deeper.

By this time, we had plenty of help in the way of men and artillery and it was decided to get back the ground we had lost. Just before dawn, our guns laid a barrage of shells on the enemy lines and a couple of freshly arrived regiments went over. After a bit of a fight, our men got back the lost ground and took some prisoners. The shelling on both sides was heavy afterwards and continued nearly all day. We stayed, expecting to be attacked again but I suppose they (must have) thought better of it, for they made no attempts. They had already paid dearly for holding the captured ground for only a few hours. One or two of the Germans we captured could speak English and said the firing had been so heavy, they thought that we had had a great many more machine-guns holding them back when they were attacking.

BRIGADIER ADDRESSES THE MEN

Before it got dark, we were relieved and went back to the Villers au Bois huts, all of us being dead beat and in need of a good rest. Just before we got to the village we were met by the Brigadier on horseback. He spoke to us and said:

'Cheer up, men! I am proud of you for the way you have carried on, under very trying circumstances. It's the first time that you have lost ground and there can be honour in the way ground's lost as there is the way ground is captured, so don't be disheartened!'

THE FINAL ROLL CALL

Arriving in the huts we removed our packs, laid down anywhere we could and went fast asleep. None of us attempted to remove our equipment, eat, drink or do anything else, we just flopped down and went to sleep. Waking up next morning, we shaved, washed and cleaned up ourselves generally. After breakfast we were marched off to some other huts, about six miles away. We were very few. At the new huts, we sorted ourselves out in our companies, for at Villa a Bois we had been all jumbled up together. The battalion Sergeant Major formed us up and called the roll. Name after name was called with no one to answer it and it was then we missed many familiar voices, answering: 'Here, Sir!' Calling the roll after a scrap is a sad affair. If, on calling out a name, no one answers to it, enquiries are made of the men present if they know what happened. Perhaps someone saw the men killed or wounded and then all details are taken as to when, where and what particular part of the man was hit. Then, if he had been wounded, the question would be asked, did he get to a dressing station and which one and were his wounds severe or slight? And so on … This went on until the whole roll had been called and we all were silent, thinking of the chaps that had gone under. Men who, only a few days ago, went with us into the line with cheerful faces, joking with one another and now, to have the unpleasant task of informing his friends at home that he had been killed …

A TOAST WITH THE COMPANY SERGEANT MAJOR

We were not allowed to ponder and think of these things, everything was done to take our minds off of the sad affair and we did our best to try and forget it. We were so few in our company that our company sergeant major was able to treat each man to a drink of champagne. He was a regular good sort to his men, but as a soldier all the time a strict one for discipline and routine. He felt the loss of his men more, I believe, than we did. We had another visit from the Brigadier and he said much about the same as he did on the last occasion, except that he hoped we would always keep the good reputation we got whilst holding Vimy Ridge.

CHAPTER FIVE
ROAD TO THE SOMME

The time Harry's Division spent marching about the French countryside described in this chapter was in preparation for mobile warfare, which the British Army expected to follow once a breakthrough had been achieved at the Somme. The Division was not involved in the initial fighting, which turned into a deadly trench warfare battle of attrition rather than breaking out into open ground. The Somme was one of the deadliest battles fought by the British Army, and the opening day of the battle, 1 July 1916, resulted in almost 60,000 casualties, of which almost 20,000 were killed, with little ground gained. Open, mobile warfare would not come about for another two years, until the late summer of 1918.

THE PLATOON OFFICER'S BATMAN

After about two weeks stay, we moved off to another part where again we had huts to live in. They were erected in a small wood on the outskirts of a village. The ground was higher than that around, and on the lower ground, not far away, was an aerodrome. From our camp we could watch the comings and goings of the planes which were busy day and night. We had several pay days since leaving the line. Rations were more and cigarettes were plentiful, so everyone was more or less contented. When we were at Vimy Ridge, our platoon officer's servant, or batman, was taken out of the line on a stretcher after a bad dose of trench fever. He was ill for some time over in France and eventually sent to a hospital in England. Wanting another man to take his place, the officer asked the CSM (Company Sergeant-Major) if he knew of a likely man that would suit. Recommending me, the officer asked if I would care for the job. Learning of what I was supposed to do and coming to an arrangement, I accepted.

My pay was to be half-a-crown a week. My duties as a servant were to see to all the officer's underwear, as regards washing and mending; to keep his equipment, boots and uniform clean and tidy, and to maintain his living quarters. Each morning I called him up, having had ready his clothes, washing and shaving things. After attending to the officer's wants, I was free to go and get my own self ready for parade. It was quite a scramble and, more often than not, my breakfast was eaten cold. In other ways, however, I was privileged to miss duties I used to get when I was not an officer's batman. When we were moving from place to place, I had to hunt round the village, or wherever we were going to stay, looking for living quarters for the officer. Having found a place, I had to find all the transport lines, where the horses and wagons are kept and find my officer's sleeping bag (which was one of perhaps twenty, all packed on top of one another). These sleeping bags, or valises, were supposed to weigh no more than ninety pounds, but I think everyone went over this weight and they wanted some lifting! Sometimes it had to be carried a good distance, it was all according to how far the transport lines were from the regiment. It was no joke to hump this valise three or four hundred yards, after doing a good days march.

Getting it to the quarters and unpacking it, the next job was to find a utensil suitable to serve as a wash basin and a chair or a box or something else to stand the basin on. As there were sometimes over a dozen officers to the regiment with each one's servant hunting and striving to find things for his comfort, it was a rush to see who could get the best of things. Sometimes, I was able to get hold of a proper bowl but this was very rare. More often, empty biscuit tins had to serve or sometimes a pail either metal or canvas. Then when the weather was cold, a fire was needed and I would be on the hunt to beg, borrow or otherwise get a brazier for the officers' place.

A PLATOON OFFICER CALLED HOPE

I took a liking to my officer. He was good sort, though I must say all our officers were some of the best. My officer seemed to be on good terms with all he came into contact with. His name was Hope and he came from South Africa. He was of medium height, thick set and about thirty years of age with a ruddy complexion. He was always cheerful, very active and took an interest in the men under his command. Should a man get into a scrape about his duties, the officer was always glad to try and get the man off the punishment. He liked to mix with the men and often joined in the games of football, and other sports such as running and jumping. More than once he came and joined us when we were having tea, sharing in whatever we might have and chatting away with the best of us.

We were interested in his experiences whilst he was in Africa. He was something to do with a cable company out there and worked at a station some distance from the town. When war broke out, he volunteered for service as a soldier in Africa. They would not accept him as they said he was doing more good by remaining at his present job. He used to stay two or three weeks at a time at the station and then would be relieved by another man. Some weeks after war had been declared, the other man had relieved him when the next day some German soldiers captured the station. They did as much damage to it as they could; took all the people prisoner, ill-treated them and moved them about from place to place until some of our men were able to free them. Mr Hope, again, attempted to get enlisted as a soldier but was refused. So he travelled to England and joined up there. After doing some training, he was attached to us. Soon after he joined us, he got up a concert for his men and we had had a jolly evening together! To make it more interesting, he raffled several articles amongst us. He had a box of fifty cigarettes, a pipe in a case and a leather waist belt. The name of the articles was written on pieces of paper and mixed with other blank papers, which were all put into a cap, and then each of us picked out a paper. Those that picked a paper with a name on it had the article mentioned. I got the belt.

MAKING PLUM PUDDING AND A BATMAN'S CHORES

There was little to do whilst we were at this camp and I seldom went on parade. I noticed that the other batmen kept away, so I took it for granted that I could do the same. I busied myself, making the officer's quarters as comfortable as I could, kept out of sight until the men had gone on a route march and then wondered around, amusing myself. Sometimes, I would go over to the officers' mess kitchen and help prepare the food. One day, I went over there and they were in a bit of trouble about making a plum pudding. They had all the things to make it but all the saucepans were in use. I offered to help them out if they would give me a piece when it was cooked. They agreed to this and I got a fire going, found an empty cartridge tin, converted it to a saucepan and, in a short time had some water boiling. Mixing the pudding materials, I tied them in a cloth and dumped it in the boiling water. The pudding turned out good and I got the piece as promised!

If the officer was in need of anything such as polish, brushes, towels, soap or cigarettes, I used to go to the village to get them. Another thing was, if there was time, I used to take the officer's underwear to a woman in the village to have it washed. Money was given to me to pay for these things and any change over was, as a rule, given to me. When I had the time to spare, I used to watch the aerodrome and became very interested in the comings and goings of the aeroplanes.

MOVING OUT TO A SECRET DESTINATION

Whilst at this camp, I believe we had some reinforcements join us to make up for those lost at Vimy Ridge. We had inspections of different sorts, one of them being for clothes and equipment. There were quite a lot of things issued to the men and, after we had changed the old for the new, we looked quite smart! Only about a week passed here and then one evening, orders were read out to the effect that we were moving on next day. This move was to be a route march lasting three weeks or more and the destination was kept secret. There was a lot of guessing as to where we were making for. Some said one

place, some said another until we were apt to go to all parts of France and Belgium if their guesses were right! Anyway, next morning everyone was busy round the camp cleaning up and we batmen were running about, collecting washing and things for our own officers, besides attending to our own wants. All valises had to be at transport lines at a certain time and having carried them there, we had to help pack the wagon. The weather being fine and very warm, I took the liberty of packing some of my own things in with the officer's, for it's surprising how heavy a pack gets on a long march!

THE ROUTE MARCH

About dinnertime, we marched off and I, for one, wasn't feeling fit. Most of the chaps felt the same way, I suppose on account of us serving so long in the trenches and not getting enough exercise. This half-day's march was only a short one, compared with the distances we were about to cover in the next three weeks. We marched until dusk, putting up at a village for the night. There was the usual scramble, getting things for the officers followed by another busy morning, packing and getting ready to move off. Starting at about eight in the morning, we marched up until about four in the afternoon. Our mess carts travelled with us and cooked our food as they went along. We would march for about an hour and then get five minutes rest, this arrangement being kept up all through the following days. At dinnertime we got one hour. Tea, we had at the end of the day's march! Each day, we travelled a little extra distance than the day before until we were marching from seven in the morning until about six at night. The actual marching was bad enough, but what was more trying was the heat. The sun was shining all the time and we felt the heat a great deal as there was next to nothing in the way of shade on the country roads. Some men fell ill and had to go to hospital. This kind of thing went on during the early stages of the march until it was decided that we start earlier, before the sun got too hot.

Pros and cons of being a batman
The new arrangement was that we started at dawn and finished at about two o'clock in the afternoon. This was much better for us but we were still affected by the heat. I used to envy the other chaps who, as soon as the day's march was done, could throw off their packs and tunics, loosen their boots and cool off. They were free to do as they liked, could lay down and rest or go and have a nice cold water wash. We batmen would perhaps have to go to the other side of the village, struggle back with our loads, get everything ready for the officers' use and not until then, were we free to go and find our cold tea and whatever was to eat. After this, I was content to remove my boots and stretch out on the grass for an hour or more. I was glad of one thing; I didn't have to go on guard like the other men. I felt sorry for these men! After doing a hard day's march, they had to go on guard duty from six in the evening and kept on until we moved off next morning. Then another day's march before they could get a good night's sleep! It must have been very trying for them.

I noticed, as we went along from day to day that the dialect of the French people altered. At our starting place, I could converse with the people and make myself understood when I wanted anything. But after about a week on the road, it was difficult to understand, or be understood, when trying to converse. We passed through some very nice scenery and quaint villages and would have enjoyed them better if it had not been so hot travelling. We slept in all kinds of places, sometimes in the houses, at other times in barns, stables and outhouses. After a time, more of us used to lie out in the open, it was much cooler!

Lieutenant Hope becomes Acting Adjutant
We had been on the march for perhaps a week or more, when my boss was made acting adjutant. His appointment qualified him to ride horseback, so now, besides my other duties, I had to get his pony from the transport lines and bring it to him in time for commencing the day's march. After the march, I took the pony back. Thank goodness the care of the pony was another man's job at the horse lines!

The French civilians
At the farms we stopped at, the farmers were well respected by the farm labourers, both men and

133

women. Women farm-workers were quite a common sight. Whether this had always been so, or only since the war began, I don't know. But they were hard working people, working equally as hard as the men. After the day's work was done, it was the custom for all the labourers to go to the farm-house and get a jug of drink of some sort. It was wine, most likely, for I think beer was not drank a lot by the French people. These people would all go to the house in a bunch and when the farmer appeared, would remove their hats if they were men and the women would bow. For the jugs being filled they would say thank you, bow again saying good night and tramp off to their homes. Nearly every-one wore wooden clogs stuffed with straw and not a few of the women smoked pipes. Most of the troops were smokers of cigarettes and if we were issued tobacco, as we some times were, we used to give it to the French people. They liked it better than that sold in French shops and I didn't wonder at it for I have tried some, it was awful stuff to smoke! What amused me were the French children smoking! No matter what part we travelled, always there would be the cry of the children:

'Souvenir, Monsieur! Chocola ... cigarette, s'il vous plait!'

It was a common sight to see quite young children smoking as young as eight or nine years old; and swearing too, if we spoke to them sharp and told them to go away!

Plate 28
The day's work done, the farmer gives his workers some refreshments

Passing out with the heat

The last part of our march was the worst. The heat was almost unbearable. Even the nights were so hot that we could not sleep in comfort and a lot of men were sick in consequence. Day after day, starting about dawn, we would march, march, march, in the sweltering heat, our clothes damp with sweat until it penetrated right through to the straps of the equipment. Sweat would run down our faces and drip on to the road. We were continually mopping our faces and other parts, until the handkerchief would hold no more, then we'd hang it from the back of our caps to cover the neck until it was dry. We were not the only regiment taking this march, for as we went along, we saw dozens of men belonging to other regiments, overcome by the heat, stretched out at the side of the lanes. Quite a lot of our chaps had to fall out, I being one of them. I had felt the heat all along, but on this particular day, I felt it more. More than once, I had been on the point of falling out when the five minutes came for rest and saved me from bringing discredit on to the regiment. In a way, the march was a test of stamina and discipline between the several regiments taking part and it got us accustomed to marching long distances. It was expected that in the next battle we had, the enemy would be put on the run and we were to be made fit enough to be able to follow up the advantage gained.

We had been marching one day and the heat was terrible. I stuck it out until about three o'clock,

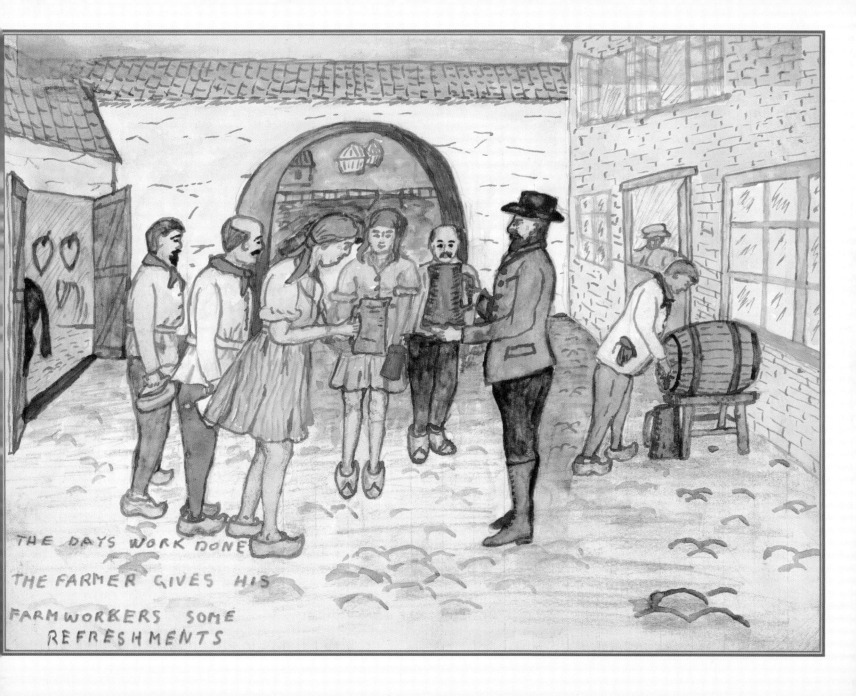

THE DAYS WORK DONE
THE FARMER GIVES HIS
FARM WORKERS SOME
REFRESHMENTS

walking like one in a dream. My legs seemed to move of their own accord and I kept bumping into my neighbours. I believe I could have lasted out till the rest came but for some reason, the regiment came to a halt and it was then that I came over dizzy. My legs gave way and down I went! I was helped to the side of the road and the regiment went on. It was some minutes before I could find the energy to remove my pack. When I did, I found the regiment was out of sight and all along the road were men, overcome by the heat or with blistered feet. There were dozens of us, some were really ill and had to be carted away in ambulances to hospital. The doctor of each regiment, with stretcher-bearers, came along attending to us. Those who were not too bad were told to rest awhile and catch up with their regiment later. What a relief to lie on the cool grass and rest! I lay there for about an hour when one of our officers, a new addition to us who had only been with the regiment a few weeks, came along gathering up us stragglers.

LOST ON THE MARCH TO THE SOMME

He had already had half a dozen men who had fallen out with sore feet or sickness. We travelled very slowly, pausing every now and again to pick up another man to join our little party, until we were about twenty strong. We travelled along through one village and then another, expecting at each one to find our regiment. We had got to a lonely hilly part and came to a place where several roads met. Here,

we halted for a rest and the officer was in doubt which way to turn. He studied a map he carried and said the village we were to go to was only about a half-to-a mile away, but which road to take he didn't know! There was no village in sight, although we couldn't see far on account of woodlands and clumps of trees dotted about all over the place. We talked it over and decided to split up our party to search for the village and the regiment. Going off in twos and threes, whoever found the village was to signal to the others that we would all go together. After searching for a time we found out that our regiment had turned off down a lane running parallel to the road we were on that we had passed about a mile back. Making our signal, we all got together again to decide what we should do. I was feeling much better myself but some of the others were looking fed up and didn't feel inclined to move anywhere. The question was should we retrace our steps a mile to the lane or go across country that was much shorter to travel. Going by road was a better choice for those with blistered feet but it would take us three or four times longer. We put it to the vote and cross-country won. We crossed turnip, potato and wheat fields and did the men who had the sore feet swear! I'll say they did! All our feet were sore, but more so after slipping and stubbing them over ploughed fields! We spotted the lane we wanted at last but to get on to it we had to slide down a steep embankment some twenty feet high. All up the sides were growing bushes of the prickly sort that scratched our hands and faces and caught in our equipment and rifles; swear words abounded!

REUNITED WITH THE REGIMENT

In about half an hour, we came upon the regiment who had just about finished tea and were lying about, resting. My first thought was to find my officer and explain things but on making enquiries to his whereabouts, I learned that he also had been overcome by the sun and had been sent to hospital so that was that! Having a good wash in some water that was almost ice cold, I had tea and found a nice spot under some fruit trees to rest along with some more of the chaps. We talked about the march and the things that had happened on the way, wondering what it was all about. Why were we doing it? There were no plans for moving off next morning like we normally did, so we kept awake later than usual. When we did go to sleep, we just spread our groundsheets on the grass, covered ourselves with our overcoats and slept until morning. After breakfast, all of us who had fallen out on the march had to parade and be examined by the doctor. There were quite a number of us. Those with sore feet were attended to, given new socks and told to rest the feet as much as possible. Us with the touch of the sun were told to get in the shade and not move about too much. These orders were not hard to do, for most of us felt we could do with a rest and we made the most of it. It was a pretty little farm where we were staying and we had few duties to do for the whole week we were here. By the end of this time, we cripples were well enough to get going again. So we bid good bye to our resting-place and were on the march again.

THE POSITION ORDER OF MARCHING

My officer had now returned to his duty and things went on as usual. The heat by now was not quite so bad but hot enough to make travelling unpleasant. I usually marched with my platoon which was at the rear of the regiment, but now orders were that officers, batmen, signallers, stretcher- bearers and runners were to march up in front. I found this position much better for marching, as there was not a lot of dust. Also we could hear and march to the drum; a thing we couldn't do at the rear, for half the time we couldn't hear the taps! The position now was first the band, numbering about twenty, then came our little crowd (say another twenty), behind us came the colonel on his horse accompanied by the adjutant and then followed the regiment in its different companies.

A SPANISH ONION

At one of the places we stopped at, I managed to get hold of a nice large Spanish onion (which I'm rather fond of). I got it in rather a hurry and was due to parade for marching. I had not time to put the onion in my pack, so I wedged it between my pack and shrapnel helmet, where I thought it would be quite safe. Getting on the road, we had marched some miles when, my pack straps becoming uncomfortable, I tried to ease myself by jolting my pack up a bit. As I jolted my pack up, the back straps loosened enough to allow my onion to roll from my helmet, out on to the road. The man behind, seeing it fall out, managed to pick it up and handed it back to me. The scramble for the onion disorganised the ranks for a bit and the colonel called me a few choice names! I felt rather uncomfortable with all eyes upon me and the men grinning at my expense, with the prospect of getting a reprimand when we halted for not securing my equipment better. I was soon put at ease, for on glancing round, I saw the colonel laughing at the incident as if it was a good joke! I got into no trouble from him, but my own officer talked rather straight to me about it and told me to be more careful.

Another day, we halted for a rest on a road with orchards each side. When we moved off, the orchard was quite a lot of fruit short! Complaints were made and we were money short next pay-day to cover the damage! We had done a lot of marching but it did us a lot of good. For months, on and off, we had been cooped up in the trenches with next-to-no exercise and that had been no good for any of us. Now, we felt as if we had had enough marching to last us quite a while and hoped that the rumour had been right that we were getting near the end of it!

BILLETING

We got to a small village where we were to stay for a fortnight, practising open warfare. The country round about was hills and dales, covered in parts with woods. We were to suppose that we had the enemy on the run and try to capture rear guards of men, guns and lorries. In order to do this we had to go out each day, scouting across country and through woods, I rather enjoyed the business, as it was something out of the usual. When we arrived at the village, as usual I found my officer a place to go and set about making him comfortable. I was going to put him in a cottage but the weather still being hot he asked me if I could manage to build him a shelter in the garden instead. I did what I could with material that I begged, borrowed or found and the result was a small tent with which the officer was pleased and said that I had done very well. This camping out was better for me, as it turned out, for my billet was at the back adjoining the garden. All I had to do in the morning was leave my billet at the farm, cross the farmyard, climb over a low wall and I was in the garden! I got hot water for shaving, a wash bowl and a chair from the cottage. It was a well-stocked garden with quite a number of fruit trees and bushes growing in it. The lady of the house gave the officer and me permission to help ourselves to any of the fruit if we cared for it. This was very nice of her and I would have some fruit even if the officer didn't.

A Strain on Anglo-French relations

Unfortunately, I couldn't say the same of the two ladies who owned the farmhouse where *we* were billeted. They were forever nagging and making complaints about the men billeted in their barns. I got on all right with them, myself. Perhaps it was because I took my officer's washing there to be done. Money was scarce with them and they were glad to receive what the officer paid. We had received no letters whilst we were on the march, so on the first night at the village when we all got our back mail and parcels, we were quite a happy party! Rations also improved in quality as well as quantity. More than once on the march, we had had to put up with a tin of bully beef and a couple of biscuits for dinner. Now, we were getting roast beef, greens and potatoes, followed by plum or currant pudding, rice and prunes. The village had about fifty cottages, one or two small shops and three estaminets. One of the estaminets was opposite our billet and, besides selling the ordinary wines, they sold rum, beer and coffee.

One trouble that we did have at the village was a scarcity of water and the orderlies had to go quite a distance to get it. There was a well in our farmyard next to the house, but the two old ladies (who were

139

sisters) guarded it and wouldn't allow us to use it if they could help it. We used it once or twice and then a padlock was put on it to prevent us using it anymore! We tried hard to get them to open up the well for us but it was no use. One day, they forgot to lock the padlock and, before they could find out their mistake, the padlock was missing without another to replace it! After that, we got water when the ladies were not in sight but what a nagging we got if they caught us! Very little of what they said could we understand – they talked so fast! What I did understand was that the old ladies were afraid that, with the well not being very large or deep, we would drain it dry. This, to our minds, was a lot of bunkum and the men thought it was very mean of the French women to try and stop us getting water so they played them up accordingly. Some of the men had wanted to buy eggs and bread but they wouldn't sell to them, saying they were saving them for market day. When *we* asked the women they refused us and even though they had a good orchard of apple trees loaded with fruit, they wouldn't sell those either. The men didn't like this kind of treatment and I am afraid the old ladies lost out through it, for eggs came from somewhere and apples were being eaten quite a lot and I expect none had been paid for!

A small donkey and cart was used for going to market and when the donkey wasn't being used, it was let loose in the orchard. Anyone venturing to enter, the donkey would attack with teeth and hooves.

The farm dog was unfriendly with us at first but with a little convincing and a meaty bone now and again, we soon made him friendly with all of us. A baker's cart delivered bread to the village every day and one day, being short in our issue, we stopped the cart to buy bread. This was something that the driver did not want as he said that he only had enough for his customers. We helped ourselves and placed the money on the cart. The driver had a lot to say about it and a few of his customers had to wait while he went for some more bread.

A QUIET GAME OF BRAG WITH SULLIVAN AND A FEED FOR THE FOWLS

We had been out one morning, practising and returned at about two o'clock. We had dinner and expected that we were done for the day. Most of the chaps in our billet got out their playing cards and started a game of brag. One chap by the name of Sullivan had had several drinks before he joined in and luck seemed to be against him at the game. He lost what money he had, borrowed some more and was losing that when the orderly corporal came up with our rations for the next day. The food was issued out to each man and all of us, except for Sullivan, put it away in a safe place. He was so excited over the game that they were playing, (anxious to get back the money he had lost, I suppose) that instead of putting his rations away, he just placed them on a box behind him and went on playing. Meanwhile, some fowls came along and started eating Sullivan's rations without him noticing it. They had almost finished the bread and cheese, the butter was in the dirt and a half-tin of jam had been knocked over and covered in dirt as well, before someone noticed what was going on.

'Whose rations are these?'

When Sullivan looked around and saw the remains of his rations, My! Didn't he swear!

He chased the fowls around the yard and set us all laughing at the way he chased first one fowl and then another, swearing all the time. No more card games were played but we all stood around and gave advice to Sullivan, cheering him on in his efforts to catch the chickens. He got tired of this at last and started calling us some fancy names for laughing at him. We told him it was his own fault and suggested that he should go to the farmhouse and ask for some more bread and butter and other things to replace what the fowls had eaten. He decided to do it and picking up what was left of his bread and cheese, he carried it over to the farmhouse to show the ladies to ask them to replace it with some more. We all followed him to see how he got on, expecting to see some fun. Sullivan didn't know a word of French and the ladies spoke no English.

Getting to the door, Sullivan knocked (the door was in two halves, the top and bottom halves opened independently.) After he knocked, the top half opened and one of the old ladies asked in French what did Sullivan want. Sullivan started to tell her in English what her fowls had done and all the lady did was look at him, wondering what he was talking about. This tickled our fancy and we had to laugh. But this riled both Sullivan and the old lady and each started talking at the other as loud as they could. We, who were looking on, thought it funny and laughed more than ever. At this, the door shut with a bang and Sullivan was left standing there with the bread still in his hand.

We kidded him on to have another try, so he knocked again. And again, the lady came to the door to find Sullivan speaking in English telling her how her fowls had eaten and spoilt his rations and what was she going to do in the way of replacing them. The lady replied: 'Je n'e compris!'

'No *compree*?' asked Sullivan. '*Compree* this: Your so-and-so fowls have had my so-and-so grub and this is all that's left!'

He held up the bread towards the lady to show her and she, thinking he was offering the bread to her to feed the chickens, took it from his hand, said 'Thank you', went in and shut the door! We roared with laughter. For a minute, Sullivan was speechless, then he knocked on the door shouting:

'WHAT ABOUT MY RATIONS!'

The lady came to the door again, looking angry and told Sullivan to go away. Sullivan didn't, instead he started arguing about the rations again. She stood it for a time and then the old woman reached behind the door, picked up a broom and started clouting

Overleaf

Plate 29
A quiet game of Brag and a feed for the fowls

Plate 30
We kid Sullivan to ask for more

A QUIET GAME OF BRAG
AND A FEED FOR FOWLS

WE KID SALAVAN
TO ASK FOR MORE

Sullivan over the head with it until he got out of her reach. We couldn't get him to have another try, so we all put something towards Sullivan's lost rations and made sure this time, that he put them in a safe place.

Afterwards, we all went about our different ways while Sullivan made for the wine shop and had several drinks. Half an hour later, orders came for us to parade and go out again, practising open warfare. We paraded in the lane and Sullivan turned up the worst for drink. We hid his condition from the officer and the NCOs by holding him steady while standing still, but when we got on the march he couldn't walk straight and kept bumping into the men on either side of him. This wasn't noticed until an NCO told Sullivan to get in step. Sullivan couldn't manage and he told the NCO that he *was* in step and that it was the men in front who were wrong. The outcome was that Sullivan got a punishment and a stoppage of his pay.

OPEN WARFARE PRACTICE

We marched about four miles from the village until we got into some wild open country and halted. It was then explained to us what we were supposed to do. The idea was that a rear guard of the enemy, who were supposed to be in retreat, were in ambush somewhere in some woods or in odd places round about, set to hold us up or delay us as much as possible. They were supposed to have machine-guns but what they really had was a tin with stones inside which they

were rattling to represent a gun being fired. In all, we had about two miles to cover across fields, ditches, through woods and growing corn and we were to go in open formation, keeping out of sight as much as possible and with the least noise. Before starting, scouts were picked with each scout having one or two runners or messengers to take back news to the main body of anything found. I acted as a scout and with others, we got about three hundred yards before the main body followed us. We scouts had been supplied with rifle, compass, several bombs and a notebook and our job was to try and surprise and capture any of the enemy that we came across. The enemy were to do the same with us. Officers with the different parties acted as judges over which side gained the most points.

My runners and I took quite an interest in our job and we managed to get right through the enemy, finishing up within fifty yards of the spot where we were supposed to be if we had read the compass correctly. It was difficult to move without noise in the woods but I managed to spot a gun and crew. To distract their attention, I threw a large stone into a bush and while they went to investigate, I got behind their position unseen and captured the gun (or tin can) leaving two men in charge. Going on, we came out of the wood on to a narrow lane on the other side of which was a cornfield. We crossed this and came upon another gun party, well on the alert but not in our direction. We worked our way around until we were near enough to throw our bombs and in theory we killed the lot. (Our bombs were tufts of grass). One of the party wouldn't stay dead after the officer had given his decision, but kept snapping his rifle at us until one of his own party tripped him up and he went on his back. This finished our practice and we all got into marching formation to return to the village. Every day, we went scouting and practiced different things in the surrounding country. The weather stayed hot and the water problem was getting worse.

FINAL MARCH TO THE SOMME

After perhaps a fortnight or three weeks, the regiment received orders to move on and we marched in stages towards the Somme. We would march all day and then stop at some village or other, where we might stay for just the night, while at others we could stay from one day to a fortnight. My officer was again acting as adjutant and I did no guards or parades. The other men only had to do short route marches with the rest of the time taken up with lectures. At the last village we stayed in before getting to the Somme, I was billeted at headquarters, with the staff and my officer next door in a small farmhouse. This was rather handy for me as all I had to do, on getting up, was to go next door to call the officer. I could get all his requirements such as shaving water, clothes and things ready and then go and have breakfast. After breakfast, I would tidy myself up and once I had got

the pony from the horse lines and helped the officer to mount, I was free to go about my job.

A FRENCH LADY'S GARDEN

Once I had tidied the officer's bedding, clothes and equipment, this soon done I used to go into the garden and chat with the lady of the house. She was a middle-aged lady and quite nice. I liked her very much. Her garden, of which she was proud, was I think the best I had seen in France. Most gardens were used for vegetables and fruit only but this one was nothing else but flowers and it was good to sit there, smoking and reading a book or chatting (with difficulty) to the lady. It reminded me of the gardens at home. There were wallflowers, marigolds, cornflowers, hollyhocks, daisies and pansies all jumbled together and the scent from them was good. The lady could speak a little English and, with the aid of an English/French dictionary, we managed to get along fairly well. We talked about all kinds of things from the war news to our home affairs. The lady told me that in the fore part of the war, German cavalry had passed through the village on scouting expeditions but hadn't stayed long. They had demanded all kinds of things from the local inhabitants and had forced the blacksmith to shoe some of their horses. They had overpowered and assaulted the blacksmith's daughter as well as other females of the village. The appearance of the Germans had been unexpected and before any French soldiers could get to the village, the Germans had gone back the way they had come.

CHAPTER SIX
SOMME

Harry's Division, the 47th (London) Division, was moved to the Somme sector in early September 1916, some two months after the start of the major summer offensive of 1916 known as the Battle of the Somme. The Division was nominated to take part in an attack on 15 September that later came to be known as the Battle of Flers-Courcelette. This was a major attack by ten divisions with the aim of breaking through the German lines toward Bapaume and ending the slogging stalemate that had developed in the overall battle. This attack was to be supported by tanks, a new, secret weapon to be used for the first time. The attack was a significant success and moved the British line almost three miles forward. On that day, almost as much ground was captured as had been taken in previous two months of fighting

146

ALBERT AND THE RUINED BASILICA

After about three weeks, we moved off to a town by the name of Albert. It was in range of the enemy guns and hundreds of shells were fired into it, at all different times, both day and night. It was a large town and had some fine buildings in it. The civil population had deserted the place, but there were hundreds of troops, horses, guns and wagons passing through, at all hours, and a good many got caught under the falling buildings when the shells exploded on them. For the number of shells it was surprising how few casualties there were. One building in particular caught our attention as soon as we arrived. It looked almost new and was very high, compared to the other buildings. It had a kind of tower attached to it and on the top was a guilded figure of a woman with her arms outstretched above her head. Held in her hands was a small child. The statue, which weighed some tons, was originally upright, but shells had weakened the base of the statue so that it now hung over at right angles to the building and seemed on the point of falling every second down on to the road some hundreds of feet below. It was a landmark for miles around and had been hanging like this for months.

Day after day, fresh troops came along until the basements of the town were crammed full, these being the only places safe from the shells that fell on the town. Our regiment was billeted in cellars but not many of us stayed there, we were all for getting out in the street in the sunshine. All the time we were dodging for cover, but we preferred this to being cooped up in a cellar all the time. One day, a lot of our chaps were sitting about on heaps of bricks near their cellars when a shower of shells came over. Before all could get under cover, they had exploded round about killing and wounding several men. One of the wounded was our head cook. He was an old service man and had come out with the first regiment. He was not badly wounded but I guess his soldiering was over, anyway, he never came back to us.

MORE REINFORCEMENTS LEAD TO ENCAMPMENTS OUTSIDE TOWN

Troops, troops and still more troops, they came in thousands until the town would hold no more and then camps were made in the open fields outside. Tents and marquees sprung up until the place looked like a huge fair. We stayed several days in the town and then moved off out into the open amongst the tents. There were hundreds of them all shapes and sizes. They were used principally for foodstuffs, medical supplies and ammunition. We got shelled while here and we had next to no protection. Dead and wounded were continually being carted away and if a horse got killed it was buried just where it lay, with a notice above saying 'a horse buried here'. If this was not done, the men from artillery, who were putting guns all over the place, were likely to dig up the horse when they were making gun emplacements. The camp covered miles of ground, and mixed between the tents were the troops, horses and guns which were being continually fired upon, and temporary hospitals. Troops had to make their own shelters in which to sleep under, that's if they could get any sleep, the place was all of a buzz with activity round the clock. The regiment stayed two days and then, late in the evening, moved off up to the line, leaving my officer and myself behind. We had all guessed that something big was coming off for weeks, but what it was we didn't know. Now at the last moment we were told that an attempt was to be made all along the line to get the enemy dislodged from the trenches and on the run. One or two surprises were promised and everyone was wondering what they were.

REPLACING THE WOUNDED ADJUTANT

My officer had his quarters in one of the smaller tents along with officers of other regiments and officers of the cavalry. I had orders to hang round about and on no account to go away. The sky became dull and cloudy and when the sun went down, everywhere was pitch dark. Later on it began to rain, but not heavy. Before the ground got too wet, I pitched a shelter made out of two ground sheets and prepared for a sleep. This was between eleven and twelve o'clock. Before turning in I reported to my officer, who was busy looking at some maps, and told him where I was in case he should need me.

'All right, get along,' he said, 'but be ready at a moment's notice to move off up the line or some other place.'

I got under my shelter and was on the point of going to sleep when the officer came and said:

'Come on, get up, we are to go up to the line at once.'

He explained that the regiment had taken over their position and soon after, the adjutant had got shot in the arm pretty badly, and we had to go round and take his place as soon as possible. Round I went gathering up the maps, papers and things, then I got myself ready and off we went. We had quite a trouble to get out of the camp it was so dark. We slid down holes, tripped over tent poles, walked into horses and guns and eventually found ourselves on a road. Firing guns were making a terrific din, round about, and not a few enemy shells were coming over also. Streams of motors and lorries were passing up and down the road loaded, in nearly every case, with shells. These were piled up in stacks at intervals, all along the road. Every stack had several guns nearby. We tramped along dodging shell holes and several times nearly got run down with motors or gun carriages.

SEARCH FOR THE 47TH DIVISION HQ AT TRENCH WOOD

The ground was all strange to us, it was raining steadily, and very dark. We kept on until we came to a fork road and here we halted to enquire the way. Everyone seemed too busy to help us and like ourselves, strangers to the district. At last some lorries halted near us and we enquired of the driver where

47th Divisional Headquarters were. He pointed out the road we were to take, trying to tell us what the headquarters looked like and the distance we were to go, but before we could get anything clear he had to move off. We got the impression that headquarters was in a kind of cave, dug out of the chalk, a little off the road, on the right hand side and about a mile in distance. Anyway, we had something to go on.

The further we went, the road got worse and worse. Soon it was a sloppy, chalky path with shell holes everywhere. How the drivers managed to keep to the road was wonderful. Most of them travelled at a trot or gallop, all the time shouting 'Gid up … get out of the way,' swearing at this, that and the other, and all intent on getting rid of their loads as quickly as possible. Shells burst now and again on the road and over would go the horses, sometimes the lorry. Speedily, these would be dragged off the road by scores of men and dumped into the fields and ditches at the sides of the road. Soon, we were splashed from head to foot in mud and had a job to find a sound piece of road to walk on. We kept going and were on the lookout for anything that might be a cave. We saw some places that were used for men's quarters, dug out of the chalk banks but they were not the ones we were looking for. We enquired again and again, each one we asked telling us to try here or try there. Trying them all, the last man said:

'Perhaps it's in the next lot of caves higher up the road.'

HARRY SEES A TANK
Getting on the road again, we continued our way. The traffic was getting more and more and guns were more in evidence on their way to take up positions ready for the attack commencing at dawn. The rain stopped and the moon shone through the clouds now and again. This made it better for travelling and we were able to see a bit better. We were all the time jumping out of the way of the lorries and things and I, for one, was all of a sweat, hot and tired. Getting some definite news of our destination, we were making our way towards it, when a contraption, which I took to be a tractor pulling a big gun, nearly ran over me. I had never seen or heard of anything like it.

'What is it?' I asked the officer.

'Oh, that's one of the surprises,' he said. 'It's what is called a tank.'

'Tank!' I said, gazing at it.

Whilst I looked, it kind of slewed round, left the road and waddled off across the fields.

'There's quite a few of them things,' said the officer, 'and good results are expected of them. Anyway, they will be a surprise for the enemy.'

BRIGADE HQ AND MEN OF THE SIGNAL CORPS
At last we managed to find our divisional headquarters, but we didn't stay. A note had been left to the effect that when we reported ourselves we were to go to Brigade headquarters, which was a short distance

Plate 31 The ruined Basilica at Albert

further along the road. These headquarters were in the remains of what had been a good-sized house. A little of the walls still stood whole, and these were strengthened with stacks of sandbags, railway lines, wood and iron girders, and were like a little fort. The place was like a beehive. Telephones rang every few seconds, orders were being given and written messages sent by the score. Standing about were men of the Signal Corps waiting to be sent off to repair or make a new telephone line.

Outside on the road, guns, shells, horses and men were still pouring along, each going to an allotted place. Enemy shells exploded on the road frequently making large holes, but hardly had the smoke cleared away when gangs of men would fill in the hole with stones, taken from the heaps kept at the side of the road. My officer had gone below somewhere for some orders and was away for some time. When he returned he said he had nothing to do till the attacks commenced, so what about getting something to eat and drink at the cookhouse attached to the house. We went along and was given a nice steak each, bread and butter and a large mug of coffee.

Going away again the officer told me to make myself comfortable and not go away from where I was in case he wanted me. It only wanted a couple or more hours to dawn and the commencement of the attack, so I lay down on the floor and tried to snatch some sleep. Hardly had I got down when some gas shells came over and we all had to don our gas masks. Our guns were now firing like mad, but with all the noise and gas mask on, I fell asleep. It seemed I had slept about five minutes when my officer woke me and said:

'Come along, we are to go up the line and be there when they go over the top.'

TO THE FRONT AND DELVILLE WOOD

The front line was not a great distance away and we had bullets buzzing by us almost as soon as we left the headquarters. We didn't trouble to go by trench until we were nearly at the front line. Our guns were placed at all unlikely places, and still more were being placed in position until at times, they were wheel to wheel in rows of dozens. The gunners were being hit by bullets and were carted away to dressing stations or dugouts in the trenches. We were lucky to get along without getting hit. Getting to the front line, we reported ourselves and stood with the troops to wait for the signal to go over the top. We had about half an hour to wait and everyone was busy with their own thoughts and each one had a serious look about his face. The enemy's lines were being heavily shelled and not a few came our way. Our trenches were crowded with men, and in places it was difficult to get along. Some of the men had to carry a shovel, others a pick or a bag of bombs. The gunners had a machine-gun to carry, followed by their crew with loads of ammunition. Stretcher-bearers and first aid men were also here, but they commenced their job after the men had gone over.

WAITING FOR THE COMMAND

Waiting for the second to go over is a nerve trying business and many are glad, in a way, when the time arrives, each knowing that perhaps in the following second they may be blown to pieces or be crippled for life. It's all in the game and I never saw a man that hesitated to go over when the time arrived. Time draws nearer and nearer, a ration of rum is passed along the trench, but not everyone takes it whilst others accept two or even three issues. Not knowing what the next few hours may or minutes may do for them, a number of the men exchange home addresses with each other, so that in the event of one or other of them getting hit, a letter could be sent home stating the fact. This was thought more satisfactory to relations than the curt and short notice sent by the War Office. 'Sorry to inform you, so-and-so died in action etc.' Our line of men were some of those that were first to go over in the attack, and for miles behind us, were thousands of other men who were to carry on what we began. A regiment on our left had a wood in front of them, and it was strongly held by the enemy. They had machine-guns galore. The trenches were reinforced with concrete and had a good backing of small guns, whilst a maze of barbed wire entanglements made the task of capturing them even more difficult. On several previous occasions, our troops had attacked this wood and had been driven back with great losses. It remained to be seen how we would fare on this occasion. Our guns were certainly giving the wood a terrible hammering and it seemed impossible that anything could live through it. Trees were shattered and split, in some cases uprooted, the whole being in a fog of smoke and bursting shells.

OVER THE TOP

The time two minutes to go, was passed along from man to man and an even greater number of our guns opened fire on the enemy lines until the ground seemed to bubble and be alive with tongues of fire. Everything was now in readiness for the attack and a number of our officers were standing on top watching the effects of our shelling, including my officer and myself. The time came to advance on the enemy. A shrill blast of whistles was given and like one man, our men climbed out of the trench and passed us on the way to the enemy lines. There was little or no resistance given by the enemy troops in front of our regiment, but the shellfire that rained about our men was terrible. Great gaps were made in our advancing lines, but the men who remained still slowly advanced filling up the gaps made, capturing the first line and so went on to the second and third. Here they stayed and got busy with pick and shovel, strengthening their position, whilst others routed out and made prisoners any enemy that had been unable to get away.

1/6TH LONDON, STOKES TRENCH MORTARS AND THE WOUNDED MOUNT UP

The regiment on our left, the 6th London I believe didn't get their objective so easily. They got a certain distance towards the wood and could get no further on account of machine-gun fire. For a time we were held in check, when some Stokes trench mortars were brought into action and bombed the gun emplacements out of existence. Our troops now were able to advance and hundreds of the enemy were found hidden away in deep concrete dugouts. These were captured with little resistance, and sent under escort back to our lines.

By now the attack was in full swing and thousands of our men were making towards the enemy in line after line as far as the eye could see. The gun fire from the enemy was by now hardly noticeable in the way of field artillery, but quite a number of the larger size shells continued to drop and explode at unexpected places, making large craters in the already churned up ground. These craters were a favourite spot for the stretcher-bearers to place the wounded and attend to the wounds until such a time that they could get them to a proper dressing station. It was very seldom that a shell hole would receive another exploding shell, so that was why wounded were placed in the craters. Our men advanced over first, second and third lines of the enemy and then came the stretcher parties, picking up the dead and wounded of both our own men and enemy. Quite a few enemy stretcher-bearers and doctors were among the captured. The strange thing about these were that they all carried revolvers or automatic guns. Never at any time did our men handle firearms. The revolvers being taken away from the enemy stretcher-bearers, they were allowed to stay on in the field and do what they could for the relief of the wounded. They, like our chaps, were wonderful, doing their job, at times under heavy shellfire, with thoughts only for the wounded.

ENEMY WOUNDED

Our own killed and wounded was bad enough, but the enemy losses were terrible. They lay one on top of another, some of the bodies of both ours and the enemy were torn to shreds, different limbs laying all over the place, a dreadful sight. We felt sorry for the captured men now coming in. They walked along like they were in a daze, clothes torn and bespattered with blood and mud. Now and again could be seen a German carrying one of our chaps who had been wounded pick-a back and trying to carry on conversation with one another as they went along. There were no escorts for the prisoners, they were simply disarmed and directed to go to our rear. On arriving on a main road, they were collected together in several hundreds and marched off to some internment camp. Before doing this, each man was searched for papers that might be of value as information to us.

INTERROGATION OF PRISONERS

Our men having got their objective, stayed till early next morning, then off again they went to advance further into the enemy's positions. My officer and I were recalled to headquarters and we spent several hours there doing odd jobs. One of them was to examine and search the prisoners as they came in. My officer was at one time in German East-Africa and could speak the language. He cross-questioned them as to papers and other things whilst I run over their pockets to make sure nothing was kept. Many of them had photos of friends and relations and these they were allowed to keep, and they thanked us. One or two of the prisoners jibbed at giving up things but soon altered their tune when a service revolver was drawn and covered them. As the prisoners gave up their papers, I collected them and placed them in sandbags. These were taken away and examined by several men in headquarters. There were hundreds and hundreds of prisoners and I guess a lot of them were glad to be out of it all.

BRIEF RESPITE

Shells of the heavy kind were falling round about but they had no particular target it seemed, and they did very little damage. We had our job examining the prisoners for several hours and then we were relieved by another two officers. Going inside the headquarters for further orders, we found we wouldn't be needed for an hour or so. This gave us an opportunity to wash and have something to eat. My officer told me to stop near by in case he should need me and went off to get some sleep. I was in need of some myself, so after eating I found a corner that was fairly

Plate 32
A party of staff officers and signallers in a shell-hole, Butte de Warlencourt, Battle of Flers–Courcelette, Somme

quiet. I lay on the floor and fell asleep. I hadn't been asleep long before I was aroused by some big shells exploding quite near which were of the gas variety. Soon the air round about was quite foggy and we had to put on our masks and I fell asleep again whilst still wearing mine.

REPORTING ON THE REGIMENT'S POSITION AT FLERS

I wasn't allowed to sleep long before orders came that we were to catch up with the regiment, get a report from them regarding their position, strength and needs in the way of rations, ammunition and first aid for wounded. A few shells were falling as we set out and we had about three miles to go across country that was churned up over and over again and was very bad for travelling. The first mile wasn't so bad but the further we went so we got more and more shells. I noticed the stretcher-bearers were still busy picking up the dead and wounded and they all seemed tired out and in need of rest. They were a fine lot of men and did great work. Several times as we went along, these stretcher-bearing men would be carrying a wounded man over the terribly rough ground with difficulty when a shell would explode near enough to upset the whole lot. If they were still able, they got up, placed the wounded man back on the stretcher and carried on. For hours they did this kind of thing and it must have been very tiring, apart from taking the risks that an ordinary soldier takes.

GRIM SIGHTS OF THE BATTLEFIELD

The battlefields we passed over had plenty of dead laying on them and some gruesome sights we saw. Groups of men armed with picks and shovels were digging large graves and laying the dead in them, first taking the identification disk from the dead body. After the bodies had been covered up, a rifle was stuck upright over them as a temporary mark of a grave, this was later replaced by a rude cross with the names of the dead on it. Yet other men were going over the ground collecting equipment, rifles and ammunition, and placing them in heaps to be later collected and sent back to base for further use. We passed batteries of guns in all kind of places and they were all busy, more or less, firing the shells at the still retreating enemy. Scores of aeroplanes were flying about over head taking note of the enemy movements and signalling the information to the gunners who acted accordingly. There were also some enemy planes about, but these kept well back over their own ground and seldom come amongst our planes. Should one or more do so, there was a fight and it was chased by our own planes.

MEETING SIGNALLERS AND STAFF OFFICERS IN SHELL HOLE

Travelling over the rough ground soon made our legs and feet ache, and I for one was glad to rest in a large shell hole, which was occupied by a party of staff officers and two signallers. We saw them long before we got to them as the collars of their tunics were bright red and showed up quite plainly against the dark background of the earth. Having come up with them, my officer enquired if they knew of the whereabouts of our regiment and the best way to get to it.

'Get down in the hole, Sir! Don't stand there advertising our position for it is rather important as we have a telephone line here which is receiving news and information from our most advance positions.'

We quickly got down in the hole and for a few minutes my officer chatted to the other officers, whilst I got into conversation with the signallers who were well supplied with cigarettes, of which I had a few. These officers had evidently been tramping over the ground like we had and got sore feet, for each of them had removed their boots to ease them. We dropped into the shell hole none too soon for as we got down, a large shell exploded a short distance away and smothered us all with dirt and made us deaf for a time. One piece of dirt struck my thumb and numbed it. I thought for a moment it was gone but was glad to find it only bruised. Getting all the information we could, we scrambled out of the hole and started on our way again, the officers saying as we went: 'Don't smother us with dirt as you go!'

THE BRAVE ARMY CHAPLAIN

Going some distance we came to a road that passed along the bottom of a very steep hill. This had been cut away until it was almost perpendicular and under the shelter of this were dozens of both German and English wounded. Stretcher-bearers were bringing in the wounded and making them as comfortable as they could, and they all looked dead tired. I was surprised to see an army chaplain or parson going about among the wounded. He was a plucky chap to be so near the fighting and carrying on as he did. He went to each and every man as they were brought in, and did all he possibly could to make the man comfortable. Round his neck he had several cups hanging by string, whilst at his side he had a large water flask. Tucked under his arm was a box of cigarettes, and he went from one to another giving here a drink of water, or there a cigarette. He wrote down messages for the wounded to be sent home to their friends and also went out collecting water, clothes and bandages from off the dead lying about, for the benefit of those he was caring for. He was a great chap and I admired him. We gave up to him what water we had and asked could he direct us to the village we were looking for. He knew where it was, and as he was going in that direction in search for more water, he offered to come part way with us. He talked to the officer as we went along, praising the men and spoke of the sufferings of the wounded, and seemed very sorry for them. Getting to the end of the ridge, the parson left us to search for the precious water and directed us on our way.

CANADIAN COLONIAL TROOPS AT THE TRENCHES IN FLERS

The ground we had to cross to get to the village was being shelled rather heavily and swept at intervals with machine-guns, it being in full view of the enemy. We hid up and waited until we thought the firing was not quite so heavy and then made a dash for some trenches just in front of the village. My officer was an easy first but we both got over safely, if rather out of breath. The trench was held by some colonial troops – Canadian I believe, and they were surprised that we were able to get to them through the shelling that was going on. We stayed just long enough to get our breath back and accept a couple of cigars which the Canadians had found in a dugout when they captured the trench, and then we made our way toward our own men that were some distance away and nearer to the village. The trenches were not knocked about much but had evidently been left in a hurry by the enemy. There was German equipment, clothes, boots, and rifles lying about the trench and stacks of bombs of the tin can variety. The dugouts were deep and roomy and not a few had sleeping bunks in them. The officers' dugouts had tables and chairs also. Quite a few empty wine bottles were found as well, so the enemy appeared to have been having a decent time whilst they were here! The village was named Flers and I believe at the time we arrived, our troops had captured half the village and were busy trying to get the whole of it by bombing the enemy out with hand grenades, going from house to house to do it. The men in support were busy linking up shell holes by digging trenches in between and it was a dangerous and tiring job. I know … I've had some! *[Note: These "Colonial" troops were almost certainly from New Zealand – Harry's Battalion attacked with the New Zealand Division on their right flank and it was they who took the town of Flers. The Canadian troops were about two miles further north and there were two Divisions between Harry's Division and the Canadians.]*

LIEUTENANT HOPE'S REPORT ON FLERS IS ENTERED INTO THE RECORDS

We stayed for about an hour and then, having got the information we wanted, we set out for our return journey back to headquarters. Another dash was made across the open ground for the safety of the hill through the shrapnel and bullets, witnessed by some staff officers who were sheltering under the hill we were making for. When we joined them, we saw they were making notes of the enemy positions and also ours. They questioned my officer of what he knew and duly entered it into their books. Then, bidding us follow, they climbed up the hill to the top where a good view of the surrounding countryside could be had. There were some good strong trenches up here and had hardly been touched by shellfire. Here also, the enemy seemed to have left in a hurry. The officers were talking together and scanning the countryside through their field glasses and making notes, when we were joined by the parson chap. He said he was pleased we had returned so far safely and asked that we would not show ourselves too much because if the enemy saw us they might fire our way and so endanger the wounded men lying on the other side of the hill.

Getting down from the hill, we started back for headquarters. We had about the same experiences going back as we had in coming out, having several narrow shaves getting hit with exploding shells. Our feet and legs ached and were getting painful through continually jumping and scrambling over shell holes. Another thing was it was now getting dusk and we had difficulty in finding our bearings. I was beginning to feel hungry and hoped we would soon get to some

place where we might rest and eat. We plodded on occasionally asking burial parties if they could direct us to our headquarters, but none of them seemed to know. It was too dark now for us to recognise any landmarks, so we travelled hoping for the best, or that we might come across a road of some sort.

[Note: The Butte de Warlencourt remained in the hands of the Germans until 1917 when they withdrew to the Hindenberg Line to shorten their line on the Western Front.]

ALONG THE ROAD OUT FROM THE BATTLEFIELD
After a time we did come to a road crowded with traffic and marching troops. From here we got our right direction and found we had gone about a mile

or more out of our way. We made our way along the road and had to keep our wits about us or we would have got run down several times by lorries and guns. There was one continual stream of traffic on the road as far as we could see and when a shell exploded on or near the road, it must have done some serious damage. The travellers took it as a matter of course, with a lot of shouting and barking orders, gangs of men with the help of mules or horses, would drag the debris off the road and dump it in a ditch. Should horses get killed, they were dragged into an adjoining field. A large pit would be dug and the horse rolled into it and covered over. There was very little confusion, each man seemed to know just what was wanted and did it. Parties of men were stationed along the road doing nothing else but filling in the ruts and shell holes with stones and sand.

There were plenty of casualties along here and the Red Cross people were very busy attending to them. There were dozens of our heavy guns firing off shells and they lit up the sky with a red glow. Going past one of these batteries, we noticed the cook getting ready refreshments for the gunners, so we went over and asked if we might have some. 'Of course,' said the cook, and gave us each a large mug of cocoa and some bread and fried bacon. Whilst we ate, we chatted to the men and exchanged our different experiences and then, thanking our friend for the refreshment, we got on our way feeling much better. Eventually we got to headquarters, reported and we were told to get some rest. I don't know where my officer went, but I found a dry corner, got down and was soon asleep.

'RELIEVED' TO HIGH WOOD

Before we went to sleep, we learned that our regiment was to be relieved and coming back to a wood named High Wood, where we were to rejoin the men. About midnight we were woken up and had orders to join the regiment because it had just arrived. Feeling still very sleepy, we went to find our regiment. We were now up to our boot-tops in mud, for it had been raining heavily for some time. Getting to the wood, we found that because there was a shortage of dugouts, three regiments had their headquarters in one dugout, whilst their staff had to do their work on the stairs. My officer managed to get down somehow and sent word up that I was to keep somewhere handy in case he should want me. Here was a fine how to do! I felt tired and it was pouring with rain with no shelter. Brrr! I felt good! Well, anyway I had to do something so I went along the trench, hoping a shelter had been overlooked.

Going along, I came to a large tree that had been uprooted by shellfire and had grown on top of a bank. The roots of the tree jutted out a little beyond the bank, so I got my entrenching tool and dug out a small cave or hollow. In front I fixed my ground sheet and had for myself a fairly comfortable shelter. I had to light a candle to work by, the light of which attracted several callers who wanted to know if I had any room for them. Not one asked if I wanted any help, so I said 'no', and got on with my job. I had just enough room to lay down without my feet reaching into the trench and tried to get some sleep. I was at least in the dry, for no rain got through my shelter and I was quite content until two other chaps begged me to let them sit down in it with their legs out in the trench and rain. Hardly had they sat down when they were fast asleep. I went to sleep but was woke up by the two men trying to get further in and climbing on top of me.

'Hey, what's the game?' I wanted to know.

They told me that their legs stuck out in the trench. Everyone that came along either tripped over them or trod on them, so they were trying to get them out of the way. I told them I was sorry but the place wasn't big enough for two let alone three, why didn't they go and find or make a better place. After a bit of swearing and a few arguments they both went and I was left alone again.

ERRAND TO FIND A WOUNDED MAN

I dozed off and was woken up again by someone pulling at my legs.

'Hello, what's the matter now?' I wanted to know.

'Who are you?' a voice said.

I explained who I was and added that I was to stop where I was in case I was needed.

'Oh!' the voice answered, and off it went. About five minutes after, the same voice came and said:

'You are to come out of there and go and find a wounded man who is in some front line trench.'

Getting out of my shelter, I found an army doctor there with two men and a stretcher. The doctor said:

'I am putting you in charge of this party and I want you to go to so-and-so trench where you will find a badly wounded man. Get him and bring him in as soon as you can.'

It was still raining hard and where this particular trench was I had no idea, except it was up front. Well, orders are orders so off we went. My two men were swearing and carrying on about the rain, the war and lots of things besides, but all the time we got along somehow with the stretcher. What a time we had – raining hard, pitch dark, stumbling into shell holes and at least a mile to go! Before long, we were soaking wet to the skin and smothered from head to foot with sloppy mud. In time we came to some trenches which had some troops in them and we asked for directions.

'It's somewhere over there,' they said, and pointed into the dark.

We push on and could find no trench or anyone to ask. Rifles seemed to be going off all around us and shells and bullets buzzed just over our heads or exploded and burst in the mud round about. Now and again star shells lit up the place on all sides of us. We three seemed to be the only people about and we were lost. Going forward again, we got over a bit of

trench much knocked about. Following it along in the hopes of finding somebody, we discovered we were in the enemy lines by hearing some men gibbering away in German. We were not long in changing our direction and retraced our way back the way we had come. Getting out of the enemy lines, as we thought, we stopped and talked things over regarding our errand. While standing there talking in whispers we saw a party of men coming out our way. We wondered who they could be – Germans perhaps? We ducked down and made plans hastily to find out. We decided to get round each side and then challenge them. I got near enough to hear them talking but couldn't make anything of what they said until one of them said:

'Bugger the dixie! I've had enough of trampling about in this mud looking for a trench that ain't here!'

A CUP OF TEA IN NO-MAN'S LAND
I called out and asked: "Who are you?"

After a clicking of rifles they asked who was I and told me to show myself. I went forward, made myself known and explained my errand. My two men now came up with the stretcher and asked the other party if they knew of the trench we were looking for.

'No!' they answered. 'We're looking for the same trench ourselves! Here we are carrying a dixie of tea about for hours over this rotten mud and nobody seems to know where this so-and-so trench is! Brrr! I am fed up with it!'

We all had another go at finding the trench with no success and decided to give up and go back.

'What about this tea? Shall we sling it?' said somebody.

'No, don't throw it away, let's have a drink first!' was the chorus.

How to drink it was the next question. The dixie or boiler was a large affair, holding perhaps three or four gallons. One way was to bend over the dixie and suck it up, another was to hoist the dixie up and drink it that way. We tried but got more outside our necks than inside. Then one of us thought of using a shrapnel helmet. This served our purpose although some tea got spilt down our fronts. Having drank our fill, the rest of the tea was emptied away and we made our way back to report our unsuccessful errands. The dixie party went one way and we the other, both parties fed up with their night's work.

RETURN TO BASE
Our party slipped and slid about over the muddy ground, cursing and swearing all the time. First one of us and then another would slip up and find ourselves sitting in a shell hole partly filled with water. Then one would grumble about carrying the stretcher, 'it's time somebody else carried it', and so on. We lost our bearings for a time, but on getting to a higher bit of ground I recognised some woods we had passed on our way out. My two men were sure it was the wrong direction and they wanted to go. As

Plate 33
47th Battalion HQ in the trench at High Wood, Somme

they were going, we had an argument about it and I said:

'Well, alright, you go the way you want to. I am going this way.'

I took the stretcher and went off. I hadn't gone very far before they followed me and said perhaps I was right, they would chance it. Once past this first wood, we could see our own wood and we all recognised it. I had carried the stretcher for some time now, so I got one of the men to have a turn at it. We were near to the end of our journey now and we all felt a bit more cheerful. One man and I had just got by an extra big hole when there was a scramble and a splash. Looking round we found our other man with the stretcher had fallen in face downwards. He looked like an African. He made one or two unsuccessful attempts to get out but every time he got near the top of it he slid back down again, (the sides of the hole were like grease). We went to his help and tried to grip his out-stretched hand but we were unable to reach him from the top of the hole, and in trying to get nearer, we almost went in ourselves. In the end I suggested he put the stretcher upright so that we could grab it and pull him out. At last we had him on top again, poor chap! I felt so sorry for him, he was in such a mess. We scraped as much mud off him as we could and then got on our way.

I found the doctor who had sent us on our errand and reported that we were unable to find the wounded man. He replied that he was sorry but our journey had been for nothing. Soon after we had been sent out, a stretcher-party had brought the wounded man in and by now he was on a hospital train. On hearing this, the two men that were with me didn't have a word to say. They just gave one big sigh, turned round and vanished in the dark, leaving me standing alone in the rain. For myself, I was glad the wounded man had been brought in and cared for but couldn't get over the fact that we had trudged for hours, wet-through over the sloppy mud and all for nothing.

'Ah well, I suppose it might have been worse,' I thought to myself as I made my way to my shelter. I was feeling pretty miserable and tired and would have been glad to rest a while, but when I got to my little dugout I found it occupied by two more chaps. They had lit my candle, had helped themselves to some of my food and seemed nice and comfortable! I pointed out to them that the place was mine and I had made it for myself.

'Go on! Who are you trying to kid? We've been here all the time!' they argued.

'It's my place,' I insisted. 'And if you will examine the things in there you will find they are mine.'

This closed the argument and I got in. They stayed a while chatting about one thing and another and was sorry that they had touched my belongings and then they went off. I had something to eat, put my overcoat over me and went to sleep.

REGIMENT RESTING IN WIDE TRENCH GULLIES

When I awoke it was daylight and it was no longer raining. I got up, had a wash in a shell hole, shaved and went in search of breakfast. A little later, my officer and I moved to fresh quarters along with the regiment, who were camped or collected in a sunken road just back of the wood. Running along side the road was a wide trench or gully and it was in this that the men had made themselves as comfortable as they could. All of them looked a sight, they were covered from head to foot in mud, and the majority of them had neither washed nor shaved. All seemed intent on getting a fire going to cook by and to dry out their clothes. The last two awful days of slaughter and nerve shaking had brought a strained look to the faces of many them. My officer went in a rough kind of shelter with some others of his rank and I attached myself to a shelter that was also the cookhouse headquarters. Inside there was a large fire burning and it was not long before I took off my clothing and dried myself. Then I got busy scraping and brushing the now dry mud off my clothes so that afterwards I was feeling much better and looking tidier.

By now everyone was busy doing their best to get themselves cleaned up and in an hour or two they were looking something like their usual selves. There were many familiar faces missing, one of them being an officer who had risen from 'the ranks' and had gone over with the boys. He had been a great favourite with the men and they were very upset he had been killed on the first occasion that he wore his officer's uniform in action. Guns still blazed away but not nearly so much as before. The advance had eased up a bit but the rumour went around that it would not be for long. Around where we were camped were all kinds of ammunition, bombs and shattered guns lying about in the mud and they were gradually getting buried by men walking over them, or the wheels of lorries and guns pressing them deeper with their weight. Unfortunately some of the men built their fires over this buried ammunition and when the heat got too much they were exploding with nasty results. A few shells came our way but they exploded out in the open fields and all they did was to add a few more holes to the thousands already there.

Early in the morning it began to rain again and the weather turned chilly. Come night, we all had to find a place where we could sleep. The men fixed up shelters by stretching their ground sheets across the trench to keep them fairly dry whilst they slept, but it was a miserable business at best. Our place was covered over with some kind of roof and very little rain came through, also we had the fire. The shelter was not large and when the other four chaps, the cooks, took up their positions for the night on top of the table and biscuit boxes, I found the only room left for me was a small place on the floor. The ground was very damp but by spreading my ground sheet over it,

OUR STRETCHER
BEARER FALLS
INTO A SHELL HOLE

I thought it would be all right and it would keep me dry. I slept heavily and found when I awoke that my weight had made a hollow in the moist clay under me and where the water had run into it I was lying in a puddle. I felt very uncomfortable and cold until once again I dried my clothes and got some hot tea inside me. We stayed here two or three days and then we were ordered to take over some trenches that had been captured that day.

Daylight raid in defence of Colonial troops

We moved off in the dark, tramping it seemed for several miles along temporary-made roads and pathways that were very trying to walk on. We were continually dodging shell holes, big lorries and guns, forcing us off the road. It didn't make things pleasant, especially as one or two of the men got pushed head-long into some trenches. Our quarter master sergeant was amongst them who I believe injured his knee and had to spend some time in hospital over it. The further we marched, the more shells we got. I don't think any of us got hit until we got to a sharp turn in the road. We halted and had to wait until our guide, who had lost his whereabouts, hunted around for the right way to go. It seemed as if we stood there waiting for a very long time. All the while we were shelled with shrapnel and quite a number of us were getting either killed or wounded. Men were dropping down or crying out. The chap next to me got hit in three places. There was a lot of grousing amongst us but no panic. We removed the killed or wounded men to as safe a place as we could find and left them for the stretcher-bearers to attend.

When we got moving again, we found ourselves going along a half-filled trench until eventually we came to a small village that was very knocked about. The trenches that we had taken over were German-made and ran alongside the village street and up adjoining lanes. They had been well made and had a number of good dugouts with generally two entrances, equipped with bunks down below. We settled into our new quarters and wondered how long we were going to stay. My officer and I were attached to headquarters in a dugout down a side lane. Daylight came and we were able to look about a bit. To leave the shelter of the trenches was dangerous, as bullets and bursting shells occasionally dropped in and around the village. As the light got better so the shelling on both sides got heavier until there was quite a bombardment going on. About 11 a.m. we got the news that the enemy up ahead of us were enfilading some Colonial troops of ours on the right and it had got to be stopped by us forcing them back.

Over the top, still eating sandwiches

Round about 12.00, rations were issued for the midday meal. We had boiled bacon and bread with

Plate 34 Our stretcher-bearer falls into a shell hole, Somme a helping of tea. The men made sandwiches and were eating contentedly when urgent orders came that they were to prepare at once to go and attack the enemy, removing him at all costs. There was some grumbling at this order because most of our attacks had been carried out at early dawn or night-time and we found it a foolhardy thing to attack in daylight. Quite a few were grumbling because there had been no time to eat their rations. Preparations began with bombs, pick axes and shovels being issued out and in very short time the men were all ready to launch the attack. To look at them nobody would think that within very few minutes these men would be going to their death or be maimed for life. The best part of them were eating and the others were having a smoke and joking with one another about the unusual attack that was about to come off. A heavy barrage of shells were to be laid about the enemy lines for a few minutes and then orders were that as soon as the barrage lifted our men were to go forward and capture the enemy trenches. Things happened as arranged and the men went over, some shouting, some smoking and not a few still eating sandwiches as they advanced to the attack.

ASSISTING THE DOCTOR

Once clear of the houses, our men were met with heavy machine-gun and rifle fire and a good many fell. The surprise attack in broad daylight evidently took the enemy off his guard for he didn't put up much resistance and our men 'got their objective'. Some Welsh troops came up and helped to strengthen the captured trenches and a new trench was dug to connect up with those in the village. A few prisoners were taken and stretcher-bearers did wonderful work in getting in the dead and wounded. For some hours there was an exchange of fire but the expected counter attack never came off and gradually things quietened down. During the attack I had to run from place to place with messages and once I acted as help to the doctor. One man I helped to dress had got wounded between the thighs. Then the doctor had to get to fresh quarters where more wounded needed attention. I was called on to go with him, carrying his medical supplies. The way we had to go was being shelled heavily. Trees were felled across the road and large holes had been made, not to mention shrapnel bursting overhead. Studying the situation, the doctor noticed a lull of a few seconds in between the bursting of the shells. We counted the seconds and planned to make short dashes, throwing our selves flat on the ground when the next shell was due to explode. The doctor went first and I watched him dash as fast as he could down the lane, scrambling over trees, sometimes crawling underneath them and then lying quite still. Hardly had he got down when several screaming shells would burst, it seemed, right at his side. Up again and another dash by the doctor until he got safely to trenches in the village. I now followed in the same way, handed over the chest of medical and surgical supplies to him and off he went to attend the wounded.

Gruesome sights on route back to High Wood

The regiment had evidently only been brought here to make this attack, for as soon as it was dark we all moved back again, returning the same way we had come, being relieved by another regiment. On our way back we saw some gruesome sights. We had had no idea when we'd entered the village that we were walking and climbing over hundreds of dead bodies that were half-buried under the dirt. Now as we travelled along, men were busy removing dead bodies that lay two, three and four deep, one on top of another from out of the trenches we had lately walked along. The enemy losses must have been terrible.

Once again we are camped at High Wood but a change had taken place in the few days we had been away. Spread everywhere now were tents of all sizes and shapes, horses, lorries, field kitchens, guns and thousands of troops taking up a space of a square mile. We could hardly believe it was the same place and war seemed miles away. I was sent on an errand to our transport lines, perhaps a mile away. To get to them I had to pass through a wood where I had seen hundreds of men tearing up trees to clear a road right

through. I thought nothing of it at the time but was surprised a few days later when I went that way again to find a double track of railway lines with engines and trucks running along them. The trucks were loaded with all kinds of war material to help along the advance that was still going successfully. Over the next fortnight, we made several moves in these back areas and rain came down on a quite a lot of days so that we got wet through and into a bad mess with the mud. A number of men who had been posted as missing turned up and rejoined us having got mixed with other regiments and detained until their own regiment could be found.

Leaving the Somme

We were moved back towards the town of Albert. It was a fair distance to go so some kind friend allowed us to ride in lorries. We were put in tents, had a hot meal awaiting us and a number of coal fires. We all got busy drying our things and generally cleaned ourselves up. Then just as we were about to retire for the night, we were mustered together and a speech was made to the effect that the heads were pleased with the way in which we had carried on. Sympathy was shown for those who had been killed and we were told that on the next day we would be leaving. The following morning we marched into Albert and stayed for a few hours before going to the outskirts of town where we boarded a train on route for Belgium.

CHAPTER SEVEN
YPRES

Harry's Division was assigned to the Ypres salient sector after leaving the Somme battlefield. This was one of the most uncomfortable areas of the front – it is very flat with a high water table, and the drainage system had been totally disrupted by the shell-fire and turmoil. Consequently, it was always wet and muddy, and much of the trench-line consisted of vulnerable breastworks built up above ground level. Harry spent an uncomfortable winter of 1916/1917 and spring of 1917 in the sector, with the regular duties of sentry, raiding, mining, training, preparing for the next battle and going on working parties. The attack on Messines Ridge took place in early June 1917, and was the opening phase of the Third Battle of Ypres, known to the soldiers as the Battle of Passchendaele, a hill-top village northeast of Ypres that was taken at the end of the battle in November 1917. The attack on Messines Ridge was considered a significant success and was initiated by the detonation of a large number of huge mines, followed by a rapid infantry attack. Much territory was taken, including the high ground used by the Germans for observation into the rear area south of Ypres. It established a secure jumping-off point for the main battle, which formally started at the end of July 1917.

To St Elloir and a gift of smoking material
Getting into Belgium, we noticed at once the different dialect although dress, manners and customs were much the same as the French. We found that most of the people could speak some English and we could make ourselves understood. We had a march lasting some days, halting only at night at some village or other to sleep. The last village we stopped at named St Elloir [St-Eloi], we stayed at for perhaps a week. The regiment was split up in platoons and they were placed a good distance apart – a good ten minutes walk in some cases. It was whilst here that my officer received a packing case full of smoking material to be distributed amongst the men. This job he handed over to me saying I must get rid of this lot as quickly as possible as there would be no knowing when we would be on the move again. I carted the stuff all about the place. The tobacco was not a good brand and most of the chaps seemed to be well supplied already. There were cigarettes and also packets of pipe tobacco. The cigarettes I managed to get rid of but I had dozens of packets of tobacco left on my hands. About half a mile away was a good crowd of men working at a quarry, so I borrowed a bicycle and took the tobacco to them. They were glad to have it and so that was that.

All quiet and waterlogged at the three large mine craters
Early one evening we got orders to pack up to go to the front and relieve some Australian troops. We marched for hours in pouring rain along roads, across fields and through woods, arriving at our journey's end some time in the early morning. It was still pitch dark and, learning we were in front line trenches, we were greatly surprised not to hear shells and bullets flying about. There were some but they were hardly noticed. We asked some Australians what the place was like and they said:

'It's fine. If you don't fire at the enemy, they don't fire at you.'

This seemed a strange way to us but it didn't last long after we arrived. The whole place seemed saturated with water and was full of surprises. Mud was everywhere. We had trenches running alongside a canal and trenches dug out on top of embankments thirty feet high. The embankment was about a quarter of a mile long and through the entire length of it were tunnels and sleeping berths for hundreds of men with dozens of entrances. The whole place was lit by electricity, the power being got from a dynamo driven by an oil engine. One end of our trenches came to a stop at three large mine craters. We had these but the enemy had made them in an effort to dislodge us.

Life in the semi-liquid mud
Those of us that had no duties tumbled into the beds and were soon fast asleep. We awoke next morning to find breakfast cooked for us – another surprise happening for the front line. The weather remained dull, raining on and off all the time we were in. We

wondered around looking over the place and things seemed very peaceful after coming from the Somme. All over the embankment grew small fir trees and bushes which quite hid the entrances. The fields adjoining were one lake of semi-liquid mud with gullies dug across them in an effort to drain the water off. We could walk about here if we wished with little danger of being hit as the embankment hid us from view of the enemy. The craters were about forty or fifty feet high, formed like a volcano and hollow inside. At the bottom of the hollow was formed a deep lake of water and mud – a most dismal spot to be on duty. To get to our posts we had planks of wood to walk on and we were all supplied with hip boots. Having crossed the crater, we had to climb to the top and being higher, we had a full view of the enemy front lines. In fact, we overlooked them being so much higher. The regiment was on duty at this place for months, only going a short distance away occasionally. We were never free from the mud even when the weather turned warm and the rain stopped.

Things would get very bad in the winter with the men in the craters sinking up to their waists in mud and having to be helped out to firmer ground. In some cases they had to leave their hip boots behind. It was difficult to keep our rifles free from mud and rust, the best way was to cover them completely with canvas, but in such a way that we could use them at a moment's notice. Being continually in this damp and cold area made the feet and legs painful. Quite a

few men got sent to hospital with trench feet, although we were well supplied with whale oil. We had to rub it into our legs and feet night and morning and I believe it did some good.

DUTY AT THE CRATERS AND A DANGEROUS CUP OF TEA

We usually did a spell of duty at the Craters for two days, which was quite long enough, as it was next to impossible to get any sleep. When relieved we went a short distance away to the reserve tunnels situated at the side of the canal. Here we were not troubled much in regard of duties but found the enemy snipers could reach us quite easily in some places along the path. We had plenty of water for washing purposes, but for drinking water we had to go to the canal and there was a real risk in going for it in daylight. One of our chaps got a sniper's bullet through his arm one morning. Four of us had decided to make some tea and tossed up who should get the water. It had fallen to me – I didn't waste any time. I dashed across, got the water and returned without a shot being fired at me. Another found some wood and all four of us had sat down on the ground round the fire, waiting for the water to boil. We heard one or two bullets whining about, but as we were sitting in a bend of the path, we thought we weren't seen. We had sat there chatting for quite a while when Whizz! a bullet came and passed clean through a chap's arm and stopped with a buzz in the bank behind us. We all bolted for the tunnel in quick time. The chap who was shot went to the dressing station and didn't seem put out at all except that he was white about the face.

INCREASE IN HOSTILITIES
During part of the day, we got sent work to do helping dig more tunnels. At night we walked across the fields to a road and got the rations that were brought along by our regimental transport limbers or carts. Really, we had quite an easy time compared with other places we had been at. Going across to the road and gazing around, we were surrounded by lights sent up from the trenches and the sound of guns, machine-guns and rifles were coming from all around. Once or twice we got shelled on these journeys and bullets came very close but I can't remember anyone getting hurt who were with our party. After a while, things became more lively. Our guns sent more and more shells each day. The enemy did likewise until there were short bombardments going on at all times of the day and night.

RELIEVED TO DOMINION CAMP
We got relieved for a time and went to a place about six or seven miles away called Dominion Camp. Roads were now being shelled at night so we travelled across country, it not only being safer but quicker. Most of us thought we were getting away from the mud, but what a surprise we had when we arrived at the camp of large wooden huts. Before we could get into the huts we had to wade through an expanse of

mud that covered our boot tops, with a chance of falling into some deep gullies. It was very dark, the camp being under some trees. Men carrying lanterns led us to our different huts. I got my officer fixed up and made him as comfortable as I could. I went round finding out the different places of importance after which I returned to my own hut, had something to eat and drink, rolled myself in two blankets and went to sleep along with the other twenty or more men lying on the floor. There was no room to spare when we all got down but it was warmer this way than if only a few were sleeping in the hut. I got up earlier next morning than the rest of the men and got busy attending to the wants of my officer. Having attended him, I had my own self to look after, wash, shave, clean myself and equipment, have breakfast and be ready for parade with the rest. I found I was very much pushed for time and, as I was supposed to do this kind of thing every morning, I asked my officer to excuse me the morning parade. This he agreed to and I was thankful for it. I filled in the time doing necessary jobs and also gave my help at the headquarters cookhouse. After dinner, I paraded with my company and we usually went rout marching up till about 4pm getting back just nicely to enjoy tea.

SIX MILES TO POPERINGE FOR A BATH
About twice a week we marched to the village of Poperinge, about six miles away, where we were able to get a bath and clean change of underclothes. We

Left
A section of the official war history map for the Battle of Messines Ridge, showing a number of the places that are mentioned in Harry's narrative. Troop dispositions depicted here are not necessarily accurate to the period of Harry's immediate involvement

Plate 35 The Craters at Messines Ridge, Ypres

THE CRATERS
MERSINES RIDGE
BELGIUM

had to strip off and have our bath practically in the open, with only a canvas screen round the baths, and we found it a very cold job. About twenty would bathe at one time, sprinklers being used and the water sometimes almost cold. Trains ran here occasionally and were often shelled. Here also were dumps of war material, a sawmill, one or two hospitals and washing centre for troops' underwear. Twelve miles march seemed a long way for the sake of a bath but I think all of us liked it. So far, nothing very serious was happening in the fighting line but our guns were coming up every day in increasing numbers and things were getting exciting. Occasionally a few shells would come in our direction but not near enough to do us any harm. The weather becoming brighter, the regiment was set to work draining the camp and clearing the mud away that, in spots, was a foot deep. This took a day or two and when completed we moved nearer the front to some reserve lines.

RESERVE LINES AND HQ FOUR MILES FROM FRONT AT HILL SIXTY

The reserve lines were situated in a hollow among some trees. There were some shelters of a kind and one or two low-built huts with several layers of sandbags on top. Headquarters were some distance away in a large chateau or house built of grey stone. It was knocked about a bit and here all the officers and staff were billeted. At the back were situated our field

kitchens, hidden from sight as much as possible. We got a number of small shells round about, but I only knew of two men getting wounded who got caught out in the open, carrying a dixie of water to the cookhouse. We had not much to do during the day here but we were inspected every morning by the company officer both for cleanliness in equipment and ourselves. Sometimes we were given lectures, altogether we didn't do so bad.

At night, parties of forty or fifty were marched to Hill Sixty situated in the front line. Here we had all kinds of work to do. Some would repair trenches that had been shelled and were still being shelled whilst we worked. Some more would work on drainage, whilst others would get a job erecting barbed wire entanglements or carrying different material up to the trenches. The same men did not go every night. We changed about, some going one night and the rest the next night. I didn't go as often as the others did because I went only when my officer was in charge.

RAILWAY LEVEL CROSSING OUTSIDE YPRES

To get to Hill Sixty we had a march of perhaps four miles. Our way led us towards the town of Ypres but just before getting there we turned off across some fields and got on to a railway embankment. The railway was in fairly good condition considering how near it was to the front lines. All level crossings, signal boxes or other structures had been shelled to a heap of rubble but the lines seemed capable of carrying traffic. It was only the last mile or two where the lines had been, and were still being, damaged with heavy shells. As we went along we came to great gaping holes with yards of rails and sleepers missing, and at other times rails that were twisted about like so much wire. Travelling along here in the dark and rain was no joke, especially when shells were flying about. Cursing and swearing we would be stumbling in and out of holes, falling over and picking ourselves up again until we got to some few hundred yards off the frontline. Under the embankment here were built tunnels or dugouts capable of sheltering hundreds of troops with a rough bed or bunk for each. Getting on to a stretch of road, we went along until we came to a dump or store of war materials. We carried this up to the front trenches, going backwards and forwards through trenches that flooded all the year round. We kept to this all through the night, returning back to our camp or reserve lines somewhere about six next morning.

TUNNELLING UNDER HILL SIXTY

Another job we used to get was to help in the mining of Hill Sixty. Our job was to remove the soil clear of the hill as the miners dug it out. There were dozens of galleries or tunnels dug under the hill and enemy lines, their position here being very strong. The enemy was also tunnelling under our position. All our tunnels were lit by electricity and day and night we had hundreds of men working there. Our tunnels were dug to a greater depth than the enemy's were and it some-

times happened that we could hear them working quite near. On these occasions, our miners would work quietly towards them and when near enough and at a suitable time, would either break through into the enemy tunnels, capturing the men working there and then blow the tunnel in. Or they would destroy their tunnels by exploding a small charge of explosive underneath them. The enemy blew several mines in an effort to destroy our work but very little damage was done on account, I suppose, of ours being deeper. It's a horrid feeling being in the tunnels when the mines go off, as there was always the chance that the tunnel would cave in and bury you alive. As it was, the sensation of feeling the whole earth rocking and swaying like a jelly around you was not pleasant.

IN TO YPRES THROUGH MENIN GATE AND OUT VIA LILLE GATE

Our next move was to take over some trenches to the right of Ypres. To get there we travelled at night from the Belgian chateau along the main road into Ypres, past what was the railway station, along by the Cloth Hall and out into the open again by Lille Gate. The whole town was just a heap of bricks and mortar. Every house or building was demolished with shells still bursting day and night amongst the ruins. The Cloth Hall still had part of its walls standing, but looked just a shell. Lille Gate was a relic of the old wall that at one time surrounded the town. It was about 15 feet thick and gave some

YMCA

LIEEL
GATE YPRES

protection to houses in that part of the town. On the ground, at the right side of the gate was a large bell about four feet high, half covered with rubbish. On the left, some plucky Y.M.C.A. men served hot tea, cocoa, eatables, and cigarettes and also had a few books for any that had the money to buy. The cups in use were empty milk tins. Outside the galley was a lake of water that came right to the walls. Crossing this by a narrow road, we marched single file for about a mile and a half with shells bursting around us and bullets whining about. There were trenches not far away and when the shelling got too bad we took shelter in them. All along the road was stretched wire mesh from tree to tree. Fastened on to the wire were small pieces of canvas in different shades of green, which looked at a distance like growing trees or bushes. This was put up to hide from the enemy any movements taking place on the road.

To Windy Corner by the narrow gauge railway

Getting to a part of the road called Windy Corner we crossed some marshy fields following a narrow gauge railway. This run almost up to some trenches situated on a small rise of ground covered with trees. Here we were fairly safe from rifle fire but shells had a nasty way of bursting when least expected. We stayed here for a time and were fairly comfortable. We had shelters of a kind. These protected us from the weather, but even small pieces of shrapnel found their way through. Just nearby was a spring of fresh water and it was fairly safe to light a fire to warm ourselves or do cooking. We did have a bit of bad luck one-day when getting some water. We had filled a large dixie when a shell exploded and punctured it in three or four places. None of the men got hurt but they were very scared. Wet legs and feet were a general thing with us and the weather was getting cold.

On duty at Windy Corner

To go on duty, we went to the other side of the clump of trees where it was partly trenches and part barricades. The trench was none too strong and the barricade simply hid us from view of the enemy. It certainly stopped some bullets but the smallest shells went clean through. Not a nice place to be at all! To make things a bit more uncomfortable, Fritz was throwing trench mortar shells at us. If these exploded near our barricade, that part would all collapse and we had an unhealthy time building it up again. Parties of men, about six in number, used to patrol the barricade that was about fifty or more yards long. The enemy was in a like position as us as regards the trenches and barricades and was always busy repairing them where our shells and trench mortars had knocked them about. We tried to stop them at this by firing at them but they kept well down and we only hit the shovels as they came up loaded with dirt. There

Plate 36
Some plucky YMCA men serving hot tea at the Lille Gate, Ypres

was an instance when a large gap was blown in the enemy barricade leaving a dazed and unprotected German boy in full view. He was an easy target but I couldn't bring myself to shoot. I turned away and had a go at several Germans that were running away out of danger. We had some casualties but I guess the enemy had more. Apart from us sending over three trench bombs to the enemy's one, we had our own artillery and some Belgian besides. The Belgian observation officer used to come in our lines once or twice every day and always had to show a pass before he was allowed to do so signed by the General in command.

RETURN TO BELGIAN CHATEAU TOC H HQ

After a week or two we were relieved and went back to the Belgian chateau. Since leaving here, a battery of guns had taken up position nearby and had got in some good work. It was bad from the enemy's point of view, for they sent over plane after plane to try and discover where the battery was situated. The battery was well hidden and fired very seldom during good daylight. One afternoon Fritz decided he knew where the guns were and sent over hundreds of shells in the hope of putting the guns out of action. None of the guns suffered damage but the fields round about were churned up, roads got considerable damage and one or two shells found their way into the officers' quarters. We had to get out quick from our position, as our shelters were not

proof against this kind of shelling. When things quietened down we went back again and made good any damage done.

BEDFORD HOUSE CAMP

After staying a few days at the Belgian chateau, we moved to some trenches about two miles along the line. These trenches were partly hidden by a small wood, which had a lake or large pond in the centre. In the centre of the lake was an island on which was once a house, this was now all in ruins. Thirty or fort yards away at the back of us were several batteries of English and Belgian field guns. These kept up an awful din firing over our heads, but in time we got used to it. The trenches were good, tidy and dry but not very deep with a number of fairly strong dugouts or shelters. The shelters were all one size, about five feet wide by three and a half feet high and ran under the earth for about seven feet. In these, four men had to find room to sleep. We had few duties during the day and could walk about or have our meals in peace, cooked by our field kitchens that had come with us. We could also make some good fires in the trench; we only had to go a few yards to find plenty of fuel lying about under the trees. We enjoyed ourselves whilst here and was sorry to leave the place. Each night we used to go on working parties either to Hill Sixty or up to the Craters, getting back some time early in the morning.

ACCIDENT IN THE LAKE, BEDFORD HOUSE

It was now very cold with ice about a foot thick on the lake and officers and men had some fun sliding across it until the enemy dropped a couple of shells on it and smashed it up. The same evening, having to go on a working party, I went in the wood to gather some fuel for the fire. It was our custom, when we returned from these parties, to get our issue of rum and tea, make a good fire and sit around yarning or singing till we got nice and warm. Then we would all squeeze into the dugout and sleep. I had got a load of wood and was about to return with it when I saw a nice chunky bit in the water not far from the shore. I grasped a branch of a tree growing near and with the other hand reached out to get the wood in the water. Without any warning, the branch snapped off and I took a neat dive into the lake. I rubbed the skin off my nose and chin, my helmet came off and I came up with weed, mud and dead leaves stuck all over me. The coldness of the water took my breath away and after I got out it was seconds before I could speak. Round about were men gathering wood and I got little sympathy from them. They enjoyed the jokes more than I did. One would say:

'Do you always go swimming with your clothes on?' or

'Why don't you wait for warmer weather?'

Another wanted to bet me that I wouldn't do it again. I didn't stop to argue but gathered up my wood and made a dash for the trench. Here I stripped off all my clothes and put on my overcoat, which luckily I wasn't wearing when I fell in. I covered my legs and feet with some scarves and then with the help of my mates, made a roaring fire to dry my clothes by.

My clothes were not even half-dry when orders came to parade for a working party so I asked the orderly corporal to be excused. He was sorry but said it wasn't in his power to excuse me, I should have to ask the officer in charge. I dressed again in my half-dried clothes and got on parade as names were being called. The officer called me over to him and I explained why I was late. I could hear the men chuckling and I felt rather foolish standing shivering there in front of the officer, with blood dripping off my nose and chin. He grasped the situation at once, ordered me to immediately get my clothes off and dry them, following me back to the trench to see that I did it. He also ordered me to get my face attended to. Soon after the party moved off and I sat round the fire drying my things. After they had dried I put them on, got some iodine for my chin and went to help unload the rations that had now arrived. For this I got a helping of rum and a sandbag of coke with charcoal mixed. I kept the fire going and waited until the party returned. I got chipped about my stopping behind. One said, and all agreed, that I had jumped into the water on purpose to dodge the working party. When the rum came round, they thought they should have my share but they didn't get it. They kept up the jokes at my expense until they were all ready to sleep then we turned in. A few days after, one of our bed-mates

Overleaf
Plate 37
On duty at Windy Corner, Ypres

Plate 38 An accident in the lake at Bedford House camp, Ypres

got wet through on a working party and caught a severe cold. For a couple of days he lay shivering and moaning with rheumatic pains in our dugout and then was carted off to hospital.

Going to work at Hill Sixty

After a time we moved up nearer to the lines and were quartered in the railway dugouts or tunnels. We were to be regular workers for several weeks under Hill Sixty, helping the miners in their work of tunnelling. Some of us worked by day, others worked at night and so we relieved each other. I didn't mind it at all; the worst part was travelling backwards and forwards to our work. On nearly every occasion, we had to travel under shellfire and have bullets buzzing around. There were some casualties but not many. I believe one of our officers got killed amongst them. Back at the dugouts we got few shells and no bullets at all. Out in an adjoining field was a small lake so we were well supplied with water both for drinking and washing. Had it been warmer, I guess some of us would have been swimming. To get to our job we used to tramp in single file from our dugouts, across some fields where there was a notice up which read: 'Beware of machine-guns!' We crossed dozens of times but I don't know of anyone getting hit. Arriving at the other side, we came to a fairly large farmhouse looking the worse for wear. Its thatched roof as a whole had slipped over so that one edge rested on the ground and the rest of it partly covered the ruins of the house. There were some strong cellars underneath which were used as stores and an advance dressing station. Going down below, we removed our ordinary boots and put on hip boots or waders. The boots we took off we put in numbered squares marked on the floor so that we could easily find them when we returned. Having got our hip boots on we made for the railway track and travelled along until we got to Hill Sixty. Having reported ourselves we were divided up into different parties and went to our different jobs.

Helping the miners under Hill Sixty

The tunnels in which we worked were about five feet high and about three feet wide. We worked right up front by the miner, taking the soil away as quietly as possible and putting it into sand bags. Having filled a bag, we carried it as quietly as possible to another man a few yards away. He in his turn carried it to another and so on until the bag had travelled fifty or more yards along the tunnel. At this point the bags were placed on trolleys with rubber tyred wheels running on wooden lines, all for the purpose of doing away with noise. The trolleys we pushed to the tunnel entrance where a party of men took the bags and dumped them, just as they were, into the railway cutting. There were millions of bags, piled one on top of another. The hill seemed honeycombed with tunnels running in all directions. Here and there a small room was formed at the sides of the tunnels and empty bags were stored here along with tools, explosives and some candles in case of emergency should the electric light fail. No ordinary talking was allowed whilst on the mining job and no smoking. A man was always on duty with listening phones to his ears, at all extreme ends of the tunnels. I tried them on once and could hear noises of the enemy digging and also somebody walking about overhead. The miner told me this was a German sentry in his trench. Our miners were quite satisfied whilst they could hear the enemy working, it was when they stopped work that they became nervous. For then, they guessed, the enemy was ready to explode his mine. I have heard of instances where our miners have allowed Fritz to load his mine and get it all ready for exploding but before he had done so, our men have tunnelled through and taken away the explosives. We always started work at dark and left just before daylight. We found it very warm whilst working in the tunnels but on our tramp back to our dugout, it was very cold, everything was frozen hard.

A TOT OF RUM

Before leaving the tunnels, we were each given a good tot of rum. Some men didn't drink it so passed it to someone that did. I often got two drinks like this. Before we got to our journey's end or to the farmhouse, we used to feel the effects. At times we had to fairly run to keep our balance, feeling that if we stopped we would fall down and not be able to get up again. Once, two of the men having had extra rum were in a very muddled state. They sat on the floor together to remove the hip boots and one of them was

attempting to pull the other's boots off, under the impression that they were his own. It was very funny to watch them arguing about it. How they got on I don't know, for I left them still arguing, going off with some others to our dugouts and bed.

HALIFAX CAMP

Our spell of mining work came to an end too quickly for my liking. I should have liked to continue but one night we packed up and moved to a place called Halifax Camp. It was a very dark night and the enemy were putting over an extra lot of shells. They were dropping on the roads, paths, woods and all kinds of places. I guess our transport had a rough time of it. Going along we saw several of our wagons in the ditches at the side of the road caused through, I suppose, the horses getting out of hand. I often wondered that the horses behaved so well as they did. Getting some distance away from the line, we were met by some motor lorries, which carried us the rest of the way to our camp. The camp was an extra large one and as many as three regiments billeted here at one time. Altogether I suppose there were about fifty wooden huts and a large YMCA hut where something of all sorts could be bought. They even had some daily papers and a small library. There was nothing much to do during the day but at night several lorries drove up and parties of us, carrying a pick or shovel in addition to our rifles, were carried to within a mile of the front lines. Then we would travel

the rest of the way on foot. In the line we would work all night, returning at about dawn to the lorries that were waiting and off we would go back to camp.

LEFT OF HILL SIXTY AT THE ANAUGHT TRENCHES

The next move we made was to man some trenches to the left of Hill Sixty. There were some ruins of a farm in our lines called Anaught Farm and our trenches were known by that name. These were very shallow with water in them from a few inches to a couple of feet in depth. Shelters were built of a sort, suitable only as a protection from rain. There was just a space dug out at the side of the trench covered over with a thin sheet of iron and a few sandbags. How we managed to stay here without a large number of casualties I don't know, for the ruins of the farm were a target for enemy shells at all different times. The enemy lines were five or six hundred yards away across some flooded fields. At night, parties of us were sent across here where we took up certain positions. There were three separate parties of us.

THREE NIGHT-TIME POSITIONS NEAR LONE TREE POST, WITH COCOA

One party of about forty men would go out armed with their rifles, a number of bombs each and a Lewis machine-gun to a shallow trench that led into the German lines and only about twelve yards away. To get so close, we had to go very carefully and quiet and this wanted some doing, loaded up with the things we

were carrying! Bursts of machine-gun bullets swept the ground at intervals, when we would be obliged to get into one of the shell holes for safety. As these were filled with water it was no joke, even if we were wearing hip boots. There were one or two casualties on these parties but no deaths.

The second party numbered about six. These all carried bombs as well as a rifle, with a Lewis gun accompanying the party as well. They went to a position known as Lone Tree post. It was situated a little behind the first party and a good way to the right, its purpose being to protect the first party from being attacked from the side or rear. It was also to catch any of the enemy on their way to bomb our lines, which was a favourite stunt round about here! Lone Tree post took its name from the fact that the stump of a tree stood upright on a slight rise of ground. Just behind was a large shell hole, fairly dry, and here we used to hide ourselves and keep a look out.

The third party went on patrol, composed of only two or three men. These used to wander about, finding out what they could about the enemy positions, keeping an eye on number one and two posts and occasionally trying to bomb the enemy.

TO LONE TREE POST WITH A MACHINE-GUN AND A BOMBING PARTY

Twice during the night, hot cocoa was sent round to us. This was carried in a large flat tank designed on the Thermos principle and carried on a man's back

Plate 39
Drying-out after the accident at Bedford House

by means of straps. Two of these were in use and they were supposed to have been captured off the enemy. I had been with all the different parties at different times, when one night my turn came round to go to Lone Tree post again. This time I was put in charge of the gun and was to act as machine-gunner. I didn't like this at all because I had never handled a machine-gun before and only had a faint idea how to fire one. I told the officer I knew nothing about them but it was no good, I was sent out just the same. Luckily that night I had no occasion to use the gun and we got back without any mishap. I complained about it again and was given a few lessons on how to load and fire. I had been to bombing school and somebody or other had reported that it was a machine-gun course that I had passed so I had been put in the place of the gunner who had gone sick or been wounded. The next time I went out to Lone Tree post, I wasn't troubled in mind so much about being a machine-gunner.

When we got the post, we made ourselves as comfortable as we could when a fine drizzle of rain began to fall. The night was darker than usual and each side got the idea that it was an ideal night to make a bombing raid. We saw our men first. There were about twenty of them, creeping across towards the enemy lines. Then when they got within about a hundred yards of the enemy, out came a party of German bombers on their way to our lines. Evidently, our men saw the other bombers coming,

for they all crouched down and waited for them to get nearer. Almost at the same moment, they started bombing each other. Several of the Germans went down with the rest working gradually back to their own lines, throwing bombs as they went. Our men followed them up until they had used all their bombs and then hurriedly made towards our lines. By this time, the German bombers had got back to their trench where, getting a fresh supply of bombs, started throwing them out front. Someone on the German side mistook the happening for something more serious and called upon the artillery, who began to send over hundreds of shells our way. Our artillery, seeing and hearing this bombardment going on and thinking it was a German attack, opened out for all they were worth on the German lines.

We poor blokes were stuck out in the middle of it! Gosh there was a din! For my part, I tried to make myself as small as possible while at the same time keeping a look out. We crouched there with great dobs of mud falling on top of us, shells and shrapnel screaming overhead and bullets buzzing in the top of our shell hole. It seemed like one continual bang. In the midst of it, I heard a thud just in front of me and the earth came up and spanked me on the nose and chin such a wallop it made my eyes water! A second or two afterwards, the man next to me gave a groan and fell like a dead weight on top of me. As he did so I felt a drip, drip of something on my neck.

'The chap must be wounded or killed,' I thought.

I rolled him off me and one of the other men helped me search as best we could for the injuries. We were unable to find any but the man still lay as if dead except that he was breathing. The bombardment only lasted perhaps a quarter of an hour and then died down as suddenly as it began. What a relief! We shook off us what mud and dirt we could and had another go at examining our man. While examining him, he came to with a groan and put his hand up to his head. We removed his helmet, which had a large dent in it and felt, very tenderly, a big bump on his head. His helmet had saved his life, without it his head would certainly have been crushed in. When we got back, we learned that we had had a fair amount of casualties in our lines and that the next regiment to us had fared even worse.

MORE SKIRMISHES

Next night, I went to the trench post with the Lewis gun and placed it at the extreme end of the men. In this position I was close up to the barbed wire and level with an enemy machine-gun. When this was fired, it struck sparks off the wire almost in my face. This was the night that our bombing patrol were planning to bomb this particular gun and we in the trench were not feeling very cheerful about it, having last night's scrap in mind! Anyway, the bombers came up and got as near to the gun as they could and crouched down, waiting for it to fire. As it fired, they pitched several bombs under the gun and in the trench behind and

then scampered out of harm's way to our bit of trench. The bombs went off, catching somebody in the enemy lines and put the gun out of action for we heard it no more that night. Of course, the bombing stirred up the enemy and they put up some Very Lights to try and discover our bombers. They swept the ground round about with a machine-gun hoping to catch the bombers as they made their way to our lines. Little did they know they were with us only a few yards away!

IN FULL GLARE

During the firing a light fell a few feet in front of my gun and it seemed to burn and light up the place for hours, to me. As I was in the full glare of the light I dare not move but kept as still as a statue gazing at the light until it went out. Then I almost collapsed, with sweat pouring off me, into the bottom of the trench. Why I hadn't been seen and shot a dozen times over I don't know! The only explanation I could think of was that the glare of the light had dazzled any of the enemy looking in my direction.

RAT BOMBING AND RABBIT SHOOTING

Things got normal again and the bombers left us to return to our lines. The hot cocoa came along soon after and we had a drink each. It was always a cold job here, having to keep as still and as quiet as possible. The refreshment men didn't stop long after we had been served but got back to the line as soon as they could. They hadn't been gone a minute or two when several bombs went off some way behind us near a clump of trees.

'That's done it!' we thought. 'The enemy has managed to get by us without us seeing them and are bombing our line.'

We kept a sharp look out for their return but we saw or heard nothing of them. Returning in due time, we reported things that had happened. The bombing behind us, we learned, was by our own men. They had seen a number of rats together so they had thrown bombs at them. They got into some real trouble over it at an inquiry. And some of the men who had been out up front wanted to punch their heads for scaring them like they did. At the same time, we learned that we were to be relieved some time that night. We weren't sorry. At about midday, we saw a rabbit out in front and several of us fired our rifles at it. One chap used a revolver. The rabbit got away easily and we got a reprimand for wasting ammunition.

To Dominion Camp and Brigade HQ for machine-gun training at Toc H

Being relieved, we marched to Dominion camp and Brigade Headquarters to undergo a course of machine-gun training. When I told my hut mates about it they wished it was them that was going because to go on one of these training courses was like having a holiday. Next morning with two more men, I walked to Brigade Headquarters. The place was on the outskirts of Poperinge. Having reported, we were shown our sleeping quarters and were free to do as we liked for the rest of the day. There were perhaps a hundred men from different regiments undergoing training courses for different things such as bombing, signalling and sniping as well as machine-gun. Our living quarters were huts made of wood and canvas with bunks arranged about the place. Should these all be engaged, there were hammocks slung from the ceiling for men to sleep in. We rose at seven each morning, washed, shaved and had breakfast. At eight we commenced our training with lectures. A sergeant explained and named all the parts of the Lewis gun, aided by a chart hung upon a board.

A Vimy reunion at Poperinge

At 12.00 we were dismissed till 2.05 when we had lessons up until 4.05. Then the rest of the day was our own. The weather was splendid and we almost forgot there was a war on, but not quite. Several times, some large shells fell in a field near by causing the Belgian farm people to leave their houses and seek shelter underneath, in cellars. From lectures, we got to practical training, having to build a gun up from the parts lying mixed up on a table or floor. Then we went to a range and had firing practise. The whole course took about a fortnight. On the last day, after we had finished firing for the day, a number of men from our regiment came up as a working party to repair the target butts. One man of the party that I thought I knew seemed to look at me in a kind of curious way. He looked, I thought, like the double of a man killed at the Vimy Ridge battle. After he had done his work on the range, he came over to me and asked if I was any relation to (and here he mentioned my name) killed at Vimy. I explained who I was and then it came to me that it was this chap who had actually been with us at Vimy and that he hadn't been killed after all. Each of us thought that the other had been killed. It was a pleasant meeting and we celebrated it by going to Poperinge with a dinner of eggs and chips. We had a lot to talk about … of old times and what had happened since.

AN ACCOUNT OF VIMY RIDGE

From my friend's account, it appears that after trying to beat off the enemy until most of our chaps were either killed or wounded, along with some other men he made a bid to get back to the main body in a trench behind. Getting as far as midway, he was hit by a piece of shrapnel that laid his leg open from hip to knee. This stopped him getting any further, so he took shelter in a shell hole. Whilst lying in there, the enemy caught up and passed him on their way while attempting to take the other line. The rifle and machine-gun fire was so great that they failed and had to retire. They lost a lot of men in the attack but those still able to get away were bayoneting our wounded as they lay helpless on the ground. My friend saw all this going on and as these beasts came in his direction he fully expected to be served the same. Whilst awaiting his fate he fainted. He lay unconscious for two days until he was found by stretcher- bearers and lay for a further three weeks in hospital before he could give any account of himself. In time, he was discharged from hospital and sent back to duty in England. From here, he was passed as fit and sent out again to rejoin us on active service. Since he had been away, most of the men he had known had all gone, so he was anxious that we two should be close pals again. When we rejoined the regiment he found that he had been placed with B Company so he got permission to transfer to mine which was C Company. We became fast friends and it seemed that my new-found friend could not bear to be out of my sight. Even when duties would have separated us, he would ask for permission to go with me.

ABSENT ON PARADE AND FAVOURITISM IN THE RANKS

I was still carrying on as Batman or servant when one morning, having missed the parade and dodging about the camp making myself busy, the company commander came along. He spotted me and wanted to know why I wasn't on parade. I made my excuses of being batman and not having proper time in which to carry out my duties and attend morning parade. I pointed out also that his own batman never did a drill or parade or even carried a rifle so I thought it quite all right that I could at least miss morning parade. This didn't seem to please the captain at all and he gave me orders to attend orderly room that evening. I informed my officer about it and he, while admitting that it was unfair considering the captain's batman did no ordinary chores, said that he was powerless to do anything about it because the captain was of higher rank. The time came to attend orderly room and I was surprised to find the Captain's batman there as well. I can't say I liked the chap; he gave himself too many airs, he never mixed with the other men and was generally considered a bit of a sneak! I said:

'Hallo, what are you up for?' But I got no reply. The captain came out to try our cases and spoke to his own batman first. The wind was whistling through the trees round about so that it was difficult to hear what each other said. Evidently, the captain had taken to mind what I had said to him earlier in the day and had ordered his own man to parade to answer a charge of being absent on parade without leave. When questioned, he could only make the same excuse as mine. This seemed to stump the captain so he gave his man very strong hints, almost putting the words into his mouth to say he went sick. After a minute or two, the man in a confused kind of way said: 'I went sick this morning, Sir, and was excused duty.' 'In that case you are free from any punishment and may go,' the Captain said. 'You may carry on as usual.' When my turn came I was asked:

'Did you go sick?' I admitted that I hadn't. Then I was given a short lecture about slackness and obeying orders and told that my punishment would be that I should no longer have the batman's job. I would join the ranks for ordinary duties. When I next saw my officer he knew all about it. He was sorry for me at the unfairness of the case but that perhaps it was all for the best since he was about to go away from the regiment to a trench mortar battery. My leave to England was about due and had I gone with him, I should have missed it. He had monies due to me as wages sent to my home and we parted company as officer and servant.

CHRISTMAS, 1916 IN THE TRENCHES

We again manned the reserved trenches at the lake and carried on in much the same way as we did when we were last there. It was freezing cold, with a little snow lying about. We did have hopes of spending Christmas at one of the camps way back and preparation had been made weeks before to mark this special time. Paper decorations had been arranged in the huts to brighten them up a bit with a programme of singing contests laid on and two small pigs that had been bought from a Belgian. But it was not to be. At the last moment, we learned that our Christmas was to be spent in the trenches. Almost any day now, I expected to go on leave so I didn't take much interest when I heard that the feast and concerts were being postponed until we left the trenches. Instead, the two days we spent in the trenches were livened up by the enemy shelling the guns just behind. They made a direct hit and only one of our gun crew managed to get away. He came into our trench with a wounded arm, telling us that both the gun and the gun pit had been destroyed, killing all of his five or six comrades. We gave him what help we could and took him to our MO.

AT THE WHITE CHATEAU

Later that afternoon, our officer came along and inquired after me. I was watching some shells bursting a little way off, along our trench when the officer found me. With a stern face he said: 'You are wanted at the orderly room! What have you been up to?' Not knowing of anything, I said so accordingly and made my way towards HQ two hundred yards or more along the trench. Before I had gone far, the officer, laughing, said: 'It's all right, don't worry! It's for leave!'

Now I was in all haste to get to HQ as soon as possible. To get there I had to traverse the trenches that I had just been watching getting shelled. I ducked low and ran along for all I was worth. I had almost reached the house, known as the White Chateau, used as Headquarters when a shell struck at the root of a large tree, bringing the whole thing down. In falling, it tore a gap in the trench and came to rest right across it. When the shell came I had thrown myself flat but as soon as the tree settled, I was up and climbing over it to get to the orderly room a few yards away.

DOMINION CAMP AND THE LONG JOURNEY HOME

Getting my pass and some money, with four other men I travelled to our transport lines at Dominion Camp, six or seven miles away. For a couple of the miles we got a lift on a motor lorry. Reporting ourselves, we were sent to Poperinge to have a bath and a clean change. We returned and had something to eat and drink and then had to rest content until six o'clock next morning. We were all there in good time, in fact, we were half an hour before time waiting for the train to take us from Poperinge towards home. Before boarding the train, we were searched by the military police to ensure that we were not carrying any souvenirs in the way of cartridges or bombs. We travelled all day, arriving at Le Havre rather late at night. From the train we marched to a camp where there were hundreds of men going on leave like us. We were given a meal, then two blankets were issued and we went off to tents to sleep. At about five the next morning everybody was up, hunting around for a place to wash and smarten themselves up. Having done so, we all sat down to a breakfast in a large marquee. Shortly after, we were marched off to the docks where, our papers having been examined, we boarded ship and were soon sailing for England. We had two destroyers for escort and I enjoyed the trip over very much, being on deck all the time. A good many were seasick but I'm glad to say that it didn't affect me. Arriving at Southampton, we boarded and were soon in London.

We got out at Victoria Station and a rush was made to one of the several offices on the platform to change our French and Belgian money into English. There were several refreshment buffets where everything was free. There were men and women available to answer all kinds of enquiries and conduct strangers to London to more distant parts of England. It sometimes happened that men were not able to travel to their homes that day. These were taken care of by the same people and put up until the next day all free of charge.

HOME AND POETRY

I had had no opportunity of letting my people know that I was coming home, so that when I did arrive it was a great surprise for them, almost a shock. Mother cried with joy at seeing me and bustled around to make me comfortable. Father wiped his eyes a bit, this was the only time I ever saw him cry. The news soon got round that I was home and friends came to say how pleased they were to see me. I had a busy time answering questions. I enjoyed myself with my friends and visited the separate homes of my sisters. I had a hearty welcome wherever I went and had a good time in general, visiting several theatres and Music halls.

One afternoon, the weather being wet, I tried my hand at writing poetry. It dealt with the time between when my brother-in-law and I went on a cycling holiday until the time I spent on leave.

> After working all the year
> Whilst rumours of war are in the air
> Fred and I do try our best
> To ride our bikes and take a well earned rest
>
> We started out one bright Sunday morn
> Were well on our way, for the sun got to warm
> The fresh country air, was a nice change

> From nothing but houses and smelly drains
>
> We travelled some time, without a spill
> Till we came to the village of Haverhill
> We thought at this place for the night we would stay
> But could not get lodging no matter what we pay
>
> We travelled that night till we came to a wood
> And against a tree our bikes we stood
> We lay down to sleep though not very warm
> And travelled again, early next morn
>
> We came to Northwold not far from the Wash
> And learned that War was declared on the Bosh (Bosch)
> The sky turned cloudy and it began to rain
> Whilst having tea with a very old dame
>
> It is at this place, really that our holiday begins
> So arrange to take lodging at a local inn
> We get well-cooked meals and quantity too
> With fruit pies, salads and fruit that was stewed
>
> We wonder around and had a good time
> Went catching eels though not with a line
> We looked up old friends that were almost forgot
> And health's were drank in beer made from best hops
>
> War news items we read in the paper each day
> And observe men of the village are called to the fray
> A good time we had, wished we could stay
> But pay our score and get on our way
>
> We start for home, old London town
> Stop at Epping Forest to have a lie down
> Then continue our way and what do we see
> A Territorial sentry on guard at Hackney

Our holidays now over, we return to our work
Whilst adverts almost shout, your duty not to shirk
Get into khakis and thrash the old Hun.
For the under-hand work he has begun

We read of his doings in Belgium and France
And the contemptible little army that led him a dance
We thought we would help in the fight for the right
So went to be attested one Saturday night

Now Fred is in India and I am in France
Taking a part in the big Somme advance
Some time we have had of it and soon it will be
That the War is over and for us victory.

When the time arrived for me to go back, my friends
and relations were sorry I had to go and wished me
the best of luck. A sister and her husband accompanied me to Victoria station. They waited whilst I made
enquiries about my train. To my surprise it didn't
leave until early next morning. We turned back for
home again and on the way broke our journey to go
and see a show at the London Music Hall.

'What about your pack and rifle? You can't very
well go in with them!' said my sister.
I settled this by going to the stage manager and asking
him would he take care of them whilst I saw the show.
This he was pleased to do, putting them in his office.

'But mind you come back for them!' he said.

After enjoying the show we went home, surprising
everyone who rightly thought that I was miles on my
way back to Belgium.

THE RETURN

Arising next morning I travelled alone to Victoria,
catching a 6 o'clock train. We went through much the
same performance going back as we did coming
home except that the conversation was not what the
travellers were going to do but what they had done. I
guess none of us were glad to return but we looked
forward to the time when we could go home to stay.
At Le Havre, we again spent a night under canvas
and next morning we were sorted out into different
parties for different destinations. From the camp to
the station was a good distance and part of the way
we walked over a lot of fine sand. I managed to get
some of the sand into my boots and I had an uncomfortable time until we reached the train and I was able
to get rid of it. Riding all that day and the following
night, we arrived at Poperinge and back to Belgium.

SORE FEET

One of my feet was sore and on arriving at our
Transport Lines, I removed my boot and sock to
have a look at it. It looked inflamed but I guessed a
night's rest would put it right so I didn't trouble
anymore about it. Next day, the regiment came out
of the front line and was going back to Halifax
camp. Here I joined them and got reprimanded for
not joining them the day before as the others had
done. I complained of having sore feet and had to
report sick. The doctor treated it but a large blister
formed which broke and it became worse. The next

night, working parties were picked to go up the line, I being one of them. I asked to be excused on account of my feet but as the doctor had not excused me duty, I would have to go. We got our tools, got on to some lorries that took us within a mile and a half of the line and then we got out to finish the journey on foot. The party marched off in fine style and from the first I was unable to keep the pace. Before I had gone a quarter of a mile I was left behind. The officer in charge wanted to know why I couldn't keep up with the rest. I informed he and he said:

'You had no business to start out! Fall out and make your way back to camp. And in the morning, see the doctor!'

My foot was paining me by now and I dreaded the six or seven miles I had to go to get back to camp. I went hobbling back and when I had gone perhaps a mile, a horse lorry overtook me. I shouted for the driver to stop and asked for a lift. He refused me at first as it was against orders to give lifts to troops, but when I explained that I was lame he allowed me to ride almost to the camp. I reported and was soon rolled in my blankets asleep. Next morning, my foot was so swollen that I couldn't get my boot on. On the doctor seeing it, hot dressings were put on and I was told to keep off it with excused duties. A few days later, the regiment went to front lines while I had to go to transport lines with some more sick men.

POPERINGE HOSPITAL AND FIRE IN A NEARBY BARN

Whilst there, every morning I had to attend hospital at Poperinge, otherwise we could do much as we liked. We lived in the large stores; a big hut or barn affair made of wood and canvas. There were tons of stores placed in there, tools, ammunition, harness, meat, vegetables, tinned stuff and thousands of blankets done up in rolls of fifty. The weather was very cold and it was difficult to get water because the pipes froze. We had a fire in a pail almost day and night and got plenty of rations that we cooked ourselves. At night, we got amongst the blankets where we were very comfortable.

At dusk, one evening a Belgian cow shed caught fire and we were all called out to act as firemen. We didn't get there until the place was well alight and couldn't do any good, as no water was handy. One or two cows got burnt to death and the sheds were destroyed. We had some fun watching our transport men trying to get a bull into harness. Every time it got loose and the men had to capture it on foot, he would chase them with bared teeth. The only way they could catch him was by riding another mule or horse, then he would allow them to handle him without any fuss.

HILL SIXTY FOR FOUR HOURS

My foot being well again, I was ordered to rejoin the regiment who was in the line at Hill Sixty. I travelled by daylight and after one or two narrow shaves, joined them about 4 o'clock that afternoon. They had a fairly good trench but the bottom of it was covered in sloppy mud and there were a few shelters that might stop shrapnel. They had lost one man killed and two severely wounded. I did about one hour's sentry when, at 8 o'clock we were relieved by another regiment and then marched right back to Dominion camp from where I had started that morning! Why I couldn't have waited for the regiment to come out of the line instead of going to them and then having to turn round again, I don't understand!

EERIE QUIET OF THE CRATERS

We had the usual drills and route marches, occasionally going to baths. The wonder of it was, we did not do any working parties. In the afternoons, we picked sides and played football matches. Whilst one match was in progress, an enemy plane dropped a small bomb on the pitch. There was no damage except for the hole it made. We were watching a match one day when an orderly corporal came along with orders for C company to get to the Bluff or Craters at once.

We were to reinforce the regiment already there as trouble was expected. In only a few minutes, we were on our way. Getting near the front, things were strangely quiet which was a bad sign. We all arrived, reported and were told to go to a certain tunnel to be in readiness for action at a moment's notice. It appeared that the enemy had almost completed a mine with the intention of blowing up part of our line. Our miners were aware of that and were planning the right moment to break into the enemy mine to destroy it before it could do its intended damage. They completed the mission but failed to destroy the mine completely. However they did obtain the German explosives, capturing six of their miners with one brought out dead. Best part of the enemy tunnel was still left behind and we blew it up later. No serious trouble came of it and in the end we were not wanted.

NO RATIONS AND A SUCCESSFUL BOMBING RAID

We found that we didn't get any rations so we scouted about to see what we could beg, borrow or otherwise get. I visited the miners' cook house and got a tin of pork and beans, a tin of bully beef, a half a loaf with the offer of some stew if I cared to come back later. We got through the day all right and were joined by the rest of our regiment the following night. The regiment that we were to relieve had made a bombing raid before they left. About fifty of them had gone to the enemy front line just before dawn, captured a few dozen prisoners, blew up and destroyed what they could and had returned to their own lines without losing a man. The affair had been carried out so well that after our men got back safely, the enemy still thought they were in the lines and shelled them heavily, completing the damage that our men had started.

FINAL DESTRUCTION OF THE ENEMY MINE AT THE CRATERS

The next night, our miners set about destroying the enemy mine tunnels still left. A few minutes before hand, all our men with the exception of half a dozen of us, withdrew and took shelter in the tunnel or dugout. On top of one mine crater were stationed a crew with a machine-gun and on the other crater was me with one man and a dozen or more hand grenades. The men had been withdrawn because it was reckoned that the enemy would vent his spite on our lines with a heavy bombardment after we had blown his mines up. For everyone to remain would have resulted in heavy casualties. The man that I had with me had not had much experience of active service and asked me what it was all about. I explained what I could and said:

'Don't be alarmed when the hill we are on swings and wobbles like a jelly!'

He couldn't believe this and laughed at the idea. Hardly had I explained when, with a roar and a bang, up goes our mine! We sure did swing and shake and then I laughed at the amazed look on my mate's face. For a second or two after, everything was dead quiet.

'What do we do now?' my companion wanted to know.

'Keep down as much as possible, but keep a look out for an attack!'

Then the bombardment started. I never guessed we would be shelled so heavily. The enemy sent over something of all sorts; shells, bombs, trench mortars and rifle fire. The continual explosions shook the place and in a short time we hardly recognised it, it had been so knocked about. My mate crouched down and I had to force him to get up to keep a look out. After a time he broke down altogether and cried out. He was shaking. The limit came when a shell burst and a large piece of shrapnel embedded itself an inch or two from his head, into the earth. Nothing I could do or shout at him would make him move.

The bombardment gradually eased up and we were not attacked as expected. My mate now got up, looking very ill and shaken, saying: 'Thank God!' I wasn't feeling so good myself. A minute or two after the firing had ceased an officer came to the bottom of the hill and shouted up to us:

'Are you all right up there?'

Answering that we were he said:

'Hang on a few minutes and I'll get you relieved.'

Getting down to the bottom we joined him whereupon he wanted to know who had visited us before he had.

'No one,' we replied.

He seemed surprised and said something about seeing into it.

FRITZ MAKES A RETURN VISIT TO THE CRATERS

We went to the dugout and had a tot of rum while the other men carried on with their usual duties now that the bombardment had stopped. A few days later, or rather nights, Fritz paid us a visit. He entered our lines by the Craters, bombed our men who retreated and then proceeded to blow up a tunnel. Before he could manage this properly, some of our men and an officer attacked him from two points. The officer, a good man in a scrap, ran into the full blast of gun cotton that the enemy had planted and got shell shock. The men climbed up on two different sides of the crater and proceeded to turn the enemy out by the use of bombs and rifle fire. One man, in his eagerness, got well in advance of his party and was mistaken for one of the enemy. He was shot through the head and died instantly. Since blowing up Fritz' mine, we had to man the crater left by it nightly. During the day, we hid up as near to it as was safe from being seen by the enemy. During our sentry duty, we came near to being hit by our own shells. At night, we went out further and climbed to the top of the last crater made, keeping watch on double sentry duty.

AN AUSTRALIAN SPOTS A GERMAN

To get from one crater to the other we passed through a short bit of tunnel roughly 15 yards long, which was flooded with water about a foot deep. It was freezing cold and icicles formed on moustaches or anywhere that caught the breath. Two men being relieved one night, passed through the flooded tunnel when one of them slipped and fell face down in the muddy water. Helped by his mate, he made his way

out as quickly as he could back to the sleeping quarters. On the way, in the darkest part of the tunnel, an Australian asked:

'What have you got, mate? A German?'

'Yes,' said the man, laughing. But before he had hardly got the 'yes' out, the Australian had wrought his unfortunate mate a hefty kick on the seat of his trousers. For his trouble, the Australian got a punch on the nose that sent him flying back into the dugout he came from!

THE SERGEANT IS ARRESTED

The sergeant that had failed to visit us during the bombardment had been put under arrest and my fellow sentry and I had to give our evidence. He was kept under close guard in a dugout and was so very upset that he had attempted to shoot himself. I felt sorry and managed to get a few words with him, hoping that he didn't bear any malice towards us who were called to give evidence. He replied:

'That's all right. You have nothing to worry about and I have nothing against you.'

Later when we made a move to another part of the line where the enemy had been rather active, volunteers were called for to get into the enemy lines and find just what it was all about. The sergeant prisoner asked to be one to go. This was granted and, with another, he was gone for two days and nights before he returned. We had given him up for lost or at least taken prisoner. It turned out that the information gained was very valuable to us and both men were recommended for decoration.

WAKING THE DEAF

While we were at the Craters, a couple of the enemy came over to our lines and threw three or four bombs into an ammunition trench and then bolted back again to their own lines. Close by to the explosions, six men had been sound asleep in a dugout. Immediately, five of them woke up startled and dashed out to beat off the enemy who they thought were attacking us in force. But the last one who had been stone deaf and waiting for his treatment to come through, slept on. The others let off several rounds in the direction of where the Germans might have been and then returned to the dugout. As they entered, the deaf chap finally woke up and asked:

'Did anyone call?'

When they all burst out laughing, he didn't know what it was about and wanted to be told so the others pointed to where the bombs had exploded. He went out to investigate, fell in the hole made by the bombs and came back after a while, rubbing himself. Then the others explained and the deaf chap saw the joke, laughing as heartily as the rest of them.

DICKY BUSH [DICKEBUSCH, 3 MILES SW OF YPRES] AND THE SPORTING TOURNAMENT

For the next month or two we were in and out of different trenches when the rumour got around that there was to be a big attack on our part and we would be going some miles back to rehearse it. We were relieved and went to Dicky Bush camp of huts. Because we had to remain here for two weeks, sports and competitions were got up for anyone who cared to enter with promises of money prizes. Boxing, jumping, running, shooting and bomb throwing were some of the items. Men were tried out and the day of the finals came. Everyone took an interest and the affair was going smoothly. The boxing ring was a good attraction and quite a crowd grew around to watch the events. Forty or fifty yards from the ring were a battery of Howitzer guns and at different times, the enemy tried to shell them. This day, while the boxing was going on, the enemy were putting shells over and did manage to hit one gun. Shrapnel was flying about, but still the boxing went on. It was marvellous how none of the men were hit. In the end a man, who wasn't from our regiment, got a piece of shrapnel in the head and went down. He was carried away to be attended to and the boxing still went on. The CO, hearing of the matter, sent word that the boxing was to stop. It did for five minutes and then they were at it again! He came out himself, this time and told the men if they didn't stop at once then the whole of the sports would be cancelled. That settled it and the sports stopped temporarily until the shelling had ceased.

REGIMENTAL SERGEANT MAJOR (RSM) OF 1/7TH LONDON TERRITORIALS

Some of us went into our huts and still the shelling

continued. Smoke from the bursting shells made a fog about the place, dirt was falling onto the roofs. Then there was an extra close explosion. We rushed out to see what it was and found that the shell had hit the ground and slid right under the Regimental Sergeant Major's hut, blowing half of it up. The RSM, who had been inside only a second or two before the incident, was only a few yards away when the shell exploded. No one was hurt and the RSM remarked: 'My luck must be in!'

He was a finely built man and had been a regular from a Scottish regiment. For a time, he had been thinking that it was rather a comedown to be put with our lot who were only Territorials. He had thought so right up until the Somme battle and always wore his Scots badges on his cap and uniform. But from then onwards, he took to wearing our badges and made it known that he was now proud to be an RSM of the Seventh London. The shell under the major's hut was only a kind of tester, for then a regular lot of shrapnel shells came all over the camp. The shrapnel came through the roofs and got so bad that we had to grab our equipment in a hurry and take cover in the trenches behind some farm buildings. Come dark, the shelling ceased and we returned to the huts. We slept, though we expected to be driven out again with more shells. This didn't happen again and the next day, we started on a three-week trek to go into training for the battle that was to come off at Messines Ridge.

To Messines Ridge – Air attack on observation balloons

The first two-day's march was a test march to see which Company came out best, the honours going to the company showing the least fatigue. One evening we stayed at a farm to rest for the night. Nearby were three of our observation balloons up in the air. Then just as it was getting dark an enemy plane darted out of the clouds, opened fire at a balloon and brought it down in flames. The plane went after another balloon but this was quickly pulled down out of the way and escaped. Anti-aircraft guns tried to bring the raider down but he soon got out of range.

Travelling on, we eventually came to a fair-sized village with farms dotted around about. We split up into parties and billeted at different places in the buildings. I and some others had a barn allotted to us but the weather, now being very warm, my pal Bridge and I decided to camp out in a field. The owners of the farm made us welcome and would sell us anything we needed like milk, eggs, butter etc. They made no fuss if we used the pump and altogether, they were more reasonable than a lot of people we had come across before. Some people where we were billeted before, even though there were plenty of fowls running about, had refused to sell us eggs.

Starving refugee family

Working for the farmer were a family of refugees, driven out from their own home by the enemy. I felt very sorry for them; they had lost everything having to escape in such a hurry. There were a husband and wife, aged around fifty and they had a girl and boy, aged about eleven and fourteen. The cottage that they lived in was apart from the farm and situated in the next field to where we were camped. It was in a bad state of repair and built principally of wooden struts or framework, filled in with mud. The roof leaked and there were large holes in the walls. There was practically no furniture; boxes served as tables and chairs. The family looked starved and miserable. As a rule we always used to have something left over at meal times and we used to pass this on to these people for which they were so thankful.

The rations issued to my mate and me, such as bread, cheese and butter were kept in a tin placed under our tent. Every morning we would go route marching when one particular day we came back and found our day's rations gone. There had been a heavy dew and we could trace foot-marks in the grass coming and going to the old cottage. We followed the tracks, which led us to the garden, and there under some green stuff were our rations, untouched in the tin. Seeing the boy later on, we asked him why had he taken them and he said that he was hungry but that after he took them he felt sorry for what he'd done but was too afraid to return them. We said nothing about it to anyone, returned the rations to the tent and they were never interfered with again.

'... AND A LITTLE CHILD SHALL LEAD YOU'

We had quite a busy time, marching, drilling, bomb-throwing, bayonet drill, sham attacks and finishing off the contests and sports. The whole Brigade was in training like us. One regiment had a very small man as an officer leading and some of the men were amused by this. Jokes were made at the officer's expense who knew well what was going on but took very little notice until the joke went too far. Some of the men got up a saying that ended with the words: '... And a little child shall lead you.'

A day came when the officer led the men on an extra-long march and they came back feeling tired and footsore. They had tea and were surprised at an order to fall-in for another march. When they formed up, the little officer said to them:

'Men, we are going on another route march and a little child shall lead you on horse-back.' The men came back exhausted and there were no more jokes about the officer being small after that!

A FIGHT AT ST-OMER, HARRY SEES HIS FIRST WAACs [WOMEN'S ARMY AUXILIARY CORPS]

We went to a place to practise long-distance firing and also to fire from the hip whilst advancing in the line. This was a thing we had never done before but was a common thing with the enemy. We generally use to finish our day's training at about four or five in the afternoon, then in the evening we attended concerts set up by our regiments in an aerodrome about a mile away. Once more, the CO gave a certain number of us permission to visit the town of St Omer. Every evening, we had the loan of the army wagons to travel in, the town being six or seven miles away. It was a fairly large town with wide streets, some large buildings, and a number of shops and places of amusement. It was quite a holiday for us and we enjoyed ourselves in our different ways. It was here that most of us saw our first WAACs, an army of females got up and put into active service to free men of jobs that women were capable of doing. They had evidently not been in the town very long, for a French officer enquired of me who and what they were! He spoke in French and I tried my best to explain to him in the same language but it wasn't much of a success, I'm afraid. He thanked me and went away, seeming satisfied.

On returning one evening, we were sat in the lorry having a singsong when we passed several Australians who had had too much to drink and were being quarrelsome. One stopped us and tried to force his way onto the lorry. We objected to this, as there was no room. Several more came up and entered into the argument, proposing that either we get out or they would throw us out. We invited them to try and there was a bit of a fight between us. We got out of it all right and thankfully got going again. One of the Australians then pulled up a small tree by the roots and came after us with it, ready to threaten us. Quickly, one of our men jumped out of the cart and met him halfway. They started hitting each other and within a minute or two, the Australian was on his back in the road – having enough of fighting for one day!

USE OF AERIAL PHOTOGRAPHY TO TARGET OBJECTIVES

We were now feeling fitter from our training and we were prepared for the attack we were going in for later. A large tract of ground had been marked out with small flags and tapes to represent the ground we were to capture. Everything was explained to us such as strong points, canals, marshes and trenches, and with the aid of a number of photographs taken by our airmen, we got a general idea of the actual ground we were to cover when the time came. We practised the attack over and over again, each of us having a specific job assigned to us. The weather was grand! I believe we all enjoyed the practice, although we felt a bit tired by night-time.

HARRY TRIES HIS FIRST GAME OF RUGBY

At last, the training came to an end and we moved back towards the line. Getting as far as Poperinge, we made camp under canvas and stayed a week doing nothing in particular but filled in the time playing football and other games. I got into my first and only game of rugby. I had no idea of the rules so they were roughly explained to me and we got going. When the match was over, I had the sleeve of my shirt missing, a bruise on my head where someone had kicked me, several hacks on my shins and most of the buttons missing on my uniform! I'd had a fine time! The term 'try' was part of the game. If the way I got torn to pieces was a try, goodness knows what I would have been like after a success!

EARLY MORNING YPRES, WITHIN A MILE OF FRONT LINE

Since we had been away training, hundreds of extra men and guns had been brought up and hidden at all kinds of unlikely places. Miles of railway track had been lain of both broad and narrow gauge. During the day, they were covered over with coloured stuff representing grass or earth to hide them from being spotted by enemy planes. There were heaps and heaps of shells all over the country, placed at spots where the artillery could get at them easily. One evening, we left the camp at dusk and moved up to within a mile or less of the front line. We hid up all the next day in the remains of a small village. What amused me was that, even so near to the front as this, there were two females still working on the farms and a woman driving a horse and cart, delivering the milk early in the morning. Guns of both sides were active here now, especially after dark. All roads for miles around had shells dropped on them and quite a number of horses and mules, besides men, were getting hit. During the day that we hid out at the village, the enemy brought one of our aeroplanes down.

NIGHT BEFORE THE ATTACK, WITHIN A FEW HUNDRED YARDS OF YPRES

Rather late at night, we left the village and went across the fields to some tunnels a few hundred yards from the line. It was pitch dark and several times, we marched under the muzzles of our own guns whilst they fired. The enemy trenches and back areas were being shelled heavily. In some spots, there was one continual splutter of deep, red fire where our shells were bursting. We had never been to this set of tunnels before. They were quite comfortable, with rows and rows of bunks inside where we had to stay until the time arrived for the attack. We had had extra ammunition issued to us, and had been given a small number of bombs a-piece. We got to the tunnels somewhere around 10 o'clock at night and were due to go over at six next morning. Naturally, we were all more or less excited but few of us lost any sleep over it and by midnight, most of us were fast asleep.

BOMB-SHY

There was one chap, however, who didn't sleep so well. He waited until I was asleep and then passed his bombs, of which he had a great dread, into my keeping. It appears that on one occasion when this chap had gone to practice bomb throwing, by misjudgement a few bombs had been thrown so that they rolled back to the throwers standing downhill. The result had been that several men had been killed or wounded. The sight had been an awful one and this chap could not get it out of his mind. Forever afterwards, he dreaded to be near bombs, let alone handle them. Next morning, when I noticed I had more bombs than I should have and realising where they came from, for fun I pitched them onto this chap's bunk. My I never saw him move so quickly! He was up and running like the devil was after him! We used all the persuasion we could muster but he would not take charge of those bombs and I believe that they were left behind when we moved out.

FINAL ORDERS AND INTO POSITIONS, WITH EMPTY STOMACHS

We were all aroused early on the morning of the attack. Final orders were given to us with a general idea of what to do and what we could expect when we arrived at our starting-off trenches and afterwards. We had had little to eat and drink this morning, which caused some grumbling until it was explained there was a reason for it and everyone quietened down. The reason given was that there was sure to be some casualties where an operation would be necessary and a full stomach was harmful to the patient undergoing surgery.

We moved up front with the least possible noise. Some of us took up our positions a few yards to the rear of the front trench in a newly dug trench; others went beyond the front line and hid up in shell holes in as near a straight line as they could. All the time this was going on, our guns were hammering away at the enemy lines while the enemy dropped their shells around us. Most of the enemy shells fell in and near our front line that was practically empty of men. My pal, Bridge, kept by me and seemed content. Our jobs in the attack were to be the same and, if everything went well, we had no need to part company. We had been told to make for some dugouts and machine-gun nests alongside of the canal. We had some bombs each and were to bomb the enemy out of these places.

TEN MINUTES TO ZERO

We had mined under Hill Sixty for a year or more and now, in this morning of the attack, it was to be exploded and to act as a signal for the commencement. None of our men were put too near it. We were a good thousand yards away and felt the effects quite plainly. We had none too much room in our trench as we waited quietly for the signal. Orders were now and again passed from man to man along the trench and we were all getting keyed up and kind of excited, as the time drew near for the start. From about ten minutes to zero, the time passed along at minute intervals. You could hear the mumble of the men's voices, passing the time along:

'Ten minutes to go…'

'Nine…'

'Eight…'

'Seven...'

This got on my nerves and I wished they wouldn't do it. Some rum was passed along for any that cared for it, but both my pal and I refused it. At last, the one minute to go message was passed along and we all got ready to clamber out and make a dash at the enemy lines. There had been a lull in the firing up until this last minute, but now there were thousands of shells flying about and the air was full of clouds, dust and smoke. It was difficult to see far around.

HILL SIXTY GOES UP

With a roar and a rumble Hill Sixty went up and the ground we were on rocked and trembled so that we could hardly stand. Some that were halfway out of the trench were shook back again. My pal being rather short had some trouble in getting out and I had to give him some help. There were some that only got a few yards when they were hit, but the most of us went forward in a rough line in much the same way as we had practised a few weeks before. The ground was rough to travel over and now and again, we tripped or got stopped by barbed wire. We came to the enemy front line almost before we knew it, but there were no men there. Jumping this, we made for the second line where we were met by shrapnel and machine-gun fire and lost some men. The others pressed on, taking the trench and capturing any of the enemy left in it. Our line of men was within a few yards of it when several aero-

planes came buzzing along just above our heads. It seemed we only had to reach up to touch the wheels. Just at this moment, my pal and I ran into a bunch of barbed wire. He made his way round to the right, I went to the left, intending to join each other on the other side. But it was not to be. The enemy were shelling the aeroplanes just above our heads and I got a piece of shrapnel into my right shoulder. In the excitement, I didn't realise I was wounded. I felt the thump, but I've had thumps before, hurting as much. Several times, lumps of dirt have struck me and I've only had a bruise. I continued on, shouting to my pal, who was waiting for me to catch up:

'I'm coming...'

Before I could get to him, my rifle dropped from my hand and it was then, when I attempted to pick it up again, that I found I couldn't. For the first time, I noticed blood on my hand and realised I was wounded. I had no wish to go any further, so pointing to my shoulder and signalling to my pal to go on, I turned round and walked back to our lines. I dumped my bombs, stood my rifle on a fire step and tried to get some idea of the extent of the damage. It wasn't very painful but it had numbed the whole arm and it was almost useless. Some stretcher-bearers were nearby but as I was just about to call out for their help, a volley of shells came over and they scattered. I scattered too, but in the opposite direction. Another shell came near and instead of exploding in the usual way with a terrific bang, gave a kind of loud pop and cracks appeared all over it. From the cracks, issued clouds of smoke. Some men nearby called: 'GAS!'

Then they promptly moved away, putting on their gas helmets. I tried to put mine on, but found that I couldn't manage it with one hand. Shells were falling thick and heavy and more of our men were coming up to carry on the attack, so I looked round for a spot of safety and to get out of the men's way. I found an entrance to a dugout that was being used as a head-quarters for a machine-gun corp. I stayed there for a while and got trodden on once or twice before an officer came out and ordered me to get out.

'What are you doing here, anyway?' he wanted to know.

Telling him I was wounded, he said that he was sorry but that I would have to get to some other place. He sent out one of his men who I knew and we went to a dugout further along the trench. There the men helped me find my wound and put some dress-ing on. We sat smoking and chatting awhile, but found that the bleeding hadn't altogether stopped.

'Are you wounded anywhere else?' the man said. I couldn't say I was, so he had a closer look at my arm and found a wound where the shrapnel had come out. He dressed it and now that I was all right, he left me and went back to his headquarters.

There were plenty of men going along the trench while the shelling was going on, but as soon as it eased up, the men preferred to walk over the top. A lot of prisoners were now coming in, some were escorted by our men but there were more that had no escort at all. Several times, one or the other of them dodged into my dugout to seek safety from bursting shells. They didn't come far in but I could see them plainly enough. I doubt if they even saw me or knew I was there, but I got to thinking how I would be in a very awkward position if one should come right in and find me. He might take it into his head to injure me. I hunted around for a weapon and all I could find was a short stick belonging to my entrenching tool. As soon as the shelling eased up, I intended to move to a dressing station, in the meantime I was all right where I was.

PRISONERS TAKEN

I got nearer to the trench and in the light I watched the prisoners on their way back to our lines. They were of all ages and sizes and appeared to have had a rough time. Some were wounded and were being helped along, others were pressed into service, carry-ing wounded men on stretchers. There was one party of prisoners that had an officer amongst them. He objected to being hurried along the trench and being put with the ordinary soldiers. The escort gave him a push and told him, in strong language, to get along. Somehow, the officer managed to get hold of a bomb and tried to use it. The escort could have shot him, but instead, he swung up the butt of the rifle and jammed it into the prisoner's face. The prisoner went down, unconscious and his face was not a pretty sight. He didn't stay down there long; two of the other prisoners picked him up and carried him away.

AN ACCOUNT OF THE FRONT

Again, another prisoner came into the dugout for safety and with him, came his escorts and a chap from our regiment. The prisoner was quite a boy, somewhere about the age of fifteen. He had new clothes on and carried a linen bag with several kinds of eatables in it. He looked scared to death. The chap with him got chatting to me and told me what was going on up front. 'Things were going good,' he told me.

But a big obstacle had been the marshy ground and the machine-guns housed and placed in small but strong concrete forts. The shelling had made little impression on them and it was now up to the advancing troops to take these forts by dropping or pitching a bomb inside each one as they came across them. A good many of the gun crews had held on until they were killed. There had been a part of a building that had been strongly fortified called the White House. This had shown up clearly on the photographs demonstrated to us during training and had been marked as a strong point. This had eventually been taken by the troops. They had had to crawl up, from cover to cover, mostly in shell holes, until they were near enough to pitch the bombs down a stairway leading to the cellar. Even after a dozen or two bombs had exploded below amongst the enemy, their machine-guns kept up their clatter. It was not until a couple of bombs were pitched through the holes where the guns were poking out, that the enemy decided to give up.

The garrison had been large and made quite a crowd when they came out. They were taken care of by one or two escorts and were being escorted to our lines. One of the prisoners didn't keep up with the rest, to an escort's liking, and he shouted and swore at the prisoner, advancing at the same time in a threatening manner towards him with his bayonet. In self-protection, the prisoner got a grip on the rifle and looked like getting it away from the chap. The chap then started calling out for help, but although there were a number of men watching the incident going on, all they did was cheer on the two struggling men and laugh. It was not until the escort chap was losing his grip on the rifle that somebody leant a hand. This man went up and parted the two by pricking the prisoner on the seat of his trousers with the point of a bayonet. The prisoner got going after this but not before someone had given him a cigarette. He saw the joke and laughed with the rest.

BOY PRISONERS

We in the dugout were smoking, whilst talking and we had the prisoner in between us as we all sat on the floor. We could see that the poor chap was scared, the two of us talking seemed to scare the prisoner more. What his thoughts were I could only imagine! By the looks he gave us and the way he acted, he must have thought that we were going to do him some harm. He jabbered away in German to us, offering his linen bag to first one and then the other of us. Taking several articles from his pockets, he offered them. Being pressed into having the bag again, I took it and examined the contents. There was a piece of dark coloured bread, several small paper packets of compressed meat and vegetables and one or two small flat tins containing what looked like sausage meat. Lying loose in the corner were about twenty small biscuits. Having examined the things, I returned them and tried the best I could to put the poor chap at his ease. We offered him a cigarette but he shook his head, making us understand that he didn't smoke. I tried with what French I knew to converse with him, this he didn't understand. The only German word I knew was 'frau'. I tried this and the prisoner drew a photo from his pocket to show us. The photo was of two females. By now, our prisoner was more at ease and bit of colour came back into his face.

The shelling decreased and we got out, making our way back towards the canal dugouts. Reinforcements of men were waiting there to relieve the others at the front of the attack. There were advance dressing stations or hospitals and a place to check the prisoners as they came in. The place was alive with men and from across the fields round about, guns were making their way to take up new positions. I learned later that our prisoner was one of a regiment that had practically come straight from his home and put into the line to stop our advance. There were numbers of these boys among the prisoners and no doubt, they simply marched into our hands hardly knowing how they got there.

THE UNENVIABLE STRETCHER-BEARERS

We passed several of our men who had been killed by shellfire but had not been picked up yet along the trenches. One man took my particular attention because he was sitting as though asleep on a fire step. It was only by going up to him, with the object of helping that I found that he was dead. There was no wound about him; he had died from concussion. A man can die this way if shells explode quite near, without even being scratched by the flying shrapnel. The stretcher-bearers were up-front now, doing their job and I didn't envy them.

Getting to the large shelter that was being used as a dressing station by our regimental doctor, I went into have my wounds dressed. The doctor was very busy attending the wounded and he had blood splashes all down the front of his white coat that he was wearing. He was attending a man on a stretcher when I arrived. Already, the doctor had taken a number of pieces of shell from out of the man's body and was searching for more. The patient was helping the doctor by telling him where he felt the shrapnel in his body. My case not being too bad, I got the sergeant stretcher-bearer to attend me. Before starting on the job, he gave me a cup of cocoa and a couple of cigarettes. All the wounded that came in were served the same and I thought it was rather nice. Having had our wounds dressed, those of us who were able to walk were asked to go to another dressing station about a mile away. It was situated at the side of a road and motor ambulances were able to pick up the wounded and cart them to better-equipped hospitals out of the fighting zone. Prisoners were pressed into service, carrying some of the stretcher cases to this station before continuing on until they came to an internment camp. On our way to the dressing station, we had a few shells come over but most of them were directed at guns and ammunition dumps.

TOO MANY WOUNDED – THE SKILL OF THE AMBULANCE DRIVERS

Now that we had got away from the exciting parts, most of us wounded cases were feeling a little groggy. We were hungry as well, not having eaten for almost eight hours. Getting on to the road and the dressing station, we found it full up with stretcher cases with half a dozen motors loading up and taking them away. We walking cases asked the doctor what we should do and he advised us to walk to a dressing station that was still further across country,

some four miles away. This didn't sound so good but stretcher cases come first so we thought we might as well make the journey. I was in no hurry to start, so I sat on a stone at the side of a gateway where the ambulances were coming through when they loaded. I had been sitting there for some time, watching the comings and goings of cases, when one of the ambulance drivers called out that he had room beside him if I cared to go. I got up beside him and off we went. The roads were awfully bumpy with shell holes every few yards. The driver drove so as to miss the holes as much as he could, but it was still a rough time for the wounded. Several times we had shells burst near and once, we almost overturned into a ditch. Only the skill of the driver saved us. I felt myself fortunate to be able to ride, for as we went along, I saw hundreds of wounded chaps walking along the road.

FIELD HOSPITAL AT POPERINGE

We were making towards Ypres and should have passed through it by rights, but it was being shelled so heavily that the driver took a roundabout and came out on the other side of the town. After we had got passed Ypres we got very few shells and in a short time, we pulled up at a hospital compound near Poperinge made up of large tents. The stretcher cases were placed in rows on the floor and doctors got busy attending them. The most serious cases were sent right away to hospital trains and then onto hospitals that had appliances to perform operations of all kinds. We cases that were not so bad, both English and German passed in turn before a doctor who examined us redressed our wounds and then inoculated us. Most of the Germans took things calmly, but one or two made a fuss about being inoculated and screamed like children. Passing from here, we came to another tent where refreshments were given to us and we were told to have as much as we liked, it was all free. It seemed strange to find yourself standing by a group of the enemy, all busy eating and drinking together. No preferential treatment was shown, we were all served alike, and having feasted we were given some cigarettes before being passed out to a tent to await our turn to go to a proper hospital.

TRANSFERRED TO A BELGIAN HOSPITAL

There was a shortage of proper ambulances, so some of us had to travel in large army motor lorries. Our lorry carried a party of about twenty to twenty-five of us, with German and English together. We had a considerable journey to go and I was glad when it ended. My arm was now rather painful and, going over the rough roads with solid tyres didn't improve matters. I found that I was more comfortable standing up and rode that way for the whole journey. Arriving at the hospital, we passed through a crowd of Belgians who were watching the cases as they came along. Going inside before a proper doctor, a more careful inspection was carried out, bullets or shrapnel were probed for and removed. My arm was probed, but no shrapnel was found. What they did get out was a piece of strap and shirt that had got forced into the wound when I was hit. The arm being dressed again, we got the opportunity to wash ourselves and that's when I realised I must have looked a sketch! I had no cap, the sleeve of my coat was all ripped up and I had my share of mud and dust upon my clothes. This was soon altered, for after washing we were all given a clean change of clothes, handed a bowl of porridge and then straight into bed. The hospital was built at the side of a railway and we could see the hospital trains taking the loads of wounded further up the line. It was quite nice to lie in a real bed again, and I should have slept all night had it not been for the groans of the wounded.

THE COURT MARTIALLED SERGEANT

The next day, those that could, got up and had breakfast. We were made comfortable and then waited for a hospital train to take us further on. When the train came in, as I was getting on I saw the sergeant of our regiment who had been up for the court martial. His trial had not been completed. He had one hand in a bandage and looked very well otherwise. I tried to find him to have a chat but I was unable to do so. I heard later that the wound had been caused with his own rifle.

CHAPTER EIGHT
BLIGHTY

Harry experienced a remarkable change from the mud and squalor of fighting in the trenches to the kindly, clean world of the medical system in a very short period of time – it must have been quite a transformation for him. By this point in the war the medical system was very efficient at processing casualties, and Harry's recollections are fairly typical. His matter-of-fact tone in describing his transformation back to civilian life must have been written with a great deal of emotion hidden behind it. A remarkable story!

WOUNDED TAKEN TO A NEW HOSPITAL

After riding for some time, we got off the train to another hospital. It was well equipped and was able to manage any cases that came along. Most of the cases had come direct from the line and, if necessary, operations were carried out right away on entering the hospital. I stayed there for perhaps a week and a routine formed whereupon I used to get up, have the wounds dressed, breakfast and then was free to amuse myself as best as I could. The hospital was ever so busy with trains coming in twice a day either bringing the wounded in or carrying them away to the coast, en route for England. In my wanderings around the hospital, I came across a heap of clothes that had been taken off the wounded. They were all bloodstained, torn and ripped about, and mixed with them I saw one or two metal waistcoats. I had heard of these things, but this was the first I had seen of them. My arm was much easier now and I was wondering what was going to happen next. The wounds were healing up nicely but I could get no use in my arm. I had heard that slight cases like mine were sent to Le Havre, or similar places where you were given the light jobs until you recovered and then sent back to the regiment. I guessed that this would be my programme and when I was put on the train again, I thought that things were about to turn out that way.

LE HAVRE AND THE FATE OF HOSPITAL SHIPS

We did go to Le Havre, but not to a hospital. We drew up alongside a hospital ship. Immediately, the cases were taken on board, with the stretcher cases first followed by the walking cases lined up two by two. I was near the end of the queue and when there were only about fifty of us left, we were told that there was no more room. This was a real disappointment to a lot of us but we had to make the best of it. We were taken in charge and put into a hospital ward right along side of the harbour. It was a seaman's hospital and most of the cases were broken limbs. We were treated well, had good meals and were allowed to go out for walks, though we had to be back by eight o'clock and supposed to be in bed by nine.

Arising the next day, we had breakfast, wounds were dressed and out we went again until dinnertime. The weather was good and we had plenty to amuse ourselves whilst walking along the seafront. Swimming in the harbour were several men while overhead, a couple of French Blimps or airships, were on the lookout for submarines or other enemy craft. We got into conversation with a chap who pointed out to us a spot where he said that two of our hospital ships had been sunk. Although it had happened some time ago, he told us that bodies were still being washed up, among them female nurses. After these two ships had gone down, no more female nurses were used on board hospital ships.

ON BOARD THE HOSPITAL SHIP TO ENGLAND

During the early part of the morning another hospital ship had come into harbour and lay moored out in the middle. We stayed out in the open all day and come night, or rather teatime, we were told to hold ourselves in readiness to go aboard ship at about 10 o'clock. This time, we were not turned back. A meal was given us on boarding and we were given a bunk each to sleep in. Every man had a life belt, all portholes were covered up and nobody was allowed on deck. What time the ship started out I don't know, for I was asleep. But I woke up again when we were just off the Isle of Wight. Daylight was just breaking, and looking through the porthole at the land, I thought what a pretty scene it was. It was slightly misty and things seemed unreal. Trees and grass were a vivid green, in front of pure white houses that seemed to have hundreds of windows. The windows reflected the sun with a deep red colour and everything seemed very peaceful. Now that it was daylight, we were allowed on deck and I stayed there until we got to Southampton where we docked.

It was about 5 o'clock and the docks were almost deserted. As soon as the ship was safely tied up, the cases of wounded were quickly got to a hospital train, drawn up alongside. As before, the stretcher cases went first. On the deckside and platform, ladies were in charge of refreshment stalls where we could have tea, coffee or cocoa simply by asking for it. They even gave us cigarettes, pipes and tobacco if we needed them. In next to no time, the train was full up and could take no more. Those of us,

numbering a hundred or more, still waiting to board had to wait until another train was sent for us. In the meantime, we returned to the ship where breakfast was being served and afterwards, spent some time going over the ship. I was surprised at the fittings and things in general on board. To me, it seemed like a little floating town with everything that could be found at a good hotel. There were lovely pictures, wide staircases, carvings, carpets, baths, dining rooms and dance halls. We spent some time like this and then hadn't even seen half of the ship! Going back to the dining hall, we were each presented with a present with the compliments of the Shipping Company. The present consisted of a pipe, pouch, tobacco, matches and cigarettes. My, we were doing fine!

ENGLAND – TO HOSPITAL CAMP AND A VICAR CALLED TRES BON

Our train now arriving, we got off the ship and boarded the train. It was quite an ordinary train but we had carriages reserved just for us and no civil people were allowed to ride with us. We travelled along, stopping at many stations and expecting eventually to arrive in London. In this, we were mistaken! We pulled into a country station, a good many miles from London and were ordered to get out. From the station we were then taken a short distance away to a kind of hospital camp. Here, spread out in rows, were about fifty huts built of wood and canvas. In each hut were four beds with a locker or cupboard to each. Placed in front of each hut were a table and four chairs. The front sides of the huts opened upwards on hinges and were supported on struts. They were left open at all times whilst the weather was good and altogether was a nice arrangement. Every four of us, as we came in the line, were allotted a hut.

The first thing to do was to take a bath and afterwards we were given a clean change of clothes and felt the better for them! I was unable to get an ordinary shirt on and off and so I was supplied with a special sleeve. Shaving got me beaten for a time but managing to hold the razor in the right hand, I guided it with the left. Had I wished, I could have had free shaves at a barber in the camp. In fact, nearly everything was free, and all we met up with wanted to help us as much as they could. As soon as the men finished bathing, they had orders to go to the medical to be inoculated. I, being extra time in the baths, was missed and had no orders to go this time but went the following day. Returning to our huts, we found dinner served and it was quite a treat to sit down at a proper served table with a tablecloth, plates, knives and forks.

Attached to the camp was a vicar who was known as Tres Bon by one and all. He was a jolly kind of man who was forever busy doing things for the comfort of the wounded chaps at the hospital. If troubled in anyway and wanting help or advice, he was always willing to give what help he could. Most of us were without money and wished to write to our friends so he would supply us with writing material and the stamp. Concerts were got up for our benefit and games put on during the day. A YMCA hall was at the camp with plenty of papers, books and indoor games so that there was no excuse to pass a dull time while we were here! Up until now, I had had no opportunity to let my people know how I was except to send a card saying that I was wounded. It was a message sent on the field card issued by the army and no other information was allowed to be written on them except the words: 'I am well, I am sick or I am wounded.' This had been worrying me a bit until I got a reply from a letter sent from the camp. The weather remained good for the whole two weeks that we were here and then, being inoculated again, we boarded a train to arrive in London.

LONDON MILITARY HOSPITAL – GOING HOME IN THE REGULATION SUIT

At London we were met by motor ambulances and distributed to different hospitals across London. Our motor took us to a Military Hospital at Bancroft Road, Stepney that was not a great distance from my home and I was very glad of this! Getting inside, our wounds were examined and dressed and particulars were taken, then we were shown to the ward that we were to occupy. We asked permission to go out which was readily granted on condition that we promised not to get drunk or in any way cause ourselves injury, and we had to be back in the hospital by nine o'clock. This we agreed to and were soon out in the street. I made my way directly for home, about a mile away. To get there I got on a tramcar. Being now in a military hospital, like all patients I had to wear a suit of clothes supplied by them. These were composed of a rather light blue coat and trouser and a white shirt with collar attached, round which a bright red tie was fixed in a neat knot. The overcoat, if worn, was an ordinary khaki with a blue band stitched on the left arm. A military cap with regimental badge completed the outfit. This suit, I found out, was the cause of lots of things happening which were all meant for respect and kindness. The conductor on the tram came along collecting fares. When he came to me I offered mine but he smiled and said:

'That's all right, chum. Put it back in your pocket. You can ride free!'

Nearly everywhere it was like this, everyone trying to make things comfortable.

It was great to get home again and my friends all made a fuss of me, hoping my wound was not too bad and would soon be well. After that, I used to go home frequently and visited my old work-mates from the sawmill as well. The mill was very busy turning out boxes and cases for army use and I wished that I might be taking some part in it.

On the second day at the hospital, several of us were x-rayed to see that there were not any bullet or shrapnel still in us. Some did, but not I, anyway none was found near the wound. One chap from my regiment had a shrapnel ball enter his chest and it had stopped within half an inch of his heart. When it was removed, he showed it to me and said that he was going to wear it on his watch chain. We all had a great time at the hospital, every day there were invitations to country drives, concerts, music halls, whist drives and theatres. There were very few restrictions at the hospital, food of all variety was good and plenty and we could have a bath or clean clothes whenever we wished.

After a week or two, the wounds in my arm healed up and I went to another ward. The arm was still painful and I did not have much strength in it. From now on, I had massage treatment every day to try and get the strength back. It certainly was getting lots better but the improvement was slow. Never a week passed without an air raid, but no bombs were dropped near us. From our ward window, we could see into the street and, when the warning signal of approaching bombers came, we watched the people hurriedly leaving their homes to take shelter some-where safer. The hospital carried on as usual, except that the shell shock cases were removed to the basement.

Sleeping next to me in the ward was a chap, a machine-gunner, wounded in the shoulder like myself. The name was also similar to mine; Stanton. When my wounds were healed, I was advised to try and use my arm. The exercise, though painful, would be a help towards getting it better. Up until then I had had my arm in a sling, but after getting the advice I left it off. This other chap got the same advice but disregarded it. Confidently, he told me that he didn't want it better whilst he was in the army for, he said:

'I have had enough of the trenches. If my arm gets well I will be sent out again. Let them give me my discharge and then I don't mind getting the arm better!'

He had been at the hospital longer than I had, and by persisting in not trying to use his arm and keeping it in one position, it was gradually getting withered.

Convalescence with a view of the Crystal Palace

Every now and again, parties of men were sent for a couple of weeks to convalescent homes. I was sent to one at Crystal Palace along with some others and from the home we could see the glass domes or roofs quite plainly. The home had originally been a Girls' college and was a very nice place. It had a good number of rooms and in each of them were two beds and other furniture. The whole place was run on the lines of a hotel, except that we who needed it still had treatment twice a day. On the ground floor were a dining room, billiard room, kitchen and the staff offices where we amused ourselves should the weather be wet. There was also plenty of reading matter. At the rear of the house was a garden and tennis court. From here, just like the hospital, we used to get invited out to different parties and drives. We were never short of cigarettes, they were given to us wherever we went and even left at the home for us! The game of billiards was in great favour and every day, competitions were played. At the time, I knew nothing about the game so I spent a lot of time with a chap from the West Indies out in the garden. He was a well-spoken and educated chap whose parents, he said: 'owned lots of property there'. We got friendly and he and I used to play on the tennis court. The rules of the game I knew very little of, but batting the balls about was very good exercise for my arm. Sometimes I would overdo it and the arm would become numbed though it didn't last for long. As soon as I could grip the bat again we would start playing. This friend of mine was in hospital for rheumatism. He had spent only a short time in the trenches during winter and had been in hospital ever since. Our stay at the home came to an end and we again returned to the hospital.

Back to the hospital and PB

About this time in the war, we had suffered some reverses in the fighting with the loss of a good number of men. Any man thought fit enough was sent from the hospitals to rejoin their regiments.

There were quite a number of men who left our hospital this way; most of them being those that had been convalescing. Every month, a board sat at the hospital to decide who was fit enough to return to their regiments. If a man was to attend, then the letters PB were written in blue chalk across the record board at the head of the patient's bed. My bed got marked one day whilst I was away, and not knowing the meaning of it, I asked the other men in the ward what it was all about. Most of the cases in my ward were shell shock and were a decent lot of chaps. They were forever playing jokes on each other and sometimes the nurses. Here was a chance to have one on me! In answer to my inquiries, they told me that PB meant permanent base and went on to explain that I would be drafted to some place to be forever drilling like an ordinary recruit. They said that generally I would be under orders assigned to someone who had never seen the line and that had no idea what it was like! This didn't sound so good to me and I thought that I would rather get back to the line than stand for this kind of thing. They piled it on, giving instances of different cases that they knew and made out that I was in for a bad time.

Later on in the day, I found out that PB meant pending board not permanent base and I wanted to get my revenge on the jokers! They kept the joke up all day between them and when they went down to the hall for supper, I made preparations to get my own back. I knew that they played cards of an evening right up until the lights went out when the matron comes round. We were supposed to be in bed before then and that there was always a rush to get into bed when they heard the matron coming. I fixed the bedclothes to that they were unable to get in properly and, with the beds having folding legs, I fixed it that any movement on top would cause them to collapse to the floor. There was the usual rush at the last minute with all of them trying to get into bed before the matron saw them. They covered themselves up somehow and the matron noticed nothing unusual, said 'Good night,' and off went the lights. Before they could sleep properly, each man had to make his bed in the dark and it was either while doing this or after they got in that several beds went down, so I was satisfied! Of course, they wanted to know who did this, so I told them PB! They came after me in a body and chased me over the beds and threw pillows. The noise brought the matron out to see what was going on but we were all in bed before she arrived, so nobody got into trouble!

The following week I went before the board and after an examination was told that I was to have my discharge, as I was no longer fit for army service. I was both surprised and pleased at this and so were my ward mates. Discharge papers and another paper entitling me to draw a pension were given me. I had an interview with a society that helped discharged men get back to civil occupations and was measured up for a civil suit of clothes.

A few days later, dressed in civilian clothes, I took my final departure from hospital and made plans to get back to civil life again. My job was waiting for me at the sawmill but I was in no hurry to start right away. I had a week's carefree holiday and then made a start and so ended my experiences as a soldier. In all, from enlistment to discharge, I spent two years, four months and a few days.

INDEX

in there way to take up positions ready for the attack commenceing at dawn. The rain stoped, and the moon shon through the clouds now and again. This made it better for traveling. and we were able to see a bit better. We were all the time jumping out of way of the lorries and things, and I for one was all of a sweat, hot and tired. Geting some definate news, of our destination, we were makeing our way towards it, when a contraption, which I took to be a tractor hulling a big gun, nearly ran over me. I had never seen or heard of anything like it. "What is it" I asked the officer. "Oh thats one of the surprizes" he said "its what is called a tank". Tank I said, gayeing at it. Whist I looked it kind of slewed round left the road, and waddled off across the fields. "Theres quite a few of them things" said the officer, "and good results are expected of them. Anyway they will be a surprise for the enimy". At last we managed to find our divisanal headquarters, but we didnt stay. A note had been left to the effect that when we reported ourselves we were